CRUSHING IT

HOW I CRUSHED DIET CULTURE, ADDICTION & THE PATRIARCHY

Kortney Olson

To my mom, Keven.

Thank you for rearranging your insides and bringing me into this world.

Thank you for the gift of alcoholism and leading me to the 12-steps; I am forever grateful.

Finally, thank you for helping me show the world that recovery is possible.

Forever BFF's.

To my dad and Barb.

Thank you for spending your hard earned dollars bailing my ass out of trouble.

Thank you for never giving up on me, no matter how many cars I wrecked.

Finally, thank you for helping me show the world that recovery is possible.

Forever BFF's.

To Pop.

Thank you for being the fiercest matriarch and role model.

Thank you for investing in my dream.

Finally, thank you for helping me show the world that recovery is possible.

Forever BFF's.

To my Husband.

Thank you for believing in me more than anyone has ever believed in me in this world.

Thank you for co-creating my dream.

Finally, thank you for helping me show the world that recovery is possible.

Forever your golden child.

TABLE OF CONTENTS

Act Three: Diet Culture Nearly Destroyed Me

HEY GRRRL HEYYYYY!

Not to sound like a total tool, but I'm super stoked you're here. Before I go waffling on, I want you to know one thing; **You are enough**. Even if you only read this first paragraph and skip out to go deadlift or drink a glass of wine, at least I'll know you've gotten this important memo. As women, we've been told the opposite since the moment we shot out into this screwed up world. In my experience, it's the sense of not being enough that's driven me to the absolute brink of peril.

That feeling of never being good enough, no matter how many hours of cardio I did and calories I didn't have, always gnawed at the back of my brain like a starving rat who'd just rolled up on a piece of havarti cheese. It seemed like every single second of my life had been spent obsessing on how I could change or improve parts of my body to such a point that I hardly possessed a single high-quality memory, despite having some incredible experiences.

For reference, I guess you could say this book is a cross between a Million Little Pieces, and 50 Shades of Grey, but all real life (and not plagiarized). I started writing this book back in 2011, but thanks to a combination of being highly ADD and somewhat intuitive, the timing couldn't be more perfect than to be finishing this now in 2020. Besides, my story was still climaxing back then. I might point out that typing the world "climaxing" makes me feel super uncomfortable, lol. Funny coming from someone who's probably slept with more people than Charlie Sheen.

Although I'm pretty sure social media is the spawn of Satan, I did most of my growing up prior to these platforms existing. Therefore, seeing and connecting with other women who were also hating their bodies, struggling with addiction, fumbling their way through childhood trauma, or feeling utterly hopeless due to a lack of purpose, were few and far between.

I'm hoping that by the end of this book you'll feel like you have someone you can completely identify with. On top of that, I hope you walk away feeling transformed and completely ready to stop giving a shit about whether or not your skin looks like a polished, "flawless" stone.

Come to think of it, let me ask you something:

Have you ever stopped and pondered the who, what, where, and why of how this concept of us being "flawed" even came from in the first place?

Chances are this might be the first time someone has ever asked you, so is it any coincidence that you're hanging out with me right now? If you've picked up this book I imagine there are a couple of different reasons why.

Perhaps you're tired of waking up every day feeling like you'll forever be trying to fill a bottomless pit deep in your soul. I've been there. No matter how many different things I stuck in my mouth, it seemed like that void just kept getting deeper and deeper. From pills, pipes, and cocktails, to food, dicks, and gossip, no matter what I shoved in there, it never made me feel better for long.

Regardless of where you are on the happiness scale, I guarantee you'll find some enlightenment within these pages. I sure as shit would have liked to know that there is an entire world of people out there who find things attractive that I grew up hating. Or that alcoholism and addiction have nothing to do with willpower.

Whether you're simply searching for more truth in your life, knowing that Columbus couldn't have possibly discovered something that was already found, or it's to the point where you can't even see the purpose of getting out of bed most days, know that you are exactly where you're meant to be on your journey.

As much as I want to reach through these pages with my strong, fourteen inch biceps and love-squeeze you while whispering that everything is going to be okay in the end, we're simply going to have to start here with the words of my story.

And what a story it is...

Note to reader:

At the end of each lesson, you'll find some follow up questions (the f*ucking work) along with a QR code to scan which will take you to a video. My recommendation is to either discuss the questions verbally in a book club, or write down your answers in your own journal. Answering them in passing is a step in the right direction, but to get the full benefit of the work, go beyond that. Don't half-ass them like I would have, lol!

If you have the ebook or print version of this book, mark it up. Use a pen, a highlighter- whatever you need to take notes or highlight parts that resonate with you. They say if you 'think it, ink it'. By writing something down, you have a ten times higher chance of recalling the information and making it "liveable", or a reality. The videos below the questions are my commentary on lived experiences per lesson.

You are worthy of spending time on yourself. We spend most of our life answering questions or fixing shit for others. You are the most important person in your life, and you deserve to work on you.

Lastly, you'll notice there are different fonts throughout the book. If you're like me, you think a lot, so I've used an italicized font to indicate my thoughts. There are sections that are emails directly from clients/fans in the past, a font that indicates writing from my personal, private journal, and a font to indicate a public blog I used to keep.

Above all, I hope you find this worthwhile.

Love,

An insecure overachiever

LESSON 1

YOU DON'T NEED TO PAY INHERITANCE TAX

I entered this screwed-up world, ass-first. This seemingly would prove to be the metaphor for my whole life; doing shit backwards.

Like the champion she is, my mother pushed me out without the help of a c-section, so I could land right on my rear.

At eleven p.m. on a brisk, clear November night, everything seemed to be normal for a healthy baby boy; a screeching mouth bellowed below a thick mop of obsidian black hair atop a solid eight pounds six ounces of stacked, donut-looking limbs. All seemed spot-on, with the small exception of the missing wang that the doctor thought he'd seen in the scans months prior.

Maybe that's why I've always felt that I could never "fit in" or do things the "right" way?

Nonetheless, I wouldn't figure that part out until Lesson 17. So as I tell myself every day, keep showing up.

It was the start of the greatest decade in the history of modern times; The 1980's. The USA was the greatest country in the world and was busy fucking every other country with no lube to prove it. Everyone was obsessed with spandex, corvettes, Top Gun, and snorting cocaine. While working out in neon leg warmers was an obsession taking over the women of America.

"Super Stomachs" by the legendary Joanie Greggains was a household favorite, and of course, I had every crunch and side bend memorized. The Pepto-Bismol pink leotard stretched across her taut frame became my first vision board as I played that VHS tape nearly every day between the ages of seven and nine.

Submerged in layers of repression for a good two decades was the mystery of why I, at seven years old, was so aware of my body and intent on controlling it. There was an obvious explanation of course--in an environment filled with negativity and emotional strife, children internalize and create self-limiting beliefs, which tends to result in future control issues. (Or so I've been told.)

Unfortunately, like so many other people, I was raised in a house with parents who low-key hated each other. Saver vs spender. Light sleeper vs snore-er. Alcoholic vs enabler. The rage played out in constant fights complete with slamming doors, screaming, and broken artifacts. My brother Brian, eight years my senior, was my only safe haven aside from my baby blanket.

Taking off and leaving town after snatching me up as she stormed out was my Mom's way of (not) dealing with her marriage or personal issues. Along with shopping, I was her main source of misplaced happiness; a job I took more seriously than someone my age should, or any child at any age should, really. It was a job I never seemed to do well enough at either. In those days, her attention was almost always divided or completely absent, and her patience severely lacking thanks to whatever substance was her flavour of the month. I could never hold her attention for more than a few seconds unless I had done something wrong like somehow getting the gum I wasn't supposed to have from my mouth into my bangs.

By the time they divorced, my mother's alcoholism was full-blown, yet unknown. No one in the family had a clue of what alcoholism was. Instead of recognizing that she was a sick person who needed to get well, the family saw her as a bad person who needed to get good.

With undiagnosed Lyme disease looming overhead, her hair drastically started to thin and become frail, furthering her already mounting insecurities. And sadly, so were her deep-seated feelings of inadequacy and worthlessness from her father's abandonment when she was an infant. To mask her pain, she coddled any liquid chemical within close reach.

Every time she pulled that strange metal thing with the long, adjustable mechanical arms out from the kitchen drawer, I knew things were quickly about to get sideways. Whether it was a bottle of cabernet getting uncorked, a can of King Cobra getting cracked, or a glass of Bombay gin being poured, like clockwork, the hair on the back of my neck always stood straight up when the booze came out.

And when your mom has different love affairs with Mr. Cabernet, Mr. Cobra, and Mr. Bombay on a nightly basis, it doesn't take long before one parent is serving the other parent with papers.

. . . .

Slightly smaller than our family's previous thirty nine acre, five bedroom house-on-the-hill, our new, post-divorce tiny apartment left little room for me to miss a single beat of my mom's self-sabotaging words and actions.

While she got ready for her date with yet another strange new man, I rehearsed the lyrics from my favourite song off my first cassette tape across the hall. Wearing her three inch bright-yellow pumps on the bottom, and over-sized frizzy espresso wig on the top, I noticed how much nicer my legs looked in heels as I stood in front of her flimsy, wall-mounted full-length mirror.

After several attempts at nailing a difficult line from "Bust A Move" by Young M.C., I stopped listening to my voice and tuned into hers. Forgetting about my potential future as the first white girl rapper, I started towards the bathroom to watch her apply her makeup while she loudly cursed the bags under her eyes. It seemed that my mom's goal of trying to like what she saw in her reflection was now going to be my very own.

Wondering if I would ever be as brave as her, I watched in awe while she twirled a pencil eyeliner directly in the flame of her lime green Bic lighter. Like she was blowing out a birthday candle, my mom exhaled forcefully on the stick before pulling down her eyelid and applied a thick line without a single flinch or a blink.

"Do you put that black stuff on your eyes to hide the bags, Mom?" I asked.

Patiently waiting for an answer and not getting a reply, I kept the conversation going to avoid the deafening silence.

"I don't see bags, Mom."

More silence.

"Mom, what are wrinkles?" I inquired again as she squeezed the white bottle of Afrin up her nose. Knowing that she always gave two pumps, I waited patiently for her to reply.

"Mom?"

"Yes, Kortney Kay!" she abruptly interjected. "I'm trying to make myself look presentable for my date! Speaking of, I might be back late, so don't wait up, ok?"

"Can I come?" I asked sarcastically, already knowing the answer.

"They don't allow 10-year-olds in the bar, toots," she replied with a smirk.

. . . .

During this less than fabulous time, I started the fifth grade. I arrived at my new school just in time to discover how shitty kids can be towards each other at that age. Unlike my old school where my aunt and uncle were both teachers, surrounded by friends that were so close I thought they were my actual cousins, I was now the "new girl". The boys in class called me Sasquatch for my hairy arms, legs, and upper lip, and Dorkney for wearing glasses, but it was overhearing teachers referring to me as "chunky" or "husky" that really hit the hardest during that awkward-as-fuck time.

I joined the swim team in hopes of losing weight, but felt so disgusting in my bathing suit that I could hardly bring myself to leave the locker room inside the community center. Between being deathly afraid of the black lines and open drains at the bottom of the pool (psa: don't allow your children to watch horror movies), along with the disgust I felt from the sight of my own body, every day after school turned into an overwhelming sense of anxiousness that made my skin crawl.

After a few short months of not seeing my body shrink, I decided to secede and called my mom to the rescue. While gripping my side and dragging my foot as if I'd just been shot in the leg, I put on my best performance, proving to myself that I was an exceptional liar as the coach excused me from practice. After pulling my comforting genie pants (think MC Hammer) over my suit, I found my way to the front office and bashfully asked if I could use the phone to call my mom. After pleading my case of illness, I hung up the phone with a brief sense of relief as I headed outside in the sunshine to wait for her to take me far away from the place I deeply loathed.

As I slid into the passenger seat without saying a word, I was met with a familiar look of aggravation.

"Kortney Kay, you probably just have gas!" she touted annoyingly. Not replying with my usual cheerful energy, we rode along in silence for several minutes. Shifting between first and second gear of her Suzukii Swift, she looked over at me and realised I wasn't in a good way. "How about we have Taco Bell for dinner, then swing by the store and get you a razor and some shaving gel?" she said with enthusiasm. The thought of a seven-layer burrito and hairless legs temporarily brought a smile to my face as I sheepishly shifted my body away from the window.

Following one year in a new school and a new town, one of my mom's new dates appeared to go further than just second base. After a whirlwind romance mostly in the Garberville Blue Room Bar, the laidback dope grower and my mom were madly in love just a few short months later. Faced with the prospect of having a two-hour bus ride after a half hour drive to the bus stop, I gladly supported my dad's demand to my mom, and moved north instead of south to the booming metropolis of Eureka, California. Along with his new girlfriend came two older boys and a girl, who was exactly one grade ahead of me, leading to our being thrust together as reluctant roommates.

Like Groundhog Day, I was back in unfamiliar territory without a map, a compass, or a bra. My dad had been living with his new girlfriend for about a year when I became a part of the new family unit. Due to a 7.2 earthquake that had nearly burned the town down a few months back, along with my own familiar negative self-talk and a blackout-drunk mom, I was a hot mess of curdled up, toxic anxiety. Unfortunately, my soon-to-be-stepsister, with her perky, giant breasts and junior sized waist, was only adding to my already endless cesspool of issues.

. . . .

A potential tipping point for my upcoming behaviour, came as a result of the dreaded "back to school shopping". Prior to the year starting, I reluctantly chose cheerleading as my new athletic endeavor after a couple of neighborhood girls talked me into it. As usual, I took note that my legs were much larger, and boobs way smaller than theirs. Fronting like I was a prude as opposed to being mortified by the sight of my legs, they convinced me that the skirt was just above my knees and wouldn't show too much skin. Living within a two-block radius, the three of us became fast friends.

A month quickly passed, and it was time to shop. Thanks to my new friends, I knew that the "in-kids" were wearing Bongo jeans and Vans shoes. Feeling like a third wheel on a bicycle , I jumped in the back seat and set out to the mall with high hopes along with my stepmom and her daughter. After an hour of roaming around several department stores and coming up empty handed while my stepsister scored several cute outfits, I was losing the will to live. As I felt my feet start to throb, I happened to catch a Bongo neon sign mounted on the wall above a section across the way.

"I'll be right back!" I shouted to the other two as I darted off towards it. Like a sugar-addicted kid in a candy store, I excitedly ran up to the rack and started skimming through the hangers for what I knew to be the biggest size in juniors; size thirteen. After looking through every turquoise, black, and white pair with nothing bigger than a nine, I moved onto the last, least desirable color--a fire engine red--where I finally found the lucky number.

After sprinting to the dressing room, I was brimming with hope. "Just one item?" asked the middle-aged attendant. I nodded as she handed me a piece of plastic engraved with the number "1" on it.

"Let me know if you need help finding another size or if you have any questions," she said as I thanked her and bolted off into the first open dressing room. Harnessing a ton of pent up energy, I accidentally slammed the door shut before I shucked off my sneakers without bothering to undo the laces. I hastily pulled my baggy Aladdin-style cotton pants down and nearly lost my balance as my glasses flew off my face. As I grabbed for the wall to catch myself, I caught a glimpse of my Michelin-Man marshmallow legs jiggling in the mirror. As a wave of disgust shuddered in my stomach, I looked back at the glaring red button-up jeans as I picked up my glasses and pressed on.

After unclipping them from the hanger, I noticed the waist looked remarkably small for a size thirteen, but felt certain that the legs would surely fit. I stepped one foot in and pulled them up to my knee before it quickly became apparent the pants were going no higher. I immediately felt a familiar sinking sense of dread start to impale me. Determined to dress like my new friends, I stepped my other foot inside and proceeded to pull upwards like my life depended on it. For a split second I felt hopeful, until suddenly, the pulling came to a screeching halt like the brakes on my mom's car would when she'd had too much to drink.

Gutted that they hadn't even made it to my hips, I tried one last aggressive pull as I held my breath before the sound of ripping started to emerge from the belt loops. With uncontrollable frustration and sadness, I blankly stared at the oozing reflection of fat spilling over the top of the stiff jeans which were now stuck a solid three inches above my knees. My cheeks, now the same color as the pants, burned in anger as I ripped them off and flung them at the back of the door with my foot. While I stood in the mirror with more disgust than an Englishman watching an American pour non-fat milk into a cup of tea before adding the bag, I could hear my mom's voice in my head, lamenting the fluorescent glare that made everyone look their worst in dressing rooms.

Bending down and pinching a supple chunk of flesh above my right knee, I tried to tell myself it was just the lighting, but who was I kidding? I was a disgusting, fat shit that would never own a pair of jeans as cool as these. Trying my best to not cry, I quickly got my baggy cotton pants on after meticulously hanging up the jeans to look exactly as I found them on the rack.

"How'd they fit?" the same lady asked as I handed the pants back.

"Not a massive fan," I said bashfully, knowing full well that I was lying through my teeth.

"Well, thank you for hanging them back up so perfectly! No one ever does that," she remarked in amazement.

"My mom trained me to do that!" I replied as I forgot about my misery for a split second and basked in her praise.

"Have a great day!" I said as I headed back out to find my new family and continue my self-loathing.

. . . .

Some time not long after the pernicious Bongo jeans event, I had yet another blow that sent me cascading down a mountain of disdain.

I hadn't seen my mom in what seemed like months and I hadn't been back to Southern Humboldt to see all my old friends and family for what seemed like years. It was that time of year for the Garberville Rodeo, which my cousins had asked if I could come down and attend with them. I wasn't a cowgirl and didn't know much of anything about ranch life, other than how to sit on a horse while it stood still.

Halfway to Garberville my mom asked if I'd packed my "rodeo outfit". As soon as those words rolled out of her mouth, I was reminded of the treacherous day she "surprised me" with hideous matching outfits. Cotton-candy pink boots perfectly aligned with the horrific sky-blue and pink paisley patterned panels of a jean jacket with matching pants. To celebrate our new "two-person family" post divorce, we were off to get a new family portrait with our match-game on strong.

It wasn't that I could hardly squeeze into the outfit that was

26

upsetting.

It wasn't even the completely unflattering position of sitting side-saddle on a childish horse statue that bothered me.

It was simply that my mom was annihilated, and I was still in shock.

"It doesn't fit anymore, Mom."

"That's a shame. What about the boots?"

"I didn't even think about them," I lied. I had immediately thought about throwing them away when I couldn't get them over my calves.

"Kortney Kay!" she exclaimed in that familiar tone of disappointment. The use of my middle name almost always meant I was failing.

"Those were really expensive!"

I knew they were expensive; it was why I had held onto them and that stupid outfit which was meticulously folded and set up on a shelf in my closet, despite it being a visceral reminder of the worst year of my life due to the divorce and subsequent move. I felt like a terrible daughter once again.

"Well, what are you going to wear to the rodeo?"

"I don't know," I replied defensively. "I hadn't really thought about it," I lied again.

The truth is, I had thought about it. I thought about it for several days leading up to that day. I thought about it while I lay in bed the night before. And I thought about it while I stuffed a pair of sweatpants and a baggy t-shirt in my backpack earlier that morning.

"I wish you would have thought of this before we got halfway to Garberville. Maybe your Aunt has something you can wear."

Sinking down into my seat, I could feel the springs poke through the vinyl and into the back of my fat legs every time we went over a bump.

Before I knew it, my mom was dropping me off. It had been over a year since I'd seen my cousins. I had spent a lot of time with various relatives when I was younger due to my parents working forty five minutes out of town. Some were actual aunts, uncles, and cousins, and some were just called that. My aunt was actually my mom's cousin, making her three daughters my cousins-once-removed. And of course, all of them, including my aunt, were relatively slender females.

Just like when we were younger, I was excited to stay over until such a point that I ran out of clothes or found myself hungry. When you grow up in the country surrounded by rivers, mountains, horses, ATVs, treehouses and forts, you tend to grow up dirty and often need a change of clothes. Not to mention, certainly always hungry. Regardless of how hard I tried to not get the dirtiest, I always ended up playing the hardest, then regretting it when I couldn't fit my legs into any of my cousins' clothes, neither girl or boy, child or adult. And when it came time to eat, more often than not, I'd feel ashamed to ask for food and say I wasn't hungry, only to end up sneaking crusts off their plates when no one was looking.

The night before the rodeo though, we all ate pizza while watching a movie, and no one's crust needed sneaking--I ate more than my fill. As I drifted off to sleep with a full belly, my eldest cousin dared me to enter the sheep-riding contest the next day.

"I never turn down a dare," I mumbled before fading into a food coma.

The next day, when it was time to head to the rodeo, everyone looked the part: from Wrangler jeans and Western-style brush popper shirts, right down to oversized belt buckles and cowboy hats. I was, as usual, the only oddball, still sporting my Aladdin pants.

"Do you want me to look through our closet and see if Uncle Sam or I have something you could wear?" my aunt asked.

"I'm fine wearing this!" I lied as the shame seeped through my skin.

"I can't believe she included Uncle Sam in that sentence. He probably weighs two hundred pounds and is over six feet tall. I must be an elephant," I thought.

At that moment my cousin conveniently reminded everyone, myself included, that I had promised to enter the sheep riding contest. Realising I didn't have money to pay the entry fee, I thought I might get out of it until, of course, my aunt cheerfully volunteered to cover it.

"Ok, then! Better get the camera ready for when I take home the hundred dollar cash prize for staying on the longest!" I touted confidently, yet full of shit. It seemed like with every sentence that came out of my mouth I grew more and more successful at lying. I internally gave myself a pep talk the entire thirty minute drive there, convincing myself that it couldn't be that hard. I had a donkey and a horse (with a sway back); how hard could it be to stay sitting on a sheep? By the time the sheep riding competition started, I was ravenous, but didn't have any money to buy food and was, per usual, too bashful to ask. I didn't want to be a burden since my aunt was already paying for me to enter, plus I thought I should avoid eating given that I apparently looked like I could fit in my uncle Sam's clothes.

I stood in line--the lone ranger in Aladdin pants--with all the boys in their Western gear, and watched my aunt and cousin walk off towards the bleachers. Holding our stack of registration and hold-harmless waivers, the young man in charge started shouting instructions at us as he checked for signatures.

"Ok, boys, listen up!" he shouted without looking up from the stack. "Riding a sheep ain't easy. You're gonna need to use all your leg strength to hold onto 'em. We'll lower you down onto the sheep's back, but it's gonna start thrashing around the second you touch it, so be ready. Once you get bucked off, hurry your ass up and walk to the side of the fence you're closest to."

Figuring I'd have someone to watch first, I nodded with confidence. As the young man took a breath and looked up from the stack of papers, he noticed me, and exclaimed, "Please excuse me! Boys and GIRL!" followed gallantly by, "Well, I guess you can go first young lady!" in a tone like he was doing me a favor. As I felt a lump forming in my throat, I considered withdrawing but couldn't stand the thought of chickening out.

"Those legs should be able to help you out there, Miss!" he said with a nod of approval, as he spit out his chew. With a smidgen of renewed hope, I semi-confidently put on the gloves and helmet. Feeling proud for not running off and giving any of those boys the chance to laugh, I walked up the ramp with my head held high.

Just as two men were about to lower me down onto the sheep, the guy who'd just as quickly filled me with hope, deflated my spirit, "Ahhhh, too bad you don't have jeans on though! Good luck!" Faster than the blink of an eye, I was sitting on a giant, pissed-off sheep with my hands latched onto the rope tied around its neck as it thrashed around like a wild beast that belonged to Satan. Adrenaline flooded my veins, and the next thing I knew it was over as my tailbone collided with the rock-hard ground. It felt like The Hulk had thrown a flying dragon punch with his knotted-up gargantuan green fist straight into my stomach.

Once I realised I couldn't get a sip of air into my lungs, I started to panic. Faster than my ride on that sheep, I started coughing uncontrollably, gasping on the dust filled air as I doubled over in pain. After getting past the shock, I stumbled over to the fence and looked up at a sea of Coors Light cans and laughing faces. Over the loudspeaker a voice echoed throughout the arena, "Give her a round of applause, ladies and gentlemen, Kortney Olson with one point two seconds!"

If I'd been wearing jeans, I would have at least made it to two seconds, I thought, as my eldest cousin came running up in a full-fledged laughing fit.

By the time my mom came to pick me up later that night, I was brimming with rage. I felt like I didn't belong anywhere- I never had the right clothes, the right body or the right skills to be someone— or anyone.

"It sounds like you all had fun!" she said, clearly not picking up on my vibe.

"Yeah, total blast," I uttered sarcastically.

"Before we drive up the hill, I want to stop and tan."

As we drove to the gym where the tanning beds were, I kept replaying every scene in my head from the last twenty four hours. From the springs digging into the back of my thighs, to eating too much pizza, to flying off the sheep and having to go first, to not fitting into any jeans, ever, the negative self-talk was screaming inside me. As we pulled into the parking lot, a flood of memories came rushing in from happier times when I used to take jazz dance class, before I was too horrified by my own existence to wear skin-tight clothing.

As we walked in, my mom and the woman behind the desk

enthusiastically said their hellos and exchanged small talk.

"Pam, you remember Kortney!"

"Oh, my heavens, how could I forget the sweetest girl in the world? I almost didn't recognise her though as she's gotten SO big!" Pam exclaimed with a robust tone and giant bouncing tits as she flailed her arms through the air.

"Gosh, it's been four years I think?" she said as she handed my mom two pairs of goggles.

"Nice to see you, Pam," I said as I tried to shake the fact that yet once again someone noticed how big I had gotten.

"You don't remember Pam whatsoever, do you?" my mom asked after we were both behind the closed door of tanning bed number one.

Momentarily forgetting about my sore tailbone, "Not at all," I replied as I plopped down on the hard, white plastic chair.

As she stripped down, I sorted through the pile of worn out magazines on the table next to the chair.

"I really need to get back on the wagon; Marcus and I have been eating so much with all the traveling we've been doing," she said between lathering various parts of her body in tanning lotion. After hitting the start button, she handed me a pair of goggles before crawling into the glowing tube.

"I'm not putting these on."

"It's the law, Kortney Kay! You need to protect your eyes!" she said.

"Yeah, well you never wear them, so why should I?" I replied defiantly.

"Because my eyes are already bad, and because I said so!" she said in her demanding, always right tone.

Taking the goggles out of her hand, I watched her shut the top of the machine as I kept the goggles secured around my forehead. I had plucked out the Vogue magazine from the pile and started flipping through the pages when suddenly something commanded my attention. That was the first time I ever saw her. A black and white photograph of a woman who looked nothing like Cindy or Claudia or any of the rest of them with their glowing tans and giant boobs and hair.

This woman stood on one leg like a frail, yet independently strong flamingo with the foot of her bent leg in the palm of her hand. Her cheekbones and hip bones were so deep cut that they were casting shadows. The strings of her black underwear and tank top were like fettuccine noodles, resting lightly on her pale, narrow hips and shoulders. Underneath her were the words: Calvin Klein Underwear.

With her head tipped to the left, her gaze materialised as a sense of living as both Batman and the Joker in one body. She was both the hero and the villain. She was tiny, but larger than life. As my mom lay encased in her humming, infrared cocoon, I painfully stood up and pulled off my dusty shirt and crusty pants to compare my reflection to that of this pristine, flawless woman staring back at me from inside of the magazine. As polar opposites as George W Bush Jr and Ellen DeGeneres at a baseball game together, I knew that Kate Moss and I were like Beauty and The Beast.

Despite knowing I could never look like her, I was ready to die trying.

Most of us have at least one parent that is unknowingly struggling with some kind of inner demon. Whether you're like me and have an alcoholic parent who is unaware that they're an alcoholic, or you have a parent who was physically abused by their parent, or you have a parent who grew up in poverty, thus carrying around the mindset of scarcity, it is absolutely up to us to divorce ourselves from our parent or guardian's reality and build our own.

My stepmom used to tell me growing up, "you need to be your own best parent". It never really made sense until I hit my late twenties. But ultimately I've come to realize that I need to care for myself in the way that I'd care for my delicate, innocent adolescent self. Our parents have done the best they could with the tools they've been given, and it's our responsibility to break the cycle of hurt. My mom and I are best friends today. It took time to get to a place where I could acknowledge and accept that she was dealing with her own pain unknowingly.

And that pain doesn't have to be my pain--nor does it have to be yours. We're plenty good at creating our own pain, so there's no sense in adding our parents' into the mix.

Do the F*cking Work

As I mentioned in the intro, I hate being told I *have* to do something. So, think of this 'work' as merely a suggestion. It wasn't until I put pen to paper that I started to grow in confidence. These questions are designed to help you build awareness around why you do what you do. I will say this repeatedly throughout this book: *You are worth the time and energy.*

A lot of us haven't been taught the importance of childhood development. Shit like Bowlby's attachment theory and dysfunctional family roles and the Adverse Childhood Experiences study should be taught in high school.

Whether you grew up without your basic needs not being met like food, shelter, and security, or you had a picture-perfect childhood, what experiences have you had that may have had an impact on your adult life?

What types of things did your parents say in front of you that potentially had an impact on your life?

What things didn't they say?

Until my hair started thinning and falling out after my Graves disease diagnosis, I didn't realise how much losing my hair initially impacted my self-esteem. I eventually shaved that shit off and accepted it, but it wasn't until I experienced it myself that I realised how much it would have impacted my mom's self-esteem.

What might your parent(s) have experienced in childhood (or as young adults) that they've still not dealt with that has had an impact on you?

In what ways have your parent's contributed to your current

belief systems?

In what ways have they not?

It is said that alcoholism and addiction can be linked to genetic and hereditary predispositions (nature) as well as learned behavior (nurture).

Is there anyone in your family that can't handle their drinking?

Is there anyone younger that you could potentially help prevent from developing the dis-ease of addiction? (I personally break the word disease down into the two words of 'dis' and 'ease', which translates to 'the opposite of ease'. That way, I don't associate the word to some kind of death sentence.)

Scan here for more good shit.

WHY YOU CAN'T RENT A CAR UNDER THE AGE OF 21

*A*s far as most people were concerned, I appeared to be soaring now that I was in Junior High; I was the class President, I played sports, I had straight A's, and I thought I played the sax better than Bill Clinton. But on the inside, as with most mental illnesses, I was a percolating mess of unacknowledged darkness. After my parents' divorce and the earthquake, my anxiety progressively grew from a nervous tick of blinking ultra hard, to uncontrollable movements and counting calories. It wasn't until I was in my late twenties that I realised how screwed up I was.

It was a special day which required special documentation. With their brand new thirty pound camcorder, my dad and stepmom attended our band performance at the school assembly. However, they weren't there to film me. They were there to film my stepsister's classmate, Sara Bareilles, belting out her rendition of the hottest love track of the nineties by Exposé'. As Sara swayed back and forth in her pegged light-blue denim jeans, white scooped neck t-shirt, and grey unbuttoned vest, I sat directly behind her doing anything but sitting still. Fidgeting while holding my baritone sax, it appeared as though I'd been smoking meth since the third grade.

Scan to see my cringe-worthy performance here:

Although I had settled in with my new family and was no longer an outsider, by the time I finished my freshman year of high school, I was so disgusted with my enormous legs, I wanted to cut them off. It seemed as though everything improved with the exception of my body image. Carrying on with my facade of being content and going places, I opened the refrigerator door one summer afternoon to get a drink. Every morning during the school year, my dad would wake me up with a glass of orange juice in my face while he cheerfully sang one of his made-up jingles. It was a delightful way to open my eyes until I discovered the seemingly harmless caloric trap.

As I scanned the shelves surveying my options, I bathed in the chilled air wafting out from the fridge. It was an unusually hot day for Eureka, and as usual, I had sweatpants on. Landing on the economy sized Costco cranberry juice, I ripped the gallon jug off the bottom shelf and slammed the door shut as I considered drinking straight from the bottle. Knowing my stepmom was lurking around, I took a small glass out of the cupboard and poured the juice up to the brim and slammed it back. With the refreshing bitter-sweet tang still on the back of my tongue, I poured another glass.

Right before placing the rectangular bottle back on the shelf, my inner dialogue urged me to read the nutritional label. Up until that day, it had never occurred to me that liquid contained calories. After scanning the top line in bold font, I instantly felt the nerves in my lower legs tingle. Similar to that moment when you wake up in a panic thinking you missed an alarm for your first day at a new job, I was consumed with an overwhelming sensation of fear and anger. Slamming the door shut, I headed to the bathroom to expel the toxic juice without a single thought of repercussion..

Throughout my sophomore and junior year, I continued to trudge the road of typical teenage life, with the exception of my disordered eating. By the middle of my junior year, one of my best friends, Adrianna, started to become overly concerned about my purging. I'd upped my game from heavily restricting calories to now sticking my finger down my throat. Narcing me out to the terrifying Dean of Students, Mr Hayley, I was confronted with the option of either having my parents called in about my "vomiting", or seeing a therapist. Surprisingly, after just two visits, I had built up enough awareness to realise that my actions were ineffective and a waste of time. The only thing I was truly accomplishing with purging was rotting a hole in my esophagus and decaying my teeth.

Although the short-lived therapy stopped me from developing severe bulimia and any further mouth rot, the root cause of my body image was never addressed. Unaware, I was about to find a new way to destroy my dental health *and* mental health.

. . . .

At sixteen, my senior year started out great, or so I thought. The end of my junior year I had won the nomination for the Associated Student Body President (again), had been awarded the prestigious 'Ms. Cool' award for my class (whatever that meant), and was playing gigs alongside my fellow Christian-rock band members. On track to slay my impressive short list of University admissions, chasing after my dream of becoming the first female President of the United

States, I had everything going for me except a crippling body image that even Jesus couldn't fix.

Ironically, everything changed the night of the Sadie Hawkins dance. Unknowingly, the purpose of this day (according to Google) is to empower women to take control of their lives. Evidently, encouraging girls to take charge and pick their date for a dance is the first step to controlling their destiny. From successfully training myself to pee standing up from a young age, to being the school DJ, I wanted to do, be, and say everything my older brother did. Maybe had I attended the dance with the date that I picked, instead of making the dance happen as the DJ, things would have turned out differently.

As "Stairway to Heaven" blared through the auditorium while pastel paper streamers waived aimlessly above, I started organising my CDs back into their respective cases to try and get a head start at packing up. I needed to join my friends at Adrianna's parent-free house after the dance for our first party as seniors. Feeling proud of my ability to press play on a CD player, I loaded up the last speaker into the back of my Honda Accord hatchback and headed to the party we had been planning for weeks. Up until this point, I hadn't done *that* much partying.

There was the first bottle of beer that me and three other classmates had snuck into the Garberville theatre in the fourth grade.

There was the first actual drink at twelve, thanks to my cousin's fake ID and Jack Daniels.

There was the six-pack of beer I had a couple of sips from thanks to a group of boys over the age of twenty one who had bought me and my other twelve year old friends to try and get into our pants.

There was the one Reggae on the River festival in Benbow where I'd eaten mushrooms and followed some guy around the river bar for over four hours because he was wearing only one shoe.

There was the one time I took two bong rips with my stepsister down the street at our neighbours' and thought I was going to die.

There were a handful of dances where I got *slightly* drunk.

And there was the *one* party I tagged along to with my stepsister the summer before my senior year. After joining in on snorting some kind of powder, I was compelled to talk to everyone and somehow managed to drink three overflowing red dixie cups from a keg without ever feeling buzzed.

But I digress.

Surprised to only see a few cars parked outside, I rolled up the driveway in neutral and pulled the e-brake before hopping out. Still on a natural high from earlier, I was imagining all of my friends loudly listening to 2-Pac while sloppily playing drinking games inside as I walked in the dark towards the house. Without knocking, I turned the chipped brass door handle and walked in to find a vacant living room. As I looked around wondering where the hell everyone was, I faintly heard voices out on the back patio.

Ignoring the small knot forming in my stomach, I slid the screen door open and walked through it onto the dimly lit patio. At the end of the house, in the back corner about twenty feet away, sat six of my friends, including my stepsister, under a motion sensor light. As I walked towards them, I could see everyone had a near-full bottle of beer along with a few glowing cigarettes as they sat in various lawn chairs.

"What's up y'all! Where's everyone else?" I asked as I looked around. Everyone was semi in the dark except for my best friend Adrianna, who was seated directly in the beam of the spotlight.

Through what felt like forced words, "Hey, Kort," Adrianna

replied timidly.

Feeling the intense awkward energy, I noticed something odd about her as I stared back. Realising Adrianna's eyes looked like she'd just left the ophthalmologist after having that shitty yellow dye dropped in each socket, I immediately knew that something was odd. Her vibrant jungle-green eyes were literally pitch black.

"Your eyes look like dinner plates," I remarked as I looked around at the rest of my friends.

As if I was in some kind of gang initiation, Becca, the future lawyer and most likely to be crowned Prom Queen, held up a glass pipe. "Plan's changed!" she said.

"What is it?" I asked.

"It's speed," she replied confidently.

As I stood there trying to think about what to say, I flashed back to all of those times I recalled Nancy Reagan crowing, "Just say no!" I vaguely remembered learning about the risks of this drug in the sixth grade during DARE (Drug Abuse Resistance Education) class after seeing a woman's sunken-in face, but was too preoccupied with the bad boy Jim Tizdale who got suspended from school for drinking Scope mouthwash.

Interrupting me, my sister stepped in with the assist, "You've done it before, Kort- you're not going to turn into a homeless derelict or anything."

Reading the puzzled look on my face, "At Jim's party last Summer, remember?" she said.

"I thought that was coke?" I replied as I looked around for a chair to sit on while simultaneously imagining what would happen if I just ran to my car. Feeling more uncomfortable than swallowing a moldy blueberry, I took the glass pipe out of Becca's hand and said, "Now what?"

. . . .

Discovering how much speed crushed my appetite, it only took a few months before I was using it on a regular basis. Proving myself to be resourceful, I managed to find a boyfriend who 'just so happened' to deal my drug of choice. I spent the entire rest of the year staying up for days on end. Instead of sleeping, I stayed up and aimlessly drew stars on lined paper until the sun came up.

One day after school, I found myself back in the same bathroom where I'd broken up with the cranberry juice. I'd upgraded the efficiency of my weight loss attempts, and this time instead of purging, I was trying to figure out how to clean my meth pipe after watching an experienced tweaker effortlessly do what I was about to attempt. After locking the door, I set my clean clothes on the floor, pulled a bottle of rubbing alcohol out of the cupboard, and turned on the shower for background noise. Living in a house with only two bathrooms, one of which was in my parents' bedroom and off limits, meant you had to be clever. Pulling out an empty can of Coke I'd purposely thrown into the trash the night before, I ripped the metal ring off and set it upside down on the laminate forest-green countertop next to my pipe.

After painstakingly pouring the rubbing alcohol in the concavity of the upside-down coke can, I hurriedly set the capless bottle down and proceeded to light the alcohol on fire with a match. Twirling my pipe around in the flame and causing the outside of it to be completely charred with black soot, I pulled the pipe out of the fire and proceeded to blow on it to cool the glass down. In the process of blowing and in typical Kort fashion, I managed to knock the can over and tipped the flaming alcohol out onto the countertop.

Driven by a brain working off three consecutive nights of no sleep, I was petrified I was about to burn the counter and couldn't think of a single excuse as to why I would be in the bathroom lighting shit on fire.Hastily reaching out to pick up the can, I managed to also knock the bottle of rubbing alcohol over. As I watched my freedom flash before my eyes, the flame connected to the fresh reserve of alcohol and continued to burn as it happened to stop short of the extra roll of toilet paper sitting on the edge of the counter. Still holding onto my pipe, I ripped the hand towel off the wall at full tilt and shoved it under the running shower head before tossing it over the flames.

As I caught my breath and waited for my already rapid heart rate to slow, I anticipated how bad the damage was going to be. Feeling like I was about to peel a Band-Aid off the tip of my finger that had been cut with dull scissors, I lifted the towel to find nothing was burned. I had narrowly escaped having to come up with the greatest story of the century. For a fleeting second, I considered perhaps my new lifestyle wasn't worth the weight loss until I took a fresh piece of toilet paper and freely wiped the soot from the pipe. I couldn't believe it had worked! It was like the soul of a drug addict-- a brand-new piece of clear glass beckoning to be dirtied.

I quickly smoked a bowl, turned off the shower, changed my clothes, splashed some water on my face, and headed off to pick up some more speed.

The next day at school turned out to be another Groundhog Day. This time it wasn't the tipped-off, brazen Mr. Hayley who had something to say, it was every-girl's-teacher-crush, Mr. Brizach.

After an hour of excruciating effort to keep my eyes open, the bell rang. Walking down the hallway to my locker, I felt a hand firmly grab me by the back of my shoulder and spin me around. Staring at me intently With his blue eyes that resembled the color of the diamond emoji, Mr. Brizach stared at me intently before sternly saying, "Ok, Kortney- don't bullshit me."

Catching me off guard, I replied in a tone that resembled a pubescent teenage boy with the world's worst cottonmouth, "Wha-what do you mean, coach?"

"Come back in the classroom," he demanded as he turned and walked towards his door.

Not only was Brizach the head coach of the baseball team and the upper-class science teacher, he was in charge of overseeing college admissions.

"I'm not stupid. I've closely watched your progress since your freshman year--you might have everyone else fooled, but not me. You sounded like you were talking in tongues at the last assembly, but no one said *shit* because everyone, including your friends, are in denial."

I wasn't sure which was more distracting, the comment he made earlier in class about how everyone looks at their shit before they flush it, or how vigorously my heart was pounding out the side of my neck. Before I could think of anything witty to say, he angrily pushed on.

"You've probably lost, what? Twenty? Thirty pounds since November? People gain weight during the holidays, not lose it. Furthermore, you've completely pissed on your scholarship applications and aren't even paying attention in class!"

Before I knew it, hot tears streamed down my burning cheeks as I felt a sense of surrender rush over me. After a pregnant pause, he asked the first question I'd answer honestly in a long time:

"You either have a deadly drinking problem or you're smoking meth, which is it?"

. . . .

Faced with the same shitty two options of either getting my parents involved or seeing a therapist, I found myself sitting across the desk from a drug counselor whom I'd already become acquainted with. Thanks to his on-campus drug prevention work that sadly hadn't had an impact on me, Mr Evans was shocked to see me.

"Far-out, Kort! I mean, yeah mannnnnnn- I never thought I'd have you of all people sitting in my office, dude!" he said jovially as he leaned back in his chair and kicked his tattered leather boots up on the corner of his desk.

"Yeah me either!" I said, finally feeling relieved that someone else knew about my secret.

"So, what was the catalyst?"

"It was easy to lose weight." I replied pragmatically.

"Well, I'll tell you what--I have the perfect solution. There's this guy, an ex heroin junkie who turned into a Golden Gloves boxing champion that now runs a boxing fitness class up in Arcata," he said.

As I considered the prospect of driving up to Arcata, he went on, "Plus his wife's a nun, so what could go wrong, man!" he said sarcastically.

"What more could I ask for then?" I said, smiling.

We spent the next forty minutes discussing what might trigger me to use again, what lifestyle choices I was going to make to stay safe, and what day I was going to attend my first boxing class. Before leaving, Evans gave me a metallic, mauve colored large coin with a joker embossed on one side and told me to carry that "chip" everywhere I went to remind myself of my decision of wanting to get clean. But wanting and needing are two completely different things. I wanted to get clean and be a good girl, but I needed to be thin and get more done. Need, more often than not, trumps want.

Little did I know I was going to spend the rest of my life collecting these "chips".

With just three days clean, I pulled into the farthest away parking space at the gym where Rob's class was held and switched off the ignition. Despite writing out my triggers just three days earlier, I was listening to the same music we'd listen to when passing around a pipe. Absolutely riddled with fear and anxiety, I managed to get myself out of the car and through the front door of the gym. As I stood behind a few people checking-in ahead of me, I imagined running back out to my Honda and driving straight to a dealer's house to get high.

"Maybe this is the one time not running away will make sense," I thought as someone asked if they could help me from behind the giant oak desk. After putting my information down on a piece of paper for my free week trial, a teenage girl with a face full of braces pointed in the direction of where the class was held. After thanking her, I dragged my feet down the hall and into the aerobics room where a handful of

other people were waiting for this Rob Guss guy to show. Imagining some middle-aged white guy with frizzy, light brown hair that semi resembled Richard Simmons to walk in, I was shocked when Rob suddenly appeared.

I was instantly enchanted with Rob's hip-as-fuck presence and he knew it. Growing up in Humboldt County meant next to zero exposure to Black people. Other than Laotian, Samoan and a handful of Mexicans, Humboldt County was severely lacking in diversity.

I immediately noticed that Rob had some kind of skin pigmentation happening which rendered the sides of his face, along with the tops of his hands, white as my sheets. As Rob began to talk, he scanned the room looking the group over. Once he got to me, he stopped scanning and locked eyes with me.

"Oh-KAY then!" he exclaimed with a level of excitement and enthusiasm that sent shockwaves up my legs.

"We've got a new cat in the building!" he said as he started strutting up to me with fire in his eyes.

"What's your name sugar mama?" he said while leaning on his back leg as if I had just knocked him off his feet.

While absolutely loving the attention, I replied, "Why hello! I'm Kortney with a K."

"Ok then, Miss Kortney--I like what cha workin' with!" he said as he scanned my body from head to toe before finally giving me a wink.

Feeling optimistic while standing at attention, ready to do whatever Rob said, I smiled for the first time in what felt like an eternity. Like getting free parking without shopping, I'd been validated. The teacher's pet, center of attention trap had settled like a freshly poured backyard cement driveway.

We were instructed to get a rope and warm-up. From there, I spent the next hour not thinking about anything other than boxing. I didn't think about what a failure I was. I didn't think about how fat I was. I didn't even think about wanting to get high. I was in the moment, and I felt amazing. Being athletic, I picked up on everything quickly. Being a perfectionist, I was expecting to step in the ring yesterday. I hung on to every word Rob said during that class and worked hard to impress my new mentor. After the class was over and everyone had left, Rob came up to me and said something that would change my life forever.

"Miss Kortney, you did great today. Listen, I want to make you my last prize fighter before I retire. I want to make you a world champion!" he said as he reached out and grabbed my hands with that same wild excitement in his face as when he first made eye contact. In an instant, it was like suddenly everything made sense. All of the pain and misery over the course of my life had led me to this moment. This moment right here was what it was all for! All of the hurt I experienced through childhood. All of the fear of being unlovable because I was fat. All of the time wasted becoming a temporary slave to speed. All of it was for this moment.

"How old are you anyway, Miss Kortney?" Rob asked.

"I'm seventeen!" I replied.

Not looking phased, "Well, I might be seventy two but I feel twenty one." Rob replied.

"Well I hope I feel like that when I'm seventy two! Plus, you don't look a day over forty," I said with a smirk.

While wetting his lips, Bob replied, "Look here juicy--after class next week, you can come by my joint and we'll review some videos of past fights and order you some proper equipment. You dig?"

"OK! Where do I sign up?" I excitedly replied.

Ironically and almost literally, I dug it like a grave.

. . . .

The week flew by thanks to my newfound purpose of being an aspirational world champion boxer. I rarely found myself thinking about using. Unlike previous attempts to quit where I couldn't make it past a few days without getting high, this felt like a walk in the park. Between school and meeting with Mr. Evans a few times, I shadow boxed my way towards progress.

Class came and despite being trapped in my thoughts over being a worthless fat piece of shit due to gaining some weight back, I worked hard to please Rob. Throughout the hour, Rob was focused on me like a lion stalking its prey, as if I was the only person in class. The attention helped me push through my insecurities and made me feel like I was someone truly special with a divine purpose.

After warming up on the heavy bag, Rob showed us a drill to help instill some basic footwork technique. As all eight of us stood in a line facing him, I couldn't help but marvel at the way he moved around so effortlessly. I wanted what he had so bad. After his demonstration, he walked straight towards me with his eyes on fire again. Before I could turn around as he walked past me, and without warning, Rob grabbed me by the hips and started explaining why it was important to never cross your feet in the sport of boxing.

Right then and there I felt slapped in the face with the fact that Rob wasn't just demonstrating for the class--he simply wanted to show me what it felt like to grab me from behind. I could feel that something wasn't right, but I didn't care. My entire life hadn't been right, and I was finally getting the attention and praise I was searching for. For once, I didn't feel like I was in an A/B conversation and needed to C my way out. I didn't feel like I was a burden. I didn't feel like I was looking for crust because I now owned the busiest pizza parlour in town.

With his groin pressed up against my body, he started pushing my hips towards the wall. Feeling like I was about to fall over, Rob stuck his black Adidas Superstan shoe between my feet, and gently kicked my right foot out in the direction he was pushing my hips, explaining that the left foot was to follow. Like clockwork, he continued to guide me through the entire formation of a box on the floor while reiterating that footwork was everything. Noticing a few of the woman's faces were twisted up, I suddenly felt uncomfortable.

Throughout the remainder of class, I felt a mounting surge of uncertainty about where this was all going, but quickly reassured myself that I was meant to be there. Besides, I was used to this slippery slope. Some people call it flirting and some people call it charisma. But whatever it was, it had never gotten me in trouble thus far. After all, this was my mentor and someone who had single handedly made my entire life make sense and saved me from addiction—or so I thought.

Later that day, completely ignoring the red flags my intuition started waving as I pulled in front of Rob's house, I anxiously got myself out of the car and up to the front door. Hoping Rob's wife was going to answer the door dressed in full nun attire, I knocked in my usual care-free jingle: bom, bom, bom-bom-bom, bom, bom. Seconds after knocking, the redwood door swung open and there stood Rob, now wearing a fresh tracksuit. Catching that familiar look in his eyes, I once again considered running back to my car, yet stood frozen like a windshield in the dead of winter.

Holding a glass of something that smelled more pungent than the flaming rubbing alcohol that almost caught my bathroom on fire, Rob greeted me with his usual enthusiasm.

"Hey baby doll--come here and give me a hug." he said in a slow, hypnotic voice. While he reached his free hand around my waist to pull me inside, he quietly said, "I'm so proud of you," by my ear as he managed to shut the door and not spill anything out of his goblet. As soon as I heard the door shut, his hand dropped from my waist to my ass where he let it rest for a second before whispering in my ear, "That's my champ."

As if my mom had just cracked open a can of King Cobra at seven am, the hair stood up on the back of my neck. Seemingly having lost all ability to use my words, I started to pull backwards after a few seconds.

That should be a clear enough signal that he crossed a line, right? I thought.

Sensing my distaste, Rob acted like everything was fine and pressed on.

"Here honey bear, come sit on the couch while I get this tape on," he said as he took my hand and walked me across the tile floor entryway and into the living room. Motioning for me to sit down on the weathered, brown leather couch, I nervously took his direction and sat down on the edge of the couch. Within seconds, Rob handed me the goblet and said, "Here sweetie, take a sip." As I stared at the glass, I questioned whether or not alcohol was remotely as bad or addictive as speed. The dealers we used to hang around always tried to get us to drink, but we never wanted to mess up our high.

I never had a problem with it previously, and Mr. Evans never asked or talked about it in our sessions. Plus, Rob beat heroin so it must be fine, I thought.

I reached out and gently took the glass out of his hand as if I was handling an explosive that was capable of blowing up if mishandled. As I lifted the cup to my mouth, I could smell the sharpness of something fucking awful. I had tried rum, vodka, gin, and whiskey before, but nothing that smelled as bad as this. Like the good people-pleasing sheep that I was, I took a gulp from the cup anyway while Rob watched with an approving stare.

"Wow!" I shouted after catching my breath. "What is that?" I asked.

"That's Remy, baby! Some straight up gangster shit right there," he said as he gave me that now creepy wink again while wetting his lips. I took another gulp of Remy and instantly felt myself calm down while Rob pushed a VHS tape in the VCR with his white finger. As he walked from the TV over to the couch, he paused at the coffee table and picked up an ashtray that had an unlit joint sitting inside. As I started questioning Rob's role as a mentor, he pulled the joint out and lit it.

I mean, heroin is a really bad drug. If he managed to get off it, and become a professional boxer, plus marry a Nun, I guess he knows best, I thought as I watched him take a long drag off the joint before handing it to me.

Knowing that the one time I smoked pot I thought I was going to die, I decided to just take a tiny hit. As I tried to inhale as soft as possible, I started coughing halfway through. After he stopped laughing, Rob said to go again. After successfully taking a hit, I handed the joint back to Rob as I watched him hit it several times without taking a breath. As he laid back in the opposite corner of the couch with his legs stretched out and a sinister grin on his face, he remarked that the joint came from the ground and that I'd be fine.

As I started coughing again, Rob reached out and grabbed his goblet glass again and handed it to me in what I thought was a gesture of good will, or maybe he was afraid I was going to disturb his wife. I took another pull and handed the glass back to Rob, "Your turn, coach!" After putting his hand up, Rob said, "I poured that for you, champ," as his eyes were halfway shut. Continuing to hit his joint a few more times, I settled back into the couch as I started to feel completely at ease.

"Ok, now let's review this particular fight," Rob said as he reached out and picked up the remote control off the coffee table. After pressing play, he slid over to practically sit in my lap. As he fast-forwarded through the first couple of rounds, I could feel myself start to leave the room on some kind of high I'd never experienced before.

It wasn't anything like mushrooms.

It wasn't anything like speed.

It wasn't anything like the bong rips I'd had before.

And it wasn't anything like being up for three or four nights in a row without a wink of sleep.

With my eyes starting to grow heavy and involuntarily close, I felt my heart start racing as I tried with all my might to lift my eyes back up. Although sitting right next to me, Rob's voice sounded like it was in the far off distance as he talked about the girl in the white trunks advancing in the right way, and how important it was that she got the girl in the red trunks up against the ropes.

The first thing I saw was the dingy, popcorn ceiling in a room that I'd never seen or been in before when I came to laying on my back. I gazed down and noticed my tube top was pulled down around my waist. The next thing that entered into my consciousness was that there was someone, with something, between my legs. Unable to speak or move, I couldn't stop Rob from sloppily kissing my mouth.

Was I kissing him back?

Why couldn't I move?

How the fuck did I get here?

"Does that feel good, champ?" he said in my ear before he pulled himself back up to his haunches. "You really wanted it. I hope it was good," he murmured in a baritone voice as he pulled himself out of me. Just like the discolouration of the sides of his face and his hands, my eyes made contact with the brown spotted dick.

Whether it was adrenaline or Jesus finally showing up, I started moving my toes and fingertips as he started groping my breasts and kissing my neck. The sound of him slurping and sucking on my skin was repulsive.

Fucking say something, champ.

I felt like a blood-curdling scream without a larynx.

With every lingering shroud of will power in my body, I opened my mouth and pushed out the words, "I have to go!" as I shoved him back with my feet and arms with all the might I could muster. Rob sat back on his butt and said, "OK, baby---you sure you're OK to drive?" I'd already had my shirt pulled on and was nearly done pulling my sweats back on. "I'm fine," I murmured as I thought about looking for my underwear, but couldn't spend an extra second in his presence. In a blur, I grabbed my bag and stumbled out the front door in a state of absolute and utter confusion, rage, disgust and regret.

He never pleaded with me to not tell anyone what happened as I was leaving, and he never once tried calling in the three weeks that followed when I didn't show up for class.

It was clearly my fault.

I drank too much.

I led him on.

I passed out.

And there I was.

And here I am.

Somewhere I didn't want to be, inside someone's skin I couldn't stand.

. . . .

In a lot of states, you can't even rent a car before the age of twenty five, let alone before the age of twenty one. The simple reason is because our brains aren't fully developed until twenty five. The decisions we make before that age can often come at a price, such as deciding that going to Rob's house for some one on one time was a good idea. Without stopping to reflect back on what decisions we've made as young people, we'll unknowingly often carry a sense of blame towards ourselves forward into adulthood.

It took me almost a decade before I could say his name without crying. After watching a video of a demonstration conducted by a pastor using a hundred dollar bill, I came to realise that my value has never changed despite the situations I've found myself in. No matter what we've experienced, our value never diminishes.

Do the F*cking Work

What types of things did you do as a kid that could have been warning signs that you had control issues? (I forgot that I used to rearrange the household furniture, on top of my bedroom set-up, on an almost monthly basis, driving my step mom crazy.)

Trauma can come in many forms, with those who inflict or incite the experience often telling you (or making you feel) that it's somehow your fault it's happened in the first place. (aka gaslighting)

What trauma have you experienced in your life that you've brushed off as "not a big deal"?

Are you aware of your 'gut feelings'?

If so, do you ignore red flags?

Why do you think that is and what can you do to change that behavior?

In what ways do you crave validation from others?

Where do you think it comes from?

Scan here for more good shit.

LESSON 3

LET YOUR ALTER EGO PROTECT YOU LONG ENOUGH TO PREVENT YOUR UNTIMELY DEATH

I'd firmly cemented the belief that everything was my fault. Still white-knuckling the pipe dream of being a world champion boxer, I miraculously made it through the longest three weeks of my life without picking up an actual pipe. Figuring waves of embarrassment, remorse, and guilt were easier to deal with than the potential of being a strung-out meth-head for the rest of my life, I shamefully showed my face in class after the hiatus.

Assuming he'd just rape and reign on like nothing happened, Rob was delightfully startled when I slouched through the glass door. As if it was just spoken into existence without words, he knew I would never be alone with him again, however, it didn't stop him from trying to grab a handful of ass or sneak one of his repulsive, slimy kisses in when no one was looking. Every time he managed to make contact, I froze. But the more I backed away from his advances, the more he stopped showing interest in turning me into his champ. Although I did learn (poorly) how to hit a speed bag, jump rope, and throw some combinations, the only thing I was *actually* mastering was the art of harbouring a festering, trauma-based resentment.

Months prior to graduating I decided that Sonoma State University was my best option. This would allow me to be with my best friend and accomplice Adrianna. After taking a scholarship sponsored trip where I visited Washington D.C. and met Diane Feinstein, I told my parents that a degree in political science just wasn't for me. Whether the sour taste in my mouth was from coming down from the drugs during the entire three day trip, or watching a homeless drug addict shit in the corner of the subway station under the Capitol, I knew I'd gotten off track and needed to find a new train to board.

Knowing my future was holding anything but bouncy, thick gorgeous hair, I decided that I needed a fresh start before my new life at college in Rohnert Park, California began. The disgust of gaining weight, along with the thought of Rob, could easily be brushed away like my baby fine hair with a simple visit to the hair salon. After returning from my D.C. trip, I decided that bleaching my hair would potentially help me get further in life. Sadly, my new look resembled Ronald McDonald more than Kate Moss, leaving my hair looking, and feeling how I was inside--dead.

In my normal fashion of doing things in reverse order, I needed my hair fixed yesterday and was due to leave tomorrow. Although my dad's favourite morning saying of "*shit*, shower, and shine" seemed like a decent methodology for life, I continued to *shower*, shit, and then semi-shine, as I failed to once again consider the consequences of my hurried decisions.

Still unaware that communication wasn't a forte of mine, as soon as the middle-aged woman opened her mouth and started speaking in a very broken English accent, I ignored the newly formed knot in my gut.

"Ahhhhhhhhhh how you do Korney?" she said. "Sorry Janelle busy today."

"That's OK. And I'm good, thanks," I lied as I crashed landed into her black swivel chair. "How are you?"

"Hair dead. Very dead," she said with a disapproving look in her eye. "Not much to fix."

"Yeah, it's pretty bad. I don't care what you do, just please try and fix it and trim off as much as you can," I said.

Snapping her cape with a crack like a matador about to square off with a bull, she flung the vinyl tropical print around my neck as she confidently replied," Yes, can."

Feeling like a body being covered at a crime scene, I noticed my diaphragm was still in knots as I sat there thinking back to standing on Rob's front doorstep. The quiet voice encouraging me to run away grew a little louder as I closed my eyes and imagined how good it would feel to get high while I waited for the matador to return.

Maybe I could just do it on the weekends from time to time? I would do anything to blow out a wall of smoke right now.

As I felt my mouth start to pool with saliva, I was suddenly ripped back into the present as the cold metal kissed the back of my neck. Feeling my heart drop an inch towards my anus, I reassured myself that she was merely cleaning up the wispy hair. Before I could push a single inquiry out, through the mirror I watched in disbelief as chunks of crunchy golden hair slid down my cape as the clippers traveled the path from the base of my neck towards my forehead repeatedly. With my head feeling like a half-peeled potato, I held back tears while I watched myself transform into a strange version of a fat Curious George.

Another eight strokes, all the while I sat frozen.

Just like every time I was bullied in a new school.

Just like the time my mom threw a lighter, CD case, and candle towards my head while in a blackout.

Just like every time she cracked a can at seven a.m.

Just like every time I stood in front of the mirror with pants stuck below my hips. And just like every time I felt Rob's hand groping my ass.

I couldn't find the words to speak and say what I felt or thought.

"Now you can grow and look pretty!" the matador exclaimed as she set the clippers down. Incapable of expressing my disappointment, I reluctantly thanked her and headed towards the front to pay.

. . . .

I arrived at the on-campus dorm that Adrianna and I were sharing with two other girls with minimal skid marks in my undies after colliding with a deer and cracking the front wheel well of my Honda. It appeared that the four of us were going to get along fine as we all took to alcohol like a fish to water. Despite being something I always turned away because I hated seeing the effects pour out from my mom, alcohol immediately showed me it's potential. After attending orientation and unpacking my car, the gates to hell swung open and ushered in a new method of takedown.

Our first afternoon was spent drinking and mingling with our new freshman peers, which seemingly set the stage for a progressive disease I had little awareness I had. Harbouring the perfect environment for mutation, I was holding inherited genes, learned behaviour, and a plethora of trauma. Every drink I had seemed to radically transform me into someone completely unfuckable with. The sweet, charming, pushover little Kortney Kay who could never find the words, took off running with her fat thighs slamming together bigger and stronger as she finally stepped out of the shadows.

I seemed to be content with my newly declared major of criminal justice, cafeteria line cook job, and getting familiar with the university gym. Thanks to a fellow classmate in my music theory class, I'd been given a brief introduction to a few exercises to keep me focused on something other than meth and feelings of shame and regret that kept sneaking into my thoughts every five minutes.

Because our new dorm mate, Kristina, was the epitome of 'daddy bought it but I got it', drinking a couple cocktails nightly became the new norm during the week.

And thanks to Rob and planting the seed of being a champion, "KO" was born.

The day of my eighteenth birthday, Adrianna joined me in visiting the closest tattoo shop. My mom had taken me to get my first tattoo of Prince's symbol a year prior, so I felt very comfortable with the idea. Plus, having a few shots of tequila helped with any second thoughts. With a slinky rayon tank top, oversized cargo pants and a black bandana affixed to my head, I sat down in the chair and explained what I wanted. Looking more like a cancer patient than a gangster, I told Aaron that I wanted a simple KO on my right shoulder.

"Yeah, ok. Do you know what type of font you want it in?"

"No. Just something bold and strong. No girly shit."

"Are you a fighter or something?"

"Yeah, I am. They're also my initials. Hopefully it keeps me from getting married."

As I sat in the chair gripping the armrest while the needle pierced my tanned skin, I thought about the countless times I was in the gym over the last few months with not a single person looking at me. Assuming it was my military haircut and lack of tits, I knew my tattoo was going to help me stay focused on my path of betterment by helping me accept my bald new identity. After paying a whopping fifty dollars in cash, Adrianna and I made our way back to the dorm to kick off my birthday party. My old-enough-to-buy-booze ex-boyfriend was on his way down from Eureka to spend the night and bring more alcohol.

By the time we got back, there was already a cluster of friends sitting on the second-floor common area drinking and playing music. Excited to show off my new tattoo, as soon as I took the last step of the stairs leading to our floor, both of our roommates, my friend from band class (who's virginity I'd somehow managed to nab), two sisters (one my age, and one older who was semi becoming my girlfriend), and my ex-boyfriend all rushed me with a variety of shot glasses filled with various spirits. In a matter of ten minutes, I'd thrown back seven shots. As the sun started to vanish and the cold air swept through the landing, everyone but my ex filtered out. With Adrianna and our two roommates off to get fast food, Nile and I chatted away on the cheap dorm couch while our knees touched.

As soon as I heard his voice, my heart did the drop straight down towards my anus. "Is this how this is gonna go down?" Jason said from the open doorway.

Shocked and muddled with disbelief, I stuttered back, "Oh my God! I didn't know you were coming down!"

"Yeah, it's called a surprise," my boyfriend muttered. "But it looks like you're busy," he said as he pulled a blunt out of his baggy jean pocket.

Pulling a lie out of thin air, I tried to remedy the situation.

"Nile was on his way down to San Francisco, so he just stopped by to say hi," I stammered.

"You're fucking lying! My boy and I have been sitting in the parking lot for about two hours."

"Yeah, and?" I said.

"We're out. Have fun with Nile and happy birthday," Jason said as he and his friend turned away from the door and walked towards the stairs.

Since my junior year of high school, I'd started building an unsavoury habit of flirting with people. Every. Single. Guy. Teachers, nerds, jocks, some girls, and even priests. This slow burn led to the inability to be physically monogamous after the 'Rob incident'. Without the common knowledge that flirting shouldn't lead to rape, I started building an aresonal of self-destructuve behaviors.

I couldn't bring myself to hurt another person's feelings by being honest, because I didn't really know what being honest felt like. It started with this one minor incident and slowly grew into a common theme of me dating two or three people at a time without their knowledge of the other person. In a man's world, it's what is referred to as 'being a player'. In a woman's world, it's referred to as 'being loose'. But in "KO's" world, it was how I masked the pain and filled the void with what I thought was "having fun".

Minutes after Jason and his friend left, I did what I knew best to try and erase the feelings of guilt and shame from lying, getting caught, and lying again. Already edging towards a blackout, I stumbled outside to our landing that was littered with disregarded old cocktails from our earlier guests and started pounding.

As soon as I opened my eyes, I knew something wasn't right. After taking a few seconds to orient myself, realising I was on the bottom bunk instead of the top, I pushed into my temple with my thumb in an attempt to make the splitting feeling subside. Still relatively drunk, I shielded my eyes from the sun shining in and attempted to stand up, but immediately collapsed onto my knees and let out a shrill.

"Jesus Christ!"

Peering over the top bunk, Adrianna looked down at me with one eye open. "You don't remember doing that?" she quietly asked.

"What?" I asked as I pinpointed where the pain was radiating from in my body.

As soon as she started pointing, I'd already looked up and saw the gaping hole in the wall. With drywall sprinkled across the low-pile pale blue carpet, I started asking questions.

Forgetting about my freshly scabbed tattoo, I started scratching my shoulder, momentarily unconcerned with the nuclear pain in my foot.

"What the fuck happened?" I asked.

"By time we got back, you were sitting on the floor sobbing. You said Jason showed up unannounced and screamed that you shouldn't be here."

"Where's Nile?"

"I think he stayed at a hotel. You were pretty scary, Kort."

I looked down at my right foot, now twice the size of my left, covered in cuts and glowing bright reddish pink, and started to get little flashes of kicking the wall repeatedly hours earlier.

"Fuck! I forgot I have a test this morning," I said as I tried to touch the side of my foot.

Realising I wasn't going to make it to class, "I don't know why I thought microeconomics was going to be easier than macro. I'm gonna fail that class anyways, so might as well drop out before the 'F' is official," I said.

When a child touches a hot stove, it learns to not repeat the process because it's painful. But in the life of a budding alcoholic/addict, touching a hot stove until the entire hand is burned completely off, is absolutely normal. With every touch, we somehow think the next time is going to be different and not continue to get worse. The (un-clinical) definition of insanity.

Predictably, from there, everything progressively got worse—and fast. A few weeks after smashing my foot, Adrianna and I packed a few gallon jugs of the cheapest wine someone else of legal age could find, and we hit the road north to Eureka for a weekend away…after having a few glasses of course. Dressed in club clothes, we left by lunchtime, so we'd be in town in time to drink with friends before we went to the one club that existed for 18+. Using the excuse of wanting to take the throbbing pain away from my broken foot, I cracked open one of the gallon jugs and poured us both a full dixie cup instead of just simply taking off my heels.

By that point, my mom was living in Ukiah after she got a job in the area. Realising I was hardly able to keep my eyes open after driving for an hour, we stopped at my mom's house for a piss knowing that she'd be at work and the house would be empty. Adrianna volunteered to drive the rest of the way as we killed off the last of the jug. An hour into the drive, she joined me in taking a nap and failed to negotiate a turn while traveling at sixty miles per hour. After driving straight off an embankment, clipping an oak tree with the driver's side wing mirror and flying through the air like the Batmobile, the car came to a rolling stop about the length of a wine bottle in front of an even bigger oak tree.

Once the car had stopped and I came-to, I looked down around in utter confusion and shock. Wearing a skirt and a small piece of cloth covering my lopsided, non-existent tits, my legs were covered in blood from shards of glass that sliced up my skin. With both windows blown out and the windshield cracked, I looked over at Adrianna blankly staring into the void.

"What the fuck happened?" I screamed.

Frozen in fear like she had just touched fingertips with the grim reaper, she tried to reply. "I. I..."

"Say it! What the fuck happened!!!!!" I screamed again.

"I don't know--I just opened my eyes and we were here," she said emotionless.

"We have to get the fuck out of here!" I frantically shouted as I grabbed my purse off the floor and shook the pieces of safety glass off.

As we stumbled through parts of squishy mud and mossy ground, I saw an older Ford truck pull off the one lane highway.

Throwing off my high heels, I tore up the ten foot embankment with my broken foot screaming in pain. Once I reached the road, the concerned older man in the truck was roughly ten feet away.

"Looks like you're gonna need a lift!" he said.

"Thank you so much for stopping. She swerved to miss a deer," I replied, lying with ease, just as Adrianna reached the road herself.

After we all got in the truck, my heart dropped after I realised I'd left the empty jug of wine and one freshly opened one in the backseat. We didn't want to leave any evidence at my mom's and foolishly threw it in the car.

"Can you give me one second, I just need to grab something out of the car."

"Are you sure you want to go back down there? We should probably get you checked out first?" he said.

Just as my hand touched the door handle and I was opening my mouth to reassure him I'd be quick, the sound of a siren came roaring up behind us.

With the CHP and an ambulance now on the scene, Adrianna and I had very different fates. After we were cleared of any major health issues, a new CHP vehicle appeared, handcuffed Adrianna, and put her in the backseat of his car and escorted her to jail. I sat freely in the front seat of the original officer's car as he drove me back to Ukiah to meet my Mom. Hysterically dipping between sobbing and laughing the entire hour drive back to Ukiah, the officer seemed genuinely concerned for my mental health. After thanking the cop and crawling into the passenger seat of my mom's car, I continued to cry as she talked with the officer outside.

"Kortney Kay- I can't believe you! You are so lucky to be alive! Most of that road is surrounded by cliffs!"

Between sobs, I gasped for air while explaining that we hadn't even drank that much whilemy mom instructed me to stick out my tongue. After placing a tiny blue pill under it, she told me to calm down or else I was really going to be hurting in a few hours. For the first time in my life, we were in reversed roles. Safe in her presence, I fell fast asleep.

. . . .

To no one's shock, after the wreck, Adrianna and I fell out with each other. The start to this failed friendship was actually lucrative for me. Her parent's insurance paid me four grand for my totaled Accord which was the same four grand I used to pay Pop, my Grandma, for the next-to-new Honda Civic that had belonged to my Grandfather, who'd just lost his year-long battle to brain cancer. Unfortunately, instead of driving an hour south to San Bruno to help out, I had spent the prior year either in a state of blackout or working out. I wouldn't realise until much later in life, that by making alcohol more important than family, I was doing exactly what my mom had done to me. I guess this is where we start to see how hurt people can hurt people.

By the time I moved out of the dorm and home to Eureka for the summer, my alcoholism was in full effect.

I started the summer working a job with the Humboldt County Roads Department. It was the perfect environment to nourish KO. The only girl amongst a team of ten men, I spent the day surrounded by blue collared jokers. I had to get up at five a.m. in order to get to work by six during the week, which was really putting a damper on my drinking plans. I found that crushing up and snorting NoDose right before doing my daily abdominal routine would help get my mind right and fired up for the day ahead. I slowly became more and more obsessed with training and joined a gym where I'd spend hours after work to lift weights. I went from doing the few things the saxophonist had shown me in the University gym, to becoming very familiar with everything else there was to play with.

Even outside of the gym, I started doing exercises everywhere I could:

Wearing ankle weights and doing calf raises while holding my stop/slow sign while working traffic control.

Hovering over the toilet and doing pulse squats every time I had to pee. Reclining my seat back in the car and doing crunches while driving.

And at night before either passing out or falling asleep, doing leg lifts in bed.

Although my drinking was becoming more and more dysfunctional, I somehow kept not getting caught. Before the summer was over, I decided to head down to my distant family's property to check out the line-up for this year's Reggae on the River festival. I'd been twice before during high school, but wasn't interested in having the full experience. I had a proper job now and only anticipated going for a few hours.

Feeling anxious about where I would find parking, I pulled off the highway in Garberville and headed to the liquor store. After easily talking some hippy into buying me a fifth of vodka, I planned on only having a few pulls off the bottle before getting down to Benbow. However, I nearly polished off the bottle by time I parked, and the rest of the night quickly became a blur.

I always had the best plans and the best intentions, but for whatever reason, things never seemed to work out. Instead of waking up at my other set of grandparents' house in Garberville, or waking up in a tent on the river, I woke up in my bedroom at my parents' house.

How the fuck did I make it back here? I thought as the familiar feeling of panic started traveling up my spine. Fully clothed, I leapt off my futon and grabbed my purse to look for my car keys. Relieved to have them, I now needed to find out what happened to my car. Briskly walking down the hallway, I heard my dad enthusiastically shout, "Morning Kort!" from the kitchen table as I paused with my hand tightly gripping the front doorknob. "Hi dad! Gotta grab something out my car--be right back!" I shouted with a smile on my face, acting like I'd just had the best night's sleep of my eighteen years while praying that my car was actually outside.

Stepping out onto the front porch, the enveloping brightness cracked open my skull and my head started pounding like a jackhammer. Although facing the wrong direction, seeing my turquoise Honda parked right in front trumped my newly formed headache.

Thank God! I thought walking around the entire car, making sure there was no visible damage. Not noticing I had side-walled the front left tire while parking, I unlocked the driver's side door to further investigate how I got back.

With my knees on the driver's side seat, I started scanning the charcoal interior of the car for clues when suddenly I made contact with not one, but four empty brown paper fast food bags on the backseat. I picked up each bag, recognising every logo before I started to formulate a possible story of what had happened. Ripping through each bag, I read the receipts of one meal per bag, indicating that I was alone in my death wish journey between Benbow and Eureka. With the highway scenery resembling something like a cross between Star Wars and Cliffhanger, it was a sheer miracle that I'd managed to make it over sixty miles, plus drive through four separate fast-food windows without killing myself or another person. Burger King, McDonalds, Taco Bell and KFC were all next to each other on

Broadway, so at least I hadn't made the drive more challenging than it already was.

I crammed three bags together and shoved them all into the fourth bag before ramming the evidence under the seat and slammed the door shut. As I went to lock the door, the flat tire caught the corner of my eye and the feeling of relief was instantly blown out with worry as

I started trying to piece together a story to tell my dad. *'How many more times was I going to have to go through this emotional whiplash?'* I thought while I walked back towards the house.

By the middle of my sophomore year, it was clear to everyone but me that I had problems. A LOT of problems.

I had replaced speed with drinking and Ephedra.

I had replaced feelings of desperation and hatred of my legs with dieting and working out.

I had replaced feelings of guilt and remorse from Rob, with sleeping with practically anyone who'd take their clothes off.

And I replaced the brain of Kortney Kay with that of K.O. by raging war on anything I could rip off the wall and throw, or challenging anyone stupid enough to look at me the wrong way.

From drinking beer in the shower at ten a.m. to get rid of a hangover, to popping a few Ephedra and pouring myself a stiff screwdriver in my coffee cup to take to class, every outing required checking out.

From the Atkins diet to the everything fat-free diet, I failed to accept that alcohol was the highest calorie dense diet I could possibly fathom. From canned vegetables to white rice with tangy BBQ sauce, I carefully followed whatever diet I was trialling with the exception of liquor.

From my fifty year-old paleontology professor who was blind in one eye and wore coke bottle glasses, to the produce delivery boy who had a tiny dick, everyone I encountered became some form of a distraction for me.

And from punching and kicking holes in the wall to knocking over the refrigerator in my on-campus apartment, I had little regard for valuing other people's property or safety when under the influence--which was daily. Even an eighty year-old grandma pushing a walker wasn't safe from threats of getting her ass handed to her when she looked at me with a stank-eye. The rage that was masking my shame was rapidly mushrooming.

With my mom now living in the next town over, we'd often try and drink together, which never turned out to be pleasant. Just like touching a hot stove and not learning the lesson, after a few calculated drinks, I'd start the expected descent towards bringing up every childhood memory I harboured of her being a horrible parent and throw it in back in her face. Between drinking with a parent and sleeping with men who were at times older than my parents, life was everything but normal for a nineteen year-old..

On the regular, I kept encountering situations I never acknowledged as unusual. Waking up on an almost daily basis at three a.m. in a sheer panic-stricken terror to dump out my purse's contents and play the game of whether or not I was in possession of my keys and license, accidentally mistaking my computer chair for my toilet and pissing on a month's worth of clean laundry, examining patches of deep blue and purple bruises across my biceps or legs from being in a fight the night before, falling down a flight of stairs, or straining back against three grown men kicking me out of a bar was leaving its mark.

It was remarkable that it took so long for me to cop my own

DUI. Three other sober girls and I piled in my Civic on a warm April Sunday afternoon and headed off to the Sonoma County Fair. Similar to Adrianna, I decided to take a short nap en route, and failed to negotiate a turn. Jumping the curb and smashing into the beige brick retaining wall in front of an auto-repair shop, I knew I needed to act fast before the cops showed up.

I'd gotten away driving drunk more times than the number of people I had slept with, which was well into the triple digits.

I'd gotten away with simply paying to repair the damage done at the man's townhouse my mom was renting a room in. I let myself in by kicking the front door down and ransacked her roommates' room because I "didn't like the way he spoke to me". After leaving threats on his answering machine, I woke up to a message from my mom letting me know that I was facing felony charges of trespassing and vandalism and that I better "cool my jets".

I'd gotten away with taking any responsibility in the last car wreck I was in, so why not now?

Similar to when I came-to in front of a massive oak tree, I suddenly felt alert and semi sober when faced with a death delivering object in front of the bumper. Looking around at my passengers to make sure everyone was alive, I started running viable options past a checklist in my head to once again figure out how I could narrowly escape being accountable. Quickly realising that someone else taking the keys would result in an unfair penalty for them, I decided that my best option would be to start pounding the pavement away from the scene of the accident.

"Holy fuck--I'm so sorry girls. I don't even know what happened. I'm going to go walk to get help, ok?" I calmly stated.

Looking perplexed, the skinny, tall blonde all-American roommate named Christie said, "We can use my cellphone?"

"Yeah, she needs to take a beat because she's been drinking," replied Naomi from under the brim of her shitty, smartass hippy sun hat.

Before I could think of what to say next, a Santa Rosa police officer flew in the parking lot. Just as I always did, I appeared to be sober aside from the smell. After an attempt of explaining the failed turn was due to a repeated fit of sneezes and being overtired from studying for my criminal justice classes, I was blowing into a breathalyzer.

"Look--you're almost 3 times the legal limit in the afternoon and you're underage. *And* you have 3 passengers with you," the cop said as I knew my chances of getting out of this were rapidly disappearing.

"I'll make you a deal- if you agree to have your blood drawn down at the station, I won't arrest you and one of your roommates can come pick you up."

Agreeing to his "deal", he asked if I wanted to leave my car there or have it towed to campus or somewhere else. Had I known that I'd conveniently crashed in front of the shop of a future crystal meth dealer, I might have chosen a different answer.

"You can tag and leave it here" I said, holding back tears as I climbed into the back of the car without handcuffs on.

. . . .

Ego: A person's sense of self-esteem or self-importance. Also known as the part of the mind that mediates between the conscious and the unconscious and is responsible for reality testing and a sense of personal identity.

All of us have an ego. There are numerous books and publications that dive deep into the subject, but for the sake of simplicity (and because I'm not a guru-

save that shit for the professionals!), our ego drives us to obtain our basic needs (such as sexual relations, job security, and healthy relationships). But there often comes a point (ok, most always) when our ego crosses a line of being unnecessarily excessive. It's important to recognise when we are driven beyond the basic needs that our ego exists for and strive to put ourselves in a greater position of power (sexually, monetarily, or emotionally). When working through trauma, more often than not, we create an alter reality (facade) of who we truly are inside which can quickly go barreling out of manageability.

When I stop and think about how much I despised alcohol as a kid (seeing how much it scared the living shit out of me every time my mom was under the influence) to then walking straight into her shoes, I'm blown away. It's similar to a terrified son who watched his father beat on his mom as a kid, swearing to never do that, yet somehow as an adult winds up doing the exact same thing to his future wife. The patterns and behaviors we create from childhood can be completely unexpected to us.

Do the F*cking Work

Have you ever created an alter ego like KO to deal with your trauma? How were they different to the authentic you?

In what ways do you feel like you're a better person when you put mind-altering substances in your body?

Write about any "bad habits" that have progressively gotten worse over time. If you're being bold, what "bad habits" have become addictions?

Come to think of it, define addiction in your own words. (sex, gambling, sugar, food in general, drama, alcohol, drugs, over the counter drugs)

In what ways do you continue to get away with unloving behaviour, despite numerous close calls?

Scan here for more good shit.

LESSON 4

IN ORDER TO GET OVER SOMETHING, YOU MUST GO THROUGH IT—NOT AROUND IT

*L*ike driving straight across through the state of Texas, the journey of getting to rehab was long and grueling. But this road was full of anything but dull moments and straight paths. Although the whispers kept getting louder, I never stopped to consider what they might be trying to tell me. "KO" would override "Kortney Kay" with justifications as to why I should keep carrying on without help. Over the next two years, my spiraling descent from dreams of the presidency to a lifestyle of a potential drug felon was falling faster than my sixth grade girl self-esteem.

Now back home in my old stomping grounds of Eureka since deciding to "take a break" from University, I rediscovered my "friends" and was back to smoking meth in a matter of weeks. Unlike when I first started using, the effects of drinking alcohol while being high were new and exciting. I couldn't get into too much trouble my first year back due to losing my license, however, that didn't stop me from hanging out with people who would steal your wallet and help you look for it, so as long as they had a mode of transportation. It's said that you become the sum of the top five people you surround yourself with, so it wasn't long before I developed a case of sticky fingers myself.

By the second year, I was co-conspiring on home invasions and stealing from Safeway while fronting like your friendly deli clerk. Other than to tweak out on my eyebrows, I looked everywhere but the mirror for more ways to justify my actions and get more drugs. After developing a kidney infection and getting fired from Safeway for showing up in a blackout and knocking a bunch of shit off the shelves at three a.m. before my eleven a.m. shift, I could sense that things weren't going to get any better. Other than completing my mandatory drunk-driving classes, I had accomplished nothing. Clearly, this was all due to being back in Eureka, and not to me personally. So, like any smart addict does, I started planning my next geographical, which all 12-steppers will know as moving to a new location in hopes it'll solve all of our woes.

If I just removed myself from this shit-hole town, all of my problems would disappear, or so I thought. Without a second spared on taking an inventory, I failed to realise that moving from Eureka to Rohnert Park, and back to Eureka hadn't made any of my problems magically vanish. Amazingly, these assholes with drugs and drama just seemed to keep finding me. With the encouragement of one of my best friends from high school who was my co-captain of the cheerleading team, but subsequently also one of the main friends I started using with my senior year, I agreed that we should move to Eugene, Oregon. She'd been off meth for a few years while living in Florida, was holding down an adult job, and was sober-ish, only dropping ecstasy at raves on the weekends. She clearly had her shit together, and moving to a new state seemed to work well for her, so why wouldn't it work for me?

After borrowing money from our parents and finding an apartment, we decided to get one last bag of meth 'for the road'. What should have taken six hours turned into a sixteen hour drive. Stopping at every rest stop, Missy and I would unfold her AAA map and cover the inside of the bug-stained windshield for privacy in her blue Kia Sport as we passed the pipe back and forth. With a carefully constructed headlight barely hanging in place with a wrapped bungee cord and pair of white tube socks shoved underneath, Missy turned the key off on the ignition and exclaimed, "We made it!" as a half-smoked Newport hung off her dehydrated bottom lip.

I had a 'new year, new me' type of vibe for the first two weeks as I truly tried to be a good girl. As much as I felt rejuvenated being in a new state, I felt cravings to get high and lose weight just as much. Conveniently forgetting about my discovery of how many empty calories were in liquid, I started just drinking beer in an attempt to slow down my blackouts. I managed to flirt my way into a sales job at a local 24-Hour Fitness and knew I couldn't show up at three a.m. causing a scene like I did at my last place of employment that annoyingly never closed. By ten a.m. on most days, I'd already had a six-pack of Pabst Blue Ribbon down my gullet, thinking that the cheaper the beer was, the less hammered I would get.

It only took a few months before my responsible girlfriend pawned my guitar and was arrested a few cities away for stealing hundreds of boxes of Sudafed, one of the main ingredients in meth. As I stood in line at the corner liquor store to buy a pack of cigarettes, I locked eyes with my soon-to-be future ex-girlfriend. A girl who just had "that thing" about her, I couldn't resist engaging back in small talk which quickly led to more than just standing in line together.

She was a rail-thin tomboy with a mouthful of crooked teeth and a slight overbite who could take an engine apart and put it back together while blindfolded. She had two dogs, wasn't afraid of the dark, unlike me, and despite her lack of makeup and big tits, could talk her way out of a traffic ticket just by flirting with a cop. Tugging at my strings of fascination, even in her oil-stained baggy jeans, dirty fingernails and wife-beater tank top, she could play the part of a girly girl at the drop of a hat. Feeling attracted to all of these facets, there was also the fact that her dad was a meth cook and she owned a van, which was probably what I was attracted to the most.

Seeing that I couldn't afford to rent an apartment by myself, nor get across town to my new job, I figured that shacking up with Jepson in the neighbouring town of Springfield was my best option. Over the course of the next year, we managed to successfully rip off a chapter of the Hells Angels, have a handful of threesomes with a meth cook that was older than her dad, and cashed a number of social security checks made out to people who were no longer of this world. All of which, of course, was justifiable. The Hells Angels had more drugs than they could possibly ingest, the meth cook was fun (and of course screwing him wasn't as deplorable as being a prostitute in order to pay for drugs), and dead people didn't need social security checks.

After a year of living by candlelight with Jepson in a cobweb-infested dilapidated shed on the back of some tweaker's property, I managed to hustle enough money to buy the truck of a newly convicted dealer. Sitting on twenty two inch platinum rims, the high-gloss pearly white two-wheel drive Toyota truck was all I could ever ask for. With a matching white windowless camper shell, the carpet-lined bed of the truck safely harboured a dual, custom-made eighteen inch subwoofer that produced a bass so strong it made my ears ache while setting off car alarms as I sped past. More obvious than a tweaker's pupils, my new ride screamed for attention.

Still riding the immeasurable high of finally having my own vehicle again, I noticed two new voicemails on my translucent pink Nokia.

"This is Sergeant Johnson of the Springfield Police Department with an urgent message for Kortney Kay Olson. I have a dispute filed by a Eugene branch of US Bank that I need to discuss immediately. Please call me at-". Before the officer could read his number out, I swiftly deleted the message and continued onto the next one.

"Hi hun, it's mom. Wanted to let you know that I'm at Campobello for the next month or so. It's a rehab in Sebastopol. Well, I'm not entirely sure what happened but I fell down a flight of stairs. I guess I was in some kind of blackout or something? Anyways, I hope you're doing ok up there and will try calling you again when I can. Love you."

Feeling split, I stood in the outdated kitchen with emotional whiplash and briefly analysed my options. Faster than it took to make a 'Cup O Noodles', I was packing my shit and heading back to California.

. . . .

After getting back to Eureka, nothing had really changed except for the worsening of my perceptions and addictions. I paid cash for a sawed-off shotgun and started selling crystal meth as one does when they're starting over and looking for a better life. Wishing I would have researched the maintenance of owning a low-rider, I watched in horror as sparks spewed onto the highway from the rearview mirror. Feeling far from Bruce Wayne in the Batmobile, Jepson started laughing as I frantically turned down the music.

"Oh my GOD what the fuck is that noise?" I shouted before taking a long pull of straight vodka from the South Fork Mountain pop-top water bottle that was nestled between my thighs.

"It's your leaf-springs sweetheart---they're dragging on the ground. I told you this was a piece of shit!" Jepson replied over the top of the sounds of crinkling plastic.

Before I could ask her opinion on whether or not we should keep driving, the truck suddenly started cutting out. Feeling the familiar four inch drop from my heart towards my anus, I pushed down on the accelerator expecting something to happen. With the soft tissue in the back of my throat still burning from the direct hit of vodka, I watched the fat sway around above my right knee and momentarily forgot about the problems I thought I was having. Shooting sparks and running out of gas while drinking and driving and high with an illegal gun under my seat and meth on my person were hardly issues worth considering. Getting rid of the hideous subcutaneous fat on my thighs was really the most pressing issue I had to resolve.

With my adrenaline pumping, I threw the truck into neutral, flipped on the hazard lights, and aggressively pulled off the side of the freeway and onto the shoulder as rocks and dust went flying everywhere. After coming to a complete stop and switching off the ignition, I slammed the rest of the vodka as if I were pounding an ice-cold glass of water on the blazing hot sun post workout. As expected, I started slamming my fists repeatedly on the steering wheel as I shouted, "Why does this shit always happen to me!"

"Did the gas light even come on?" Jepson calmly asked.

"Fucking NO!" I screamed.

"I'm not the one who bought a piece of shit truck. No need to yell at *me*!" Jepson clamored back.

I decided to start walking towards the next town to find gas, which ironically was where all my issues had started in the first place-the birthplace of the husky Sasquatch. Looking for someone other than myself to be pissed off at, I slammed the truck door as hard as humanly possible and stormed down the highway with my air lats on display. As the effects from the vodka intensified, I stopped obsessing about my thighs chafing together and continued to kick rocks as I aggressively stormed down the redwood tree-lined stretch of road ahead of me. After a few minutes of trudging towards town, a miracle happened; my new saviour had arrived.

Standing twice my height and looking nearly twice my age, a dreadlocked hippy stepped out from his mud-covered white Ford truck. Instantly recognising he was a dope grower, I casually asked, "Whose dick do you gotta suck to get a ride around here?" I was fully in the throes of KO and ready to fight anyone who wanted a piece.

"I saw your truck back there. Where ya heading?" the man asked.

"To find gas and a stiff cocktail," I replied.

"I've got a gas can if you want to hop in. My name's Mark by the way."

"Nice to meet you Mark. My name is tattooed on my shoulder," I said as I pushed my hand into the side of my hip in an attempt to flex my shoulder and look more impressive.

In usual fashion, I had Mark eating out of my hand before he'd even stuck the nozzle in the red plastic gas can. Exchanging numbers, Mark suggested that I come out to the hills and work for him trimming weed.

"Sounds profitably exciting. I'll think about it," I said as I leaned over and grabbed the back of his neck and pulled him in for a friendly kiss. As he sat dumbfounded, I jumped out of the truck and told him I'd hold his can ransom until we meet again. Forgetting my previous attempt of tree hugging hadn't worked, I considered the prospect of living deep in the woods.

Clearly money does grow on trees--it's called weed. But meth however does not, so sounds like a winning outcome to me, I thought as I started fielding Jepson's questions about who the hippy was.

"White people with dreadlocks are so stupid. Did he at least give you any weed?" she asked.

Within forty eight hours I'd left Jesper with mutual drug friends and was parking my busted truck at my brother's house in anticipation of Mark picking me up.

My stint at being the head trimmer bitch for a massive outdoor operation lasted approximately three months before my health started rapidly deteriorating. Between contracting a case of pink eye that presented as if my tear duct had a sinus infection, and procuring yet another painful kidney infection that felt like someone had shot me through the back with an AK-47, I decided that I'd had enough of outdoor weed and forest-living life. Making sure I continued to avoid the deplorable group of gangsters I was hanging with before I skipped town, I connected with a boy who used to have a crush on me back in high school. Graduating my freshman year, he was only four years older than me but seemed to have his shit together. I figured that moving down to a smaller operation and not having to deal with other trimmers would make for a good environment to try and cut back on my using.

After another three months of failed attempts to stop sneaking meth into my life, I decided that moving in with my brother and his two small children would straighten me out. The one that was always there for me as a kid and a total square, I figured that being around my two year-old nephew and five year-old niece was enough motivation to stop fucking up. Once again, it seemed the cards were stacked against me as the immediate next door neighbour's still-living-at-home thirty year-old daughter was strung out on heroin and meth. It literally took two hours before I had a new best friend.

One night, after spending the sunny afternoon inside a dark room next door, I was higher than the Northern Lights. With paranoia setting in, I stood behind my bedroom door and listened as my brother, who was across the hall, continued to snore louder than a freight train. Concerned I might wake him, my niece, or my nephew up, I couldn't bring myself to turn the handle and walk ten feet down the hall to the bathroom. It was well past three a.m. on a Wednesday and I had zero business being awake.

CRUSHING IT

I had pushed myself past the limit of any stashed piss I'd ever stashed before. Never having experienced paranoia like this, I questioned what could have potentially been cut into the bag of crystal I smoked earlier with the neighbour. As I scanned the room for something to pee in, I tried justifying my potential action by remembering the countless times I'd seen a childhood friend or grown man piss into a bottle.

If they can do it, so can I, I thought as my gaze landed on the holy grail of emergency toilets. Half the size of a basketball and shaped like an inverted Hershey's Kiss, the glass vase was perched beautifully in a sturdy, black iron stand. Acting as some type of spiritual decoration in my wannabe spiritual, meth-filled life, sunk inside the half-filled vase sat a collection of engraved rocks amongst some random river rocks I fished out of the Eel River while high as fuck.

HOPE.

GRATITUDE.

GOD IS LOVE.

As I stood staring into the bowl, I considered bravely opening my door and walking down the hall to the bathroom one last time. I reached my hand in and pulled out the rock "hope".

I hope this works, I thought as I shook the excess water off the rock and set it down.

I fished my hand back into the warm water and felt my bladder swell as I pulled out the rock "gratitude".

I'm so grateful for this idea.

Without shaking the rock, and knowing I was edging close to the point of no return, I finally pulled out "God is Love".

CRUSHING IT

I'm sure this God person will still love me even after this is over, I thought as I decided to not bother saving the river rocks.

Leaving the vase on the ground, I quietly slid my window open and popped the corner of the screen off so I could pour the remaining rocks and water out. Briefly considering hanging my ass out the window instead, I emptied the vase and placed it back on the ground before shutting the window and blinds. I pulled off my sweats, hovered over the glass bowl and patiently waited for something to happen. Despite how bad I had to go, nothing flowed. I was too high, too overstimulated, and too paranoid to even breath. After several minutes, my legs started to shake while my forehead slightly dampened. After nearly collapsing from holding a squat for what felt close to five minutes, I finally got down on my knees over the vase and relaxed enough to let it go. After executing my pro drip-dry dismount and putting my sweats back on, the voice inside my head spoke loud enough for me to acknowledge. I knew I could no longer ignore the fact that I was an addict. I had a problem I couldn't fix on my own and I needed help.

Despite being more awake than I had ever felt in my entire life, I switched off the light and crawled onto the twin mattress to sob with my tightly clenched, ragged baby blanket. Crying on and off until the sun rose, the light filled everything in the room but my soul. Suddenly the game of having a fake ID, selling drugs, and running life in the fast lane came to a shrieking halt. Flashing back to my spiritual rocks, I knew I was meant to be doing more than doodling stars, trimming pot, and collecting ordinary stones out of the river. The day after my twenty first birthday, I told my dad everything, and shortly after, our family doctor, in hopes that he could prescribe me something stronger than hope, gratitude, and God.

I slept for three days straight after being admitted to the hospital. After breakfast on the fourth day, I was instructed to write my name on a sticker name tag and attend my first class along with the group of new residents. I anxiously walked into what looked exactly like a classroom, minus the flag, and took a seat in the front row. Feeling a sense of false pride, I noted I was the youngest person in the room. As I looked around to take everyone else's inventory, trying to figure out what brought each person into the rehab, I felt mentally insane. One second I was excited to be back in a classroom, and the next I was holding back tears. I felt more unstable than the San Andreas Faultline.

After a few minutes, a Black woman wearing scrubs and a crisp white lab coat glided into the room.

"Good morning beautiful people!" she boisterously exclaimed. "I'm the head doctor of this entire hospital and happen to be incredibly passionate about the treatment of addiction and alcoholism."

For the next thirty minutes, she talked in dire, broad terms about our odds of beating this disease, as well as what to expect over the next twenty four days while in her facility. Before concluding the session, she asked us one important question I'd never forget the answer to.

"So, tell me class--what exactly is the purpose of life? As in, what is the ultimate thing we're seeking while here on earth?" she asked.

As to be expected with a room full of fucked up people plagued by the disease addiction and coming down or sobering up, the room was deafening with a heavy silence.

"Ok, let's go! I know you're all smart enough to think of

something since you all somehow managed to not die on your way here." After another period of awkward silence, the old guy in the back corner, who I earlier had worked out was partially blind and a heroin junkie, shouted out, "To get rich or die trying!"

"Yeah, probably not, Russ--keep going," she replied.

"Happiness!" shouted the fifty-something year old next to me who looked like George Bush junior.

Shaking her head no, people kept answering.

"Finding true love?"

"Being successful?"

"Living a healthy lifestyle?"

"Finding your purpose?"

Still unsure of what month it was and semi-regretting my decision to get clean, suddenly a word popped in my head and prompted me to raise my hand up high in the teacher's pet fashion.

Without saying anything, the doctor nodded her head giving me the go-ahead.

"Is it balance?" I asked.

"YES!" the doctor exclaimed as she did a small jump in the air. After glancing at my nametag, she put me on display.

"Did you all hear Kortney?" she questioned loudly. "Get a library card and check it out--the answer is balance. Finding balance is the quest we all need to seek!"

"Love the spelling of your name," she said as she locked eyes with me again.

"Thank you!" I gushed.

As she went about talking to the class again, I sat in a pool of satisfaction as a semi-permanent grin hung on my face. For a second in time, I questioned why I was so utterly pleased with being right and causing her happiness before everyone suddenly started to get up.

"Hey Rockstar, glad to see your shining face and that you're still with us," Russ said as he walked by my desk.

"Ah, thanks, Russ," I said as I noticed his nametag. I vaguely remembered meeting him the day I arrived, but I could recall his smile making me feel welcomed.

"Balance huh--I would have never gotten that," he said with a sarcastic tone, clearly preparing for a joke. "I guess that's why I'm back here for the third time!" he said with a forced laugh.

"Third time's a charm, right?" I said batting my eyelashes as I noticed how fucked up his teeth were.

"Well, see you around kid."

Aside from group therapy and one-on-one time with our assigned therapist Pat, I attended my first AA and NA meetings while in rehab. I remember feeling like I belonged but felt completely clueless around what any of it meant.

What the hell is this 'self-will run riot' shit? Are they talking about an eighties big-hair band or something?

A middle-aged Black man was the most impressionable part for me. I wasn't sure if it was his enthusiasm and confidence that I wanted, or his shredded physique.

"Yeah y'all! It's like my disease is over in the corner doing push-ups, man! Just waiting for me to fuck up! Just over there in the corner creepin' boy! My disease be pushing, pushing, pushing," he said without taking a breath. As he continued doing push-ups in the air with his arms, I couldn't stop staring at his bulging veins which seemed to grow with every push. "All I need is one thought that I could maybe just have one drink and get away with it."

After taking a pregnant pause, he raised his hands as if he was conducting the New York Symphony and said, "But we know where that leads... one's too many," he said before the rest of the room, including Russ, finished in unison, "And a thousand's never enough!"

After the twenty eight day spin-dry, I had the longest amassed amount of time of being clean and sober since I was seventeen. In the spirit of practicing balance, I had some amazing breakthroughs, such as realising that Rob's spotted dick was not my fault and experiencing the energy in 12-step recovery rooms, and some breakdowns, such as finding a way to fuck the partially blind heroin junkie. (Of course I did)

Sometimes quickly, sometimes slowly. Some habits die hard so long as we don't die along the way.

. . . .

In order to get over something, we have to actually face it. I can't tell you the amount of times I've tried to bypass doing the work (examining my own shit) to heal. To be fair, up until I was in my mid-twenties, I was incapable of acknowledging that I was masking my hurt with substances. But it's said that "AA/NA is the last house on the block", meaning that once you admit that you're an addict/alcoholic (or that you're struggling with an addiction such as sugar), you can't unknowingly go back and drink or use like you used to because you know you're screwing up.

No matter how many different things you put into your mouth, forms of drama you distract yourself with, or people you try to fix, your problems will not go away for long. You might temporarily find reprieve from having to think about them, but just like Schwarzenegger, they'll be back.

Do the F*cking Work

When your internal voice of reason (i.e. your consciousness, higher self, or spirit) has tried to raise awareness of your trauma, have you tried distracting yourself with external things such as food, drama, sex, alcohol or drugs?

If so, how's that working out for you?

What are the things you distract yourself with the most?

Have you contemplated reaching out for help to tackle your trauma or do you see it as a sign of weakness?

In what ways do you justify your behaviour that you know isn't worth writing home about?

If you've attempted to seek help/guidance, have you felt like you keep failing at overcoming the issue?

The term balance is tricky, hence why the head doctor of the rehab believes it is the ultimate quest for humans. How do you balance celebrating weight loss in your visceral organs to ease the stress of them operating properly, but not trigger yourself into wanting more of a certain look? How do you express yourself sexually, undo stigmas around women liking sex and work to free, but not give impressionable tweens that sex sells? How do you stand in your strength but refrain from batting your eyelashes at your husband to kindly take the garbage out in the dark on a freezing cold night, or open the new jar of pickles that seems to be stuck? How do you care about women's rights but at the same time appreciate and recognise the pressures from unique issues that men face?

What's your take on the term 'balance'?

Do you feel like you are always out of balance with things in your life?

If you're struggling with dependency of some sort (especially chemical), I encourage you to answer these questions:

What is your dependency history?

How has this dependency occupied your mind?

What triggers cause you to return to your dependency?

Scan here for more good shit.

Kortney Olson's Journal Entries
St. Helena Hospital

Jan 3, 2003
Chemical Dependency History
First drink: I was 13 with my Cousin. Jack Daniels. Straight
shots. I vividly remember waking up the next morning feeling like
shit. She had bought the bottle with a fake ID.
Junior High: Random weekend partying, mostly drinking.
Smoked my first cigarettes.
Marlboros were only $2.10 a pack!
Age 15: first line of speed and diet pills
Age 16: first time frying on mushrooms at Reggae on the River.
Age 17: first time trying acid. Also, when I heavily became
involved with speed.
Age 17: first time trying ecstasy.
Age 20: first time trying heroin, and last.
I could see how the "experimenting" started to turn into a safety
net for using over the years.

Rough guesses for number of uses:
Ecstasy: 5 times
Heroin: 1 time
Mushrooms: 6 times
Acid: 3 times
Speed: 1,000 x 10
Alcohol: 1,000 x 10
Valium/Vicodin: 7 times
Diet pills: 1,000 x 10
I see the similarities.

Jan 9, 2003
Step One Written Work
1. Preoccupation with chemicals: I would hide my drugs (crystal)
all over the place.
Especially after I started selling it, I would try and think of clever
places in case I ever got pulled over. I cut a hole in my fanny bag
under the zipper where I would stash my "shit" (very common
street name). Driving around with alcohol became a little bit
sketchier after I got my DUI. That didn't stop me from
transporting open containers though. For example, I would
empty a bottle of vodka into a water bottle since they were the
same color. I would totally look forward to smoking dope after
eating a lot, as I am fantasizing about right this second.
2. Attempts to control use: I moved up to Eugene, Oregon from
Eureka to try and get cleaned up. After a week or two, I already
had all the connections I needed. I tried switching from hard
liquor to beer, thinking that I would not black our, or drink as
fast.
Moving out to the woods after getting to Eugene so I wouldn't
have phone access, or a car to hook myself up. I just ended up
hitch-hiking. I tried switching over to diet pills to control my
eating rather than doing speed. That lasted about a week. Trying
to smoke weed instead of speed did not help either. That lasted
about 3 days at the most.
3. Kinds, amounts, and frequency of use: Whiskey was one of my
favorites. I could drink at least a pint daily. I could smoke, or at
least would want to smoke a half to a full gram of crystal a day. I
would drink at least a 6 pack of cheap beer to get my
carbohydrates daily.
4. Effects on physical health: I would wake up with such a bad
hangover at times, that I would see double, feel my heart beating
in my temples and my lower back would ache where my kidneys
are. I would smoke so much dope that the inside lining of my lips
would peel off in thick sheets. From over all abuse with hemicals

my hair started thinning and falling out, tremors, dental work increased (I had 5 cavities filled this last visit), scars from "picking", taste buds numbed, pre-ulcers and holes inside my nose started to form.

5. Effects in sexuality and life: My sexual relationships increased 10-fold. I lost my self-worth. I thought I liked to have sex, but I think it is a deeper issue that that. (Pat underlined and put a star next to this sentence) I contracted a STD, which is curable with a drinkable shot of Zithromax. Who knows, I might even have HIV. I did in fact discover that I have a sexual desire for women on top of men.

6. Effects of social life and friends: My social life definitely revolved around mostly to only other tweakers at one point. I was too paranoid to be around anyone else who didn't use. My Best Friend Adriana would cry herself to sleep at night one summer because she didn't even know who I was anymore. I built-up a lot of anger. I bashed, broke, split and ruined a lot of things all the time to try and release my anger. It never helped. It just started the entire shitty circle all over again.

7. Social life and friends: I was hanging around people who were felons, had warrants out for the arrests, were/are theirs. These types of people would steal the jewelry off their dead Grandmother in her casket. I have had numerous friends and ex boyfriends reject me after I started to try and get clean because I had hurt them too many times. I quite working out, and started smoking cigarettes.

8. Effects on family: My stepsister and I no longer talk. She is also a dope head. I've caused my parents a lot of financial difficulty. My parents have recently been fighting because my stepsister and I have been fighting.

9. Effects on spiritual life: My entire theory, belief, faith in god had been trampled.

Because I was sinning so much, I did not want to be associated with God. Because of my disassociation with God, I quit playing music for him too.

10. Effects on work: I quit going to school- alcohol. I got fired from Safeway- dope. I got fired from 24 Hr Fitness in Eugene-dope. My dream job down the drain.

11. Finances: I pulled a tweaker stunt and cashed $2,000 worth of stolen checks.

They all got returned and came straight out of my reserve line at a 19.2% interest rate.

Overall, I know I've spent at least $10,000 in alcohol and crystal meth alone. I lost over

$12,000 in wrecked vehicles due to alcohol.

12. Insane behavior: I peed on all of my clean clothes thinking my computer chair was my toilet in my door room! I used to get a rush from flashing cops. Especially giving them the full moon. I've been kicked out of Kinko's, Scandinavia, restaurants, and pool halls for starting fights with anyone who looked at me the wrong way. Including an 80-year-old man with a walker.

13. Destructive behavior: When I moved out of my dorm my freshman year in college I owed $280 in damages done to the apartment. My sophomore year, $940, not including the $219 from kicking in my Mom's apartment door and punching a hole in her room-mates door because I didn't 'like him'. I broke my hand punching the floor out of anger because I couldn't do a headstand after several attempts. I broke my foot by kicking the wall barefoot.

14. Accidents: My Best Friend drove my Honda off a 15-foot embankment. We should have died because we just missed hitting a tree, twice. From the money I collected from her insurance, I bought my Grandfather's Honda after he died from a brain tumor, and drove that into a 4 foot high retainer wall. Drove down to San Francisco after being up for 5 days and almost wrecked tragically.

Jan 9, 2003
Today was a good day. I am still having cravings unfortunately.
In order for me to kick these cravings in the face, I need to start
upping my workouts. I know this disease will kill me. I can't
waste any more time. I have to do this while I am still young. I
can't lose anymore hair, time, and teeth.
I'm trying to work on forgiveness and understanding. I can't
change my mom. Even without the alcohol she will always be the
same person deep down. I can't change her. I wish I could go to
a real N.A. Meeting right now.
90 meetings in 90 days is definitely something I need to take
advantage of.
I'll see you in the Purple Rain, Pat!

Jan 11, 2003
Triggers for meth:
A. Doodling on paper while talking on the phone
B. BIC lighters
C. Propane tanks
D. Dropping wax
E. Talking to old friends, shit!
F. Plucking my eyebrows
G. Certain clothes
H. My glasses case
I. Mirrors that aren't hung up
J. Grease soundtrack
K. Straws, especially the ones on the juice boxes here!
L. Air fresheners (the glass ones you can blow into a pipe)
M. Playing cards, seeing people play solitaire

Jan 5, 2003
'Anger Survivor' Step 2
1. I kept trying to get high. No matter how much I was doing, I
wasn't getting high. I also kept trying to sell drugs to make

money. I only ended up doing more, and hurting myself financially.

2. Hiding my stash in random, bizarre places.

3. The angry, wounded, and sad part only got worse through my addiction. The only part I Felt successful in was keeping thin.

4. My faith in God.

5. N/A

6. N/A

7. By being dishonest and committing sin after sin. Mostly by letting God out of my life completely for that time.

8. God the Father, God the Son, and God the Holy Spirit. I call God 'heshe'

9. Because who else can I trust? Who else besides myself am I living for?

A Relapse Exercise For the acting-out survivor: Getting and staying safe.

1. When I am feeling unsafe, I can go to > my dad

2. When I feel unsafe, I can always call > my dad

3. If I cannot reach my first choice, I can also call > my Brother

4. One thing I can do when I feel full of rage is to > hit a punching bag

5. One thing I can do when I am flooded with fear is to > hold my blanket and pray to God.

6. One thing I can do when I am flooded with sadness is > to cry

7. I know that I need to take care of that wounded part of me because > if I don't I will relapse

8. I know that hurting myself is not an option because > it does not heal the pain.

9. I know that drinking and using drugs only make things worse because > it only temporarily numbs the pain.

10. The trigger for my current pain is > my mom and self image.

Forgiving Myself For My Relapse

1. One reason I should forgive myself for relapsing is > because I am only human, born to make mistakes.

2. One thing I learned from my relapse is > cross addiction is a bitch

3. In looking back on it I believe that the trigger for my relapse was > ignorance

4. One thing I might have done other than relapse is > learned more about my disease.

5. I am going to strengthen my recovery program by > following the program to the fullest.

Staying Safe Worksheet

1. When I feel unsafe, I know I can call > my dad

2. I need to learn to put my own needs first because > I am the most important

3. I need to be assertive because > no other way of communication is as effective.

4. Something I did recently that I was not very assertive about was > talking to Mindy

5. It might have gone better if I could have been assertive because > now I don't want to smile at her.

6. An example of an internal boundary I need to set is > left blank.

7. An example of an external boundary I need to set is > left blank.

8. The person I am really angry at is > myself

9. I am angry at this person because > I feel like a failure

10. I need to express my anger directly because > holding it in is very unhealthy

11. Admitting that I suffer from the disease of addiction helps my recovery because > I can reach out and know that I am not alone.

12. I know that I am powerless over drugs and alcohol because > my life became unmanageable.

*13. I know that I am also powerless over other people because >
I am only in control of myself*

*14. I know that I need to work a recovery program that includes a
12 step support group because > that community (of other
addicts) are who's going to get me through this.*

*15. Two ways I have learned to take care of myself are > good
sleep, exercise and food.*

*16. An example of how I can be passive-aggressive is > to
pretend nothing bothers me.*

*17. I know that being direct is a better way to manage my feelings
because > there is no room for misunderstandings.*

*18. I now know that being able to ask for help is a strength, not a
liability, because > I am not as strong as I think I am.*

19. I need to ask for help around > affirming myself.

*20. Over controlling is a relapse symptom because >
codependency.*

21. When I am feeling unsafe, a place I can go to is > my dad.

*22. When I am flooding with bad feelings, one thing I can do to
help myself is > to workout*

*23. When I am having a flashback, one thing i can do to help
myself is > beat my monkey up*

24. I like the way I am learning to > be honest

Jan 16, 2003

*Today was a huge step in my recovery. Group really helped me
out a lot. It really made sense when you (Pat) commented on my
calmness/inner peace shining through.*

*Today's session really validated everything you councilors have
been trying to express about how we don't have to do this alone.
It felt really good to let all of those surfacing feelings out rather
than pushing them back down. I know that the fellowship of other
addicts/alcoholics is what's going to keep me sober. I just found
out that I am not pregnant as well.*

Thank you so much for helping me Pat. You truly are an angel in disguise.

Jan 19, 2003
Today I made a conscious decision to not use or steal. Last
weekend while my parents were here we went to Walmart. I
decided I was entitled to some free Biore' face strips from out of
a box. I still have the craving/urge to '5 finger discount' from
large corporations. I feel as though I'm like Robin Hood in some
way. I steal from the rich and give to the poor. Of course I shared
my Biore strips or else I would have bad karma. Well, I'm afraid
that's not how the world works. Converting, or resuming back to
my old behaviors, I will relapse. I noticed a "rush" of
adrenaline. My voice was shaky, and I shuddered when I tried to
talk to my Dad after we left the store and got into the car. My
palms got sweaty. Those Biore strips are not worth my chance of
relapsing and probably dying.
So, this afternoon, I'm going to practice and live out the values
and morals my mom installed in me as a little girl. I'd be pissed if
someone stole from me.

Jan 21, 2003
Today was awesome! My parents were here still from yesterday
to participate in the family session, which I didn't get much out
of, but it was good to see them anyway. Also,
I SAW MY MOM!!!!!!!!!!!!!!
It was SO cool. It was the first time my mom and I have spent any
moment together both sober. Everyone loved her. Everyone
always loves her. I'll have to tell you about it later because I'm
going to bed. It's been a Long day! Ahhhhhhhh, I love that word
(bed) now!

Jan 22, 2003
On Monday in the women's group, I learned something important
from Beth the counselor. We were discussing a fellow peers

situation regarding her significant other, when Beth said something that really struck me. She said something to the effect of how unhealthy it is to be someone else's higher power. For someone to do that to you, only feeds your ego, and there is no ego involved in real love.

I'm starting to get anxious, fearful and exhausted all at the same time. Easy does it is what they say. Thanks so much for your help Pat, there really are no coincidences. I'm really going to try and make this walk in the morning haha! I'll go if you go!

Jan 23, 2003

Today was a good day. When Don was talking today, it felt really good to tell the group that I was quietly conspiring suicidal thoughts and ideas in my head. Just letting everyone know what I was thinking really helped me get rid of my disease's agenda, which for the day was apparently, death.

I now see the power in sharing.

(Pat circled the last sentence and wrote "and telling the truth!")

LESSON 5

BEFORE WE FIND PURPOSE, WE USUALLY LACK IT

Thirty five thousand dollars later and twenty eight days clean and sober (Daddy's insurance bought it, but I got it), I had a not-so-stellar exit plan from rehab to live with my cousin in Oakland, California. She'd been chatting with my dad and felt it would be a great idea for me to get away from Humboldt County. Showing her best intentions, she attended a few AL-anon meetings and gathered as many tools as possible to provide the highest level of support. I had it all planned out. I was going to get a job, go back to community college, pay off the insurmountable, ridiculous amount of debt that was keeping me up at night (a whopping four grand), and finally find my purpose in life.

Oddly, I happened to be in rehab with the owner of a used car lot from Eureka who was willing to take my truck in on trade. He happened to have a four-door Honda Accord for sale that screamed 'sophisticated'. Figuring the whole "third time's a charm" bullshit might apply to my ownership of Hondas; I just knew that having a new-to-me car would fix my problems. After getting settled into my cousin's house, I found a couple of meetings that were close by and made a stab at my new life. I was living life on what I heard described in meetings as 'the pink cloud'.

I couldn't feel more content with myself. I'd landed a job and had just picked up my ninety day chip for staying clean and sober. The night before at eighty nine days, I picked the "The 4 Agreements" back up and continued reading where I'd left off years back. As I sat and processed the concept of not taking it personally if a stranger walked up to me in the street and shot me in the foot, something fell onto my leg. Certain a spider had crawled across my flesh, I jumped off the bed and dropped the book on the hardwood floor as I danced around brushing vigorously at my crotch. Suddenly my brain pieced together that the supposed spider was actually a little drug baggie that had fallen out of the book.

As if I'd never touched a drug in my life, I picked the bag up off the floor like it was covered in rabies and scowled at the contents inside. Without so much as a thought of tasting the powder, I walked straight into my little bathroom and flushed whatever was inside down the toilet. As I stood there watching the water swirl around the bowl, I felt as if I'd been touched by God. At that moment, I knew that I was cured! My relentless obsession of pursuing thinness into the depths of hell had suddenly subsided just as quickly as it has started. Overwhelmed with joy, the taste of freedom flooded my soul as I practically skipped back out of the bathroom.

Wanting to share the news with my cousin, I tossed the book on the bed and ran down the stairs. Figuring she was out back smoking a cigarette, I headed towards the sliding glass door. As predicted, with a Marlboro light lit in one hand, and a glass of Cabernet in the other, I smiled as I stood in the doorway and listened in.

"Oh, she just came outside!" my cousin said as she made eye contact with me.

"I'm talking to your Dad!" she said as she pulled the cordless phone away from her mouth while carefully trying not to burn her bleached hair.

"Hi dad!" I shouted from the doorway.

"Yeah, I'll put her on before I go," she carried on. "Yeah, Ev--Kort's been doing *so* good! She just got her ninety-day chip today, right Kort?"

"I did!"

"Yeah, so cool bud. I knew you could do it," she said before turning her direction back to my dad.

"I feel like she deserves a glass of wine!" she exclaimed.

As soon as the word "deserves" registered in my brain, a sense of entitlement rushed over me. As I daydreamed about how it would taste, it was as if I could feel that warm humming sensation already happening as I imagined slowly sipping from a wine glass like the adult I had become.

"Here's Kort!" my cousin said interrupting my thoughts as she stamped out her cigarette and handed me the phone.

As I made small talk with my dad about my new job, I was simultaneously having thoughts on whether or not my cousin was being serious. Just as I hung up the phone, out walked two glasses of wine followed by my cousin's smiling face.

Feeling like my days of pounding Carlo Rossi out of a gallon jug and slamming warm Diet Coke mixed with Captain Morgan from a red Solo cup were far behind me, I graciously extended my hand to receive the stem of the glass.

After all, speed was my real problem and clearly I'm past that.

Not a single considered thought crossed my mind of everything the last ninety days had taught me:

"Alcohol is a drug, period!"

"One is too many and a thousand is never enough."

"It's the first drink that gets you drunk."

These were all meaningless slogans I was just regurgitating without actually connecting to what the fuck any of it meant, hence why the glass of wine was currently in my hand.

. . . .

It only took a few weeks before I stopped going to meetings and was moderately drinking on a nightly basis. I hated my job and could hardly bring myself to get out of bed. While I hurriedly ran around the outdated aged-care facility as every nurse's little bitch, I thought about how far off the track I'd gone. What made things even more unbearable, was I had no idea what the track even looked like; I felt so blocked, I couldn't even daydream the life I wanted. With my stepmom's advice running through my head, "Do what you love and the money will follow," I simultaneously thought about all of my failures.

Being the first female president failed (so far). Being a world champion boxer failed. Being an interior designer failed. Being a criminal justice major and pursuing a career in the FBI had failed. And now I was holding my breath while lumbering my fat ass around dark hallways, ducking in and out of smelly rooms delivering crusty food and shuffling paperwork. Other than the vision of having a thigh gap and finding clothes that fit, I didn't know what I loved.

Finishing up a grueling twelve-hour shift, I glanced up at the TV while clocking out. I stood watching Vice President Dick Cheney discuss weapons of mass destruction with closed captions on as the suffocating sense of fear started to encompass me. We'd been at war with Iraq for a year and nothing seemed to be getting resolved. Everything in the world seemed like it was getting worse. My debt, my weight gain, the safety of our country. Walking through the dusty automatic sliding doors and out into the dark, I could feel the tears building up behind my eyes. After furiously jabbing the key into the lock of my third Honda, I slid behind the wheel, slammed the door shut, and started crying under the light of a flickering street lamp.

I'd never felt so lost, full of despair, and crippled with fear. As hot tears uncontrollably fell into my hands, I felt like I was slipping into a black hole of nothingness. Between my shoulders rising and falling with my sobs, my thoughts shifted between how disgusting I was physically, mentally and spiritually. I had nothing to offer the world and no way of making a career. I was supposed to have had this all figured out before graduating high school and here I was at almost twenty two without a shroud of interest or hope in anything. Unsure if the void inside my chest would ever close, I drove home with the intention of just having a glass of wine.

. . . .

Waking up to an onslaught of angry replies in my text messages the next morning, I knew I needed to get back to meetings and lay off the drinking. Leaving the local 24-Hour Fitness with my cousin, I spotted a sign that the sales team was hiring. Feeling like I was robbed of the opportunity back in Oregon, I ended up taking an application and filing it out. Within a matter of months, I was one of the highest grossing salespeople in the country. Between the hustling atmosphere of sales, working with all men, and making significant money for the first time, I was on top of the world... but in a state of blackout.

Instead of finding a meeting to attend before work or during lunch, I worked out. Cardio in the mornings before work, and weights at lunch. It was far more important to my success in sales that I looked fit on the outside--no one was going to buy a membership based off of how fit I was on the inside. And after work, I found hanging out with my team members and joining the boys next door at Chevy's Bar and Grill equally as important. As my sales increased, so did my drinking. It's all about balance, right?

Crazily enough, it was unusual to find me passed out in the back of my car, sleeping on top of my laundry, because normally I would just drive myself home. And I drove everywhere drunk. Pulling stunts like reclining my passenger seat all the way back and shouting "Hold on! Just keep breathing!" to an imaginary woman in labor, who I was rushing to the hospital, as I sped down the shoulder past all the cars sitting at a complete stop on the 580 interstate with my hazard lights on during rush hour traffic, was normal. Waking up and not remembering how I got back, was also normal.

Even backing my car into a light pole and smashing my bumper in the Chevy's parking lot seemed normal. It was the poor visibility of an older car that was to blame. Along with the asshole who parked too close to me, *and* the poorly lit parking lot.

Once again, I dodged having to take a hard look in the mirror. Somehow I claimed the incident on insurance and traded in my 'piece of shit' for my first ever brand-new car, my fourth Honda. Things couldn't be that bad given the circumstances. I was working out (obsessively), had a good paying job, and wasn't smoking meth.

Despite my alcoholism worsening at exponential speeds, I kept making sales, and eventually got promoted from assistant general manager to running my own club as a general manager. After a year of drinking more than Ozzy Osbourne and Keith Richards combined, it didn't come as a surprise when I came down with a wicked chest cold at the time of my promotion. I had accepted that bad shit seemed to always happen to me and that I was doomed to continue to be the reigning champ in the game of bad timing. Unable to miss my first day on the new job, I stocked up on Robitussin and powered through.

After ten days of hacking my lungs out, I started feeling better. Making the treacherous crawl home from San Ramon to San Leandro, I pulled out the bottle of Robitussen from my purse and put it between my legs. Driving with my knees, I quickly got the childproof top off. As the smell wafted upwards, I suddenly felt my gut lurch like a second string forward trying to dribble past the star point guard of the opposing team. With both spots behind my jaw aching in anticipation from the horrendous taste, I gulped down the rest of the syrup and tossed the bottle on the floor. The familiar sense of feeling hangry instantly vanished and a slight out-of-body buzz rushed over me.

I better stop at CVS and pick up some tampons.

Should I buy another bottle of Robitussen just in case I start feeling sick again?

It's not like it's expensive--and I think CVS had a buy one, get one fifty percent off.

Better to be safe than sorry.

After being in my new role for a few months, I started finding time to suddenly want to date again. Whether I sought out William like I used to seek out meth cooks thinking I'd get free shit, or whether I was truly attracted to his personality, I started dating the main full-time bartender at Chevy's for a brief stint before things went to shit.

Waiting for William's shift to end, I sucked hard at the bottom of my third Long Island iced tea before heading to the bathroom to sneak a shot of Robitussen. After drinking nearly half the bottle while sitting in one of the stalls, I got my pants up and headed back out to the bar. Deciding that I better slow down on the drinking, I ordered a screwdriver instead of another Long Island and pondered how I ended up drinking so much despite promising myself I was only going to only have one drink.

I opened my eyes to the familiar surroundings of my bedroom. With my usual thoughts racing along with my heart pounding, I tried to piece the evening together while wondering what had happened to my date. Starting to sweat profusely, I threw the covers off my body and noticed I was still fully dressed. Stepping down onto the hardwood floor, I felt something ooze up inside my sock and nearly shit my pants thinking I had stepped on some kind of potato bug or cockroach. Forcing myself to look at the bottom of my white sock, I held my ankle in both hands, trying to figure out what I had stepped on.

Staring at a puddle of what almost looked like blood, I tried my absolute hardest to make sense of what was on the floor. Looking around, I could faintly see a small trail heading out the bedroom door leading from the puddle. In usual routine, I next scanned the room for my purse which quickly appeared across the room with some of the contents strewn around it. I then followed the trail of this red substance in little dribbles down the stairs and through the house towards the front door. Quietly unlocking the door, I poked my head outside and noticed my car was nowhere in sight.

With my heart pounding, I popped back inside and ran to the kitchen to grab a towel to wipe up the mystery substance. While I waited for the water to heat up to rinse the towel, the thought of Robitussen crept into my head. Figuring that I failed to put the lid back on properly, I felt a fleeting sense of relief as I wiped the drops up from the floor. Taking the stained towel with me, I headed upstairs to look for my phone. Wondering why I had thrown my purse across the room before getting into bed, I picked up my lip gloss and wallet off the floor.

Now picking up my purse, the empty plastic bottle of Robitussen crashed down onto the floor. Sticking my hand inside the bag, I felt the same oozing sensation as I had earlier on my foot upon awakening. Pulling out my phone, I noticed the screen was cracked and the back covered in syrup.

Fuck. Just my luck.

After waiting until it was at least eight a.m. before ringing, I reluctantly called William for answers.

"Hey KO."

"Hiiiiiiii. I didn't wake you up, did I?" I asked.

"No, I haven't really slept."

"Soooo, what happened last night? For some reason I can't remember anything!"

"Yeah. I can imagine," William replied coldly.

Unable to handle the anticipation a second longer, I pleaded for more answers.

"Was I raging?" I asked.

"You could say that," he said sarcastically.

After a few seconds of silence, he told me in detail about what happened.

While waiting for him to get off work, I conveniently passed out in my car for an hour. After several failed attempts, he managed to get me up and into his car so he could drive me home. As soon as we pulled up in front of my cousin's house, I woke up and started screaming at him. After calling him a selfish dick and a worthless piece of shit for not letting me drive home, I proceeded to overhanded-ly bash my purse on the dashboard of his Audi Quattro like I was playing whack-a-mole at the fair. Once I'd had enough, without saying anything, I let myself out and walked off towards the house.

"Oh my God--I'm so sorry!" I stammered.

"Yeah. I gotta admit--I was startled. I've never seen a girl unleash like that before."

"Did I fuck up your car at all?"

"You left a decent dent, yes."

Whether it was breaking a bottle of Robitussen or breaking yet another man's heart, I couldn't pause long enough to look at my part in why things were always turning out like an episode of Breaking Bad. All I knew was that it was always everyone else's fault.

If you had the stressful and demanding job that I did.

If your employees were as annoying as mine.

If you had as much debt.

If your legs were as disgusting as mine.

You'd probably drink too.

When Adrianna suddenly reappeared in my life, I never thought for a second that it'd bring me to a rock bottom lower than the rocks I'd pissed on in the bottom of that vase. And that was just going to lead to another bottom underneath yet another rock.

In my experience, feeling like I had zero clue as to what I was supposed to be doing with my life was the main reason why I felt like such a piece of shit. Whether it was my false sense of importance and pride, or pressure from institutions like school or society's subliminal messaging (via ads, news, and media), I always had this sense of feeling lost, hopeless and meaningless in life. Instead of being encouraged to simply show up each day and serve humanity through kindness, we're told that we need money to be successful because we live in a capitalist society.

Out of the thousands of people I've met around the world, only one or two come to mind who knew exactly what they wanted to 'be when they grew up', and stuck to that path. I'm almost forty, and I'm still trying to figure out what I want to be when I grow up. And frankly, is there anything wrong with that?

Do the F*cking Work

In what ways have you felt like you lack purpose and don't have a clue what you're supposed to be doing with your life?

What people in your life have expectations of you that you cannot fulfil?

Why are you constantly having 'bad luck'?

Analyse what part you might have played in creating the outcome.

Write about mistakes and behaviors you keep repeating over and over again, despite how many times you promise yourself you're not going to?

It wasn't until I was about to get the serenity prayer tattooed on my arm that I realised the prayer was all about acceptance. I had said the prayer in 12-step meetings at least a thousand times over the years. I couldn't believe I had just regurgitated the words without actually critically thinking about what it meant.

What things do you say in your life that you haven't consciously connected with?

Scan here for more good shit.

HUMILITY: THE ANTIDOTE FOR FEAR OF JUDGEMENT

*U*nlike myself, Adrianna had stayed in school and received a degree. She was clean, had a job, and kind of felt like home. She wasn't the only person who felt like home back in Sonoma County though. My mom was still living in the area and had been sober now for a couple of years. Figuring that transferring to a different 24-Hour Fitness and going back to having less responsibility would straighten me out, I once again packed my shit and moved north to escape myself.

Living with my gorgeous, party-animal, high-functioning, highly successful cousin and drinking myself into a nightly state of oblivion was shockingly not working out well. Although I had never asked for help, in my mind 24-Hour Fitness was guilty of pushing me into a job I didn't have the right skills for, therefore leading to my need to drink. Clearly, the fault lay with them and not me. They should have known that I found it challenging as a twenty two-year-old pushover (who could only speak her mind when she was drunk) to lead and delegate to a staff twice my age.

I'm pretty sure push-up guy from rehab had said something else in that AA meeting that hadn't quite landed yet:

Whenever I point a finger at someone else, I usually have three fingers pointing back at myself, though I tend to pretend otherwise.

Although I hadn't lived with her since I was ten, I held onto hope that maybe my mom was the one to save me, despite unconsciously knowing that I needed to save myself. I didn't know how, because, though hard to believe, I wasn't ready.

After unpacking my shit in her tiny second bedroom, I took off to meet Adrianna and her new group of friends, but, true to form, only after I'd made a pit stop at a liquor store. Showing up with a decent buzz, I walked through the front door without knocking in classic KO fashion. There were about six people I had the pleasure of meeting that night. A couple of girls, Adrianna's boyfriend, and two other guys. One guy, Billy, seemed level-headed, relatively mature, and was a softball coach, while the other, Jackson, had no head whatsoever and just got out of jail. Evidently, the level-headed guy's house was the place to be.

After a few rounds of shots, I had completely transformed into the highest unfuckable-with version of KO possible. While Christina Milian's song "Dip It Low" blared out from a shitty wireless speaker, I lost control by believing I was in control, and proceeded to slip into some kind of angry, white-girl strip tease for all to see. Pulling hard on the end of my belt and releasing the lever, I cracked the brown leather down onto the cheap laminate flooring while simultaneously dropping both knees to the ground like I was Michael Jackson.

Rocking a blend of cotton/spandex jeans, I made a figure-eight with the inside of each thigh as I slid my pants in the direction of no-headed boy who was sitting at attention on the edge of the couch. Cracking the floor as if I was trying to reach down into hell and whip Satan himself, I could sense that Adrianna's two other girlfriends were less than impressed. Hoping one of them would say something and allow me to *really* show off, I carried on for the remainder of the song with the laser-focused mission of capturing Jackson.

I never paused to consider what consequences might be lurking up ahead as I placed my hands on Jackson's knees and slid my body up and down between his legs. Just like I always pick the wrong line at the grocery store, the gas station, or security checkpoint at the airport, I always seemed to pick guys (and a few girls) who were more fucked up than I was. Like a moth to a flame burned by the fire of a Bic lighter underneath a meth pipe, I somehow managed to pick the one person who had an active meth addiction, unbeknownst to the rest of the group.

It only took another couple of hours before Jackson and I were both in the bathroom passing a pipe back and forth and making out like two fifteen year-old kids who had just snuck out of the house.

As with most addicts, there's almost always some innocent bystanders who get twisted up in the drama; after all, misery loves company. The first victim was Adrianna, followed shortly behind by Billy. It wasn't long before the other two girls stopped coming around, Adrianna and her boyfriend broke up, and the four of us were spun out on a daily basis. Jackson and I had moved into Billy's garage and miraculously managed to keep using with just one income.

We somehow spent most of our days in our new makeshift bedroom whenever I wasn't at work. Built in the sixties with no improvements, the double car garage had a single dust and cobweb infested tiny window as the sole light source. Covered with an oil stained towel that was hung up with mismatched thumbtacks, rarely did we know (or care) what time of day or night it was anyways.

Along with everything else I seemed to have forgotten in rehab, it wasn't long before the thrill of getting high quickly became lackluster. The name "crouching tiger hidden dragon" is a literal translation of a Chinese idiom which describes a place or situation that is full of unnoticed masters. An addict never goes back to their original level of tolerance. We only pick back up where we left off-- and it seemed I couldn't stop leaving off.

Jackson and I lasted another few months before one day everything changed. As people usually do after they haven't slept the night before, and the night before that, we had already gotten into an argument by nine a.m. Just like my mom used to slam the front door and leave after an aggressive feud with my dad, I slammed the door so hard I broke the frame. After several hours of staying out, I returned to my garage palace to find no one there. Not only was Jackson gone, but now Adrianna's car was parked out front with no sign of her either. Normally she'd be at work and always replied to my texts within a matter of minutes.

One p.m. turned into three p.m. and neither one of them had replied to a single text message. What started out as marginal agitation, quickly transcended into panic as I realised I only had one bowl of meth to smoke. Pouring my fifth screwdriver to calm my nerves, I tried to figure out what my next move was going to be. Bending down to put the half gallon of orange juice back in the fridge, my eye caught the nutritional box on the back of the bottle. Instead of pondering why I kept trying to put things in my mouth to change the way I felt inside, my thoughts quickly justified the calorie trap, thanks to being strapped with meth. Just as I slammed the fridge shut, Billy's flaming red hair and freckled face trudged through the front door. I knew Billy was interested in me, as most guys were after I'd leave them confused by my overly flirtatious advances. Just like Adrianna, he was a college graduate working an unfulfilling job unrelated to his degree. So, when Billy got home from work, he was happier than a pig-in-shit to join me on the couch with a cocktail and listen to my relationship drama. Stirring his ice around with his finger, Billy listened to me carrying on until suddenly my phone had dinged. Adrianna had finally messaged me back.

"What's wrong?" Billy asked, reading my face.

I read the text out loud, "Hey (dot dot dot) We're at the beach. I took the day off and left my phone in the car, sorry."

"Can you fucking believe that shit?" I said as I stood up.

"Wow!" Billy exclaimed. "I kind of felt like they might have had some weird thing going on since she and Charlie broke up, but that's pretty shitty of her to just leave you hanging like that while she hung out with your boyfriend."

"Yeah, that *she* hooked me up with!" I shrilled.

Exploding off the couch like an untrained bull terrier, I stomped my way to the kitchen to pour another drink and load the rest of my meth. As I poured my sixth screwdriver, and Billy his second, I could feel half of my face was somewhere between coming down, being high, or blacking out. Making sure I didn't spill a drop, I managed to carry the two highball glasses and pipe back to the couch. As normal as two eighty-year-old men sharing a pipe full of tobacco, Billy and I passed the glass tube back and forth as I started to momentarily feel less hammered.

"Fuck this shit--I'm going to teach these two a lesson," I said valiantly while I set the pipe down. "They fucked with the wrong bitch."

Knowing Adrianna had some personal belongings out in the garage, I flung open the interior door and scanned the space that resembled something like a scene out of the show Hoarders. Right next to a giant box of unopened fireworks sat two pairs of her shoes. Thinking on my high and drunk feet, I darted back into the kitchen and started hastily rummaging around the cupboards. Hearing the sound of slamming, Billy poked his head around the corner.

"What are you looking for?" he asked between grinding his teeth.

"You got any vinegar anywhere?" I asked.

Heading to the cupboard I hadn't opened yet, Billy pulled out a bottle of unopened white vinegar that looked like it had been there since the house was erected.

"Thanks," I hastily said as I grabbed the bottle out of his weathered hand and headed back to her shoes.

After ripping the soles up, I poured the vinegar in each shoe before taking out my lighter and burning the plastic off the tips of each shoelace, sticking them to the outside of the shoes. From there, I stormed back to the kitchen to grab a dirty cup out of the sink and headed to the bathroom with my cocktail in tow. Without shutting the door, I finished my drink before taking the empty cup to the toilet with me. Filling the cup three quarters of the way full, I set the neon yellow piss on the ground and finished peeing. After wiping with Jackson's faded chartreuse colored towel, I carefully hung it back up while my pants were still around my knees. Next, I snatched his toothbrush out of the holder.

Back at the toilet, I pulled my pants up and bent down on my knees to open the lid. Dipping his smashed bristled toothbrush in and out of the piss-filled bowl, I brushed underneath the lid of the bachelor-pad toilet with precision. After placing the brush back, I grabbed the cup of piss and once again headed back out towards the garage. Shouting for Billy to open the door, I continued walking as if I had a pipe bomb in my hand.

"Oh my GOD! What are you doing?" he asked as I walked past.

"Shut the fuck up and help me or I'll pour this on top of your head like a cooler full of Gatorade after a championship game, Coach!" I shouted as I set the cup down next to the stack of mattresses on the ground. Knowing that this was about the only other thing Jackson owned in his life, aside from a shitload of debt and his toothbrush, I was throttled to fuck it up. With the mattress and box spring stacked neatly under a pile of messed up blankets, I pushed the corner of the mattress towards the wall and shouted for Billy to hold it up while I got to work. By this point, I guess Billy knew better than to ask me any more questions.

Feeling like this was the best idea I've ever had, I picked up the purple plastic cup and poured half the piss in a straight line before stopping and switching directions. Within a matter of seconds, there was a very visible two-foot by one-foot piss stain in the shape of a cross staring back at me. Billy dropped the mattress down onto the box spring and took a step back while he laughed with hands up in the air. "Having three younger brothers, I thought I've seen it all," he said as I stared off into a void.

With my high starting to wear off and a blackout starting to wear on, a fireman's axe caught my eye.

Noticing that I was fixated on something, Billy carried on.

"I mean--I've thought about pissing on Tim's clothes in high school when he got me busted for bringing home weed, but a mattress?"

"What are you looking at?" he asked.

"Ah nothing. Just thinking," I replied with my eyes locked on the bright shiny yellow handle.

"Hey--make yourself useful and go make us another drink!" I said enthusiastically.

I figured the last thing lying around that I could fuck up was Adrianna's car.

I sat down at the wooden circular card table we played poker on and lit a cigarette while I waited for Billy to bring me another drink.

All I could think about was getting high again. I knew I didn't like being as drunk as I was, but it was better than being even remotely sober. I took a drag off my Marlboro Red and briefly thought about all of the times Adrianna and I had spent together. We were inseparable--from basketball practice and road trips, to our repeating weekend slumber party where we'd watch the same goddamn movie over and over again. Still unclear on how she blamed wrecking my car on me, she just up and replaced me with the daddy-bought-it-but-I-got-it roommate and blew me off. Then she had the nerve to just waltz back into my life and hook me up with some meth-head who she's now apparently hooked up with? That bitch.

Before I could make up another bullshit story in my head, Billy pulled me out of my thoughts by gently setting a drink down in front of me.

"Did you put any vodka in here?" I said after taking a sip.

"Yes! Jesusssssss you're a handful!" he replied back.

As if Billy had just challenged me to a chugging contest, I gulped the fresh screwdriver down and stood up like I'd just won.

"Whatever," I replied as I slammed the cup down and headed over towards the wall where an assortment of shovels hung up amid the axe.

After unhooking the axe from the wall, I tried out various grips to see what felt the best. I knew I needed to get a move on if I were going to remember any of this bashing.

"I'll be right back," I said as I headed towards the door leading out to the backyard.

"KO, where the fuck are you going with that axe?" Billy stammered as I stepped out into the brisk air.

CRUSHING IT

Unlatching the rusty lock on the wooden gate, I started towards Adrianna's silver Saturn as the anger started to boil up into my cheeks again.

How has she managed to keep the same fucking car for some many years?, I thought as I continued advancing across the brown crab grass. Before I could get another two paces forward, Billy had to go and be a hero. With all of his five foot seven ass in a full-sprint, he tackled me from behind and slammed me onto the dirt.

. . . .

Over the next two years, my sanity fell faster than a drunk girl in stilettos. All of my decisions revolved around how I could keep chasing thinness and muscularity at the same time. I had maintained an impressive washboard stomach and decided that it was smart to ensure that never changed. After being awake for a stretch of several days, I decided that getting a tattoo of a scorpion underneath my belly button would keep me from getting pregnant. Resembling artwork of a four-year-old, I continued to tell myself that getting pregnant would cause the sketch to turn into a lobster, signifying that my life was then--and only then-- a hot fucking mess.

After Jackson and Adrianna had fucked off never to be heard from again, Billy and I turned the house into a home now that he seemed to be the next logical partner to chase my non-existent dreams with. Not with the love we made, because that never happened, but instead, from the home improvement projects I apparently found therapeutic and distracting. Unlike most tweakers, who would spend countless hours doing pointless shit like separating hundreds of different sized nuts, bolts and screws only to then dump them into the same bucket when finished, I was productive as fuck. During the next seven hundred and thirty days, I bounced around from various sales jobs in between renovating Billy's mom's inherited house.

I kept up my now predictable cycle of trying to quit smoking meth by working out harder and drinking less, but as usual, Billy and I would fall off after about the three to five day mark. I steered us through a vicious cycle of trying everything from fasting with magical colon cleaning herb kits, to slurping our cravings away while on the cabbage soup diet. Nevertheless, we'd always end up with the same failed outcome—a binge dinner at our favourite restaurant, Old Mexico. With a plate of flautas, chimichangas, fajitas, chips and salsa, we'd finish two or three massive margaritas, and convince each other that we'd 'just get one bag to help us pass the feeling of being disgusting fat shits.

Billy and I were obviously "never that bad" because we'd both never shot up. People who stuck a needle in their arm were the bottom of the barrel derelicts who were homeless, toothless, repeated jailbirds. Holding onto our false pride by a thread, we still managed to somehow find every other way to ingest speed. Taking a tube of glass similar to that of a straw and heating one end in a torch until it was basically lava, then snorting a line of crystal with the non-melted end, to then blow out smoke, was somehow not as degrading as being an intravenous drug user. Just like sleeping with a drug dealer or meth cook was way more respectable than actually *being* a prostitute (at least in my tweaked out mind), because clearly snorting spilled speed off the carpet with a straw was nothing to be ashamed of.

As a productive tweaker, I started studying real estate appraisal in between staying up for days on end to conduct home improvements to boost the property value of Billy's mom's house. Using a Home Depot account attached to Billy's place of employment, we bought anything and everything needed to improve the property value of her house. The poor love had suffered a massive stroke years before Billy and I met, which rendered her unable to really speak. Along with experiencing aphasia which left her without a short-term memory, I could easily justify that his mom's house needed the makeover more than Billy's employer needed a trustworthy employee.

After many night shifts of retexturing the popcorn ceilings, ripping out the forty year old shag carpet, laying laminate wood flooring, resurfacing the kitchen cupboards, repainting the entire interior, and landscaping the front yard by pulling crabgrass out by hand at eleven p.m. at night under a spotlight, I finally talked Billy's mom into replacing the windows throughout the house to finish off the renovations. I wanted the outside surroundings of my life to look well put together since the insides were a shattered fucking mess. Although I was certain our elderly neighbours around the cul-de-sac thought it was odd to see me at such weird hours working in the dirt, their generation appreciated hard manual labor and were delighted to see the improvements happening.

After passing the test to get my appraisal license, I failed to pay the nine hundred dollars for the piece of paper, and instead spent it on shards of crystal. Another few months passed, and I was nowhere near to finding out what I was supposed to be doing with the rest of my life.

On a whim, I decided that applying for the California Highway Patrol would be my next power move. It would give me a new focus and an easy reason to get and stay clean. It wasn't quite as cool as the FBI, but it would do in a pinch.

"Hey! Do we have any stamps laying around?" I asked Billy.

"You're the one with postmasters as parents. Shouldn't you have stamps on you twenty four seven?" Billy replied. "What's gotten into you?"

"I'm going to apply with the CHP!"

"You *what?*"

"Yeah! I can be a motorcycle cop like my mom's dad was!"

"I thought your grandpa was an insurance broker before he died?"

"Yeah, that was my real grandpa. I'm talking about the soft cock that bounced out on my grandma when my mom was like a year old."

I checked the mail every day like I was six, waiting for a golden ticket from Charlie to personally visit his chocolate factory. After seemingly an eon, my acceptance letter arrived, along with a date and time to report for a physical test and initial panel interview for consideration. Knowing I would need to be somewhat forthright about my 'prior' drug use, I planned on pitching myself as the perfect top qualifying candidate since I could spot a drug addict or drunk from a mile away. Unlike the squares who'd never touched a drug in their life, I would be the perfect officer to serve my great state!

I called our friends who we'd partied with frequently in Oakland and arranged to stay at their apartment the night before. Driving to Vallejo from Oakland at eight a.m. in the morning made way more sense than fighting rush hour traffic from Santa Rosa. I was going to do everything in my power to be punctual, because you can't respect someone who disrespects your time.

After arriving at our friends', and spending an hour talking about how hard it was to stay off the meth-express train, we decided to head down to the local dive bar for a game of pool and a few beers. Although we managed to avoid talking each other into getting high, thanks to the prospect of spending the morning with cops, our beers mystically turned into a gallon of spiced rum. When my alarm went off at seven a.m., I woke up on the couch fully clothed in my shoes and still partially drunk. As a blanket of panic started pulling up over my legs, I frantically drug my ass into the bathroom to try and clean the smell off my teeth. As I quietly pulled my friend's door shut in hopes that I didn't wake them, I was hit with a wafting smell of shit.

CRUSHING IT

Jesus! I wonder which one of them shit their pants in the night?

With my head feeling like a spinning top, I flicked the bathroom light on while catching a glimpse of my swollen eyes in the mirror. Before my internal committee could start in on how disgusting I looked, another wall of putrid smell smacked me in the face.

Pulling in separate directions to undo the bottom button on my size fifteen jeans, I noticed I didn't have any underwear on. Instantly the blanket of fear got heavier as I pushed down a sensation of nausea and sat down on the plastic throne. As my nose battled the familiar scent of a sunbaked porta-shitter after a music festival, I tried to figure out where the fuck my underwear went and what happened last night. Other than a game of Twister lying on the floor, nothing had seemed out of the ordinary in the living room when I woke up.

I rarely ever puked while I was drinking, and almost never puked the next day, but today was proving otherwise. As if I were entering a sandstorm with Indian Jones by my side, I peered into the stark white bathtub with my black t-shirt safely covering my face. Examining the source of the fetid stench, I found a hardened brown turd staring back at me while I hovered over the toilet. Thinking the family Pitbull had backed one out in the tub, I forgot about my nervousness for a second while I wiped.

How and why did Jonestown take a shit in the bathtub!?

While I stood there contemplating whether or not I had the spare time to help my friends by cleaning up after their dog, I noticed my peach colored thong wadded up in the corner opposite the tub. Next to my thong, was one of two white bathrobes that had been hastily discarded on the floor? Being helpful, I picked the robe up, aiming to hang it next to its mate on the back of the door, and saw what looked like a massive skid stain. Suddenly, all of the pieces fell into place as to who actually left the surprise in the bathtub...and it wasn't the dog.

"Why are you in your bra?" Billy asked perplexedly as I walked in the front door later that afternoon.

"For some weird reason I threw up right as I was pulling onto the freeway," I replied.

"Well that sounds unpleasant."

"Yeah, not my proudest moment," I said as I thought about whether or not I should mention I wiped my ass with someone's robe in the middle of the night after shitting in their bathtub.

"So, how'd the test go?" he asked.

"I passed the physical, but they strangely seemed to frown upon the amount of times I've 'experimented' with hallucinogens," I replied sarcastically. "They told me to reapply in seven years," I said, rollingmy eyes. "Their loss, not mine. Who wants to be triple A with a gun, anyway?"

With Billy being the only source of income, I decided it was time to go back to work. The more trying to find a purpose had failed, the more I kept drinking and smoking. Despite knowing that the definition of insanity was repeating the same thing over and over again and expecting a different result, I went back to 24-Hour Fitness and bought my fifth Honda. It was only a matter of weeks before Billy and I got in a huge fight, causing me to ride off in a rage on two wheels and dump my bike into a curb to avoid slamming into the back of someone's bumper. Flying over the front handlebars, I crash landed into the pavement with my left shoulder and tore a cruciate ligament while turning my entire left side into hamburger meat. I managed to slur enough words out to convince the 7/11 employee to not call 911, and once again got away without little to no consequences.

Looking for answers everywhere but where they actually were, I kept myself sick by looking at all the ways I was different from the other fuck-ups and continued to justify myself straight towards multiple felonies.

. . . .

As human beings, we will do almost anything to belong. Our number two fear (second only to change) is being judged by other humans. We so desperately want to belong to a group or community, that we will compromise our belief systems and fuck up our wellbeing just to be "accepted". With social media setting this tinderbox aflame, this desperation for acceptance permeates every part of our lives--online and offline.

When we do stupid shit, instead of owning it, we bury it in fear of judgement. By being able to laugh at ourselves and our mistakes, we remain humble and free. Having humility doesn't translate into being humiliated. It simply means that we are neither better or worse than others. We remain neutral. We usually take ourselves so seriously, when in reality, no one else fucking cares because they've done just as much stupid shit! By not thinking you're better than others, we can accept that we are human and are no doubt going to make mistakes.

Developing the skill of being able to laugh at your past mistakes can take time. But as I wrote about in the previous chapters, we have to first acknowledge our past, then go through the work to heal. I certainly didn't get clean and sober, followed by immediately laughing at the fact that I took a shit in my friend's bathtub and proceeded to wipe my ass with their robe! I had to cry first. Then write and analyze. Then make amends. Then of course, I laughed.

Do the F*cking Work

Define the word 'humility' in your own words.

Who do you have in your life (a friend or family member) that you find yourself in a codependent relationship with? (i.e. misery loves company and breaking up is hard.)

We often think that making some kind of a change takes something more than a conscious decision to do something different. The first step in making that change is to at first admit, then accept, that you have a problem with something.

What changes do you want to make in your life?

In your opinion, what is the difference between admitting and accepting?

Why do you think you need to do both?

What things in your past can you consider laughing at that you otherwise have felt ashamed about?

Scan here for more good shit.

BEAUTY IS NOT IN THE EYE
OF ADVERTISERS

I bounced around sales jobs like a dryer sheet in the wind until I found a group of men to hire me that were nearly just as dysfunctional as I was. The auto industry was the perfect place to drink on the job, smoke meth on my lunch break, and continue to skate by without getting fired. I'd decided that Billy and I could no longer live together and continue to pretend like we were anything more than co-dependent drug addicts.

Although I wanted it and knew what I had to do, I failed miserably at staying clean and sober despite my half-assed attempts. My upper lip would curl every time I saw the word "God" on the walls inside the rooms of a 12-step recovery meeting. The thought of spending any amount of time hanging out with people who I didn't have a fucking thing in common with, was repulsive. Of course, once I randomly discovered that I had five felony charges relating to a violation of section 368(d) of the penal code, I finally decided to try everything in my power to not leave a meeting five minutes before it finished.

While trying to get Billy a job working for me in the internet sales department at the dealership, it appeared that we would go from being co-dependents to co-defendants in a matter of seconds.

"Hey Kortney, it's Todd. Is Billy down there training with you at Cadillac?" my boss asked.

"Hey Todd! No, I haven't seen him in the last hour. What's up?" I replied.

"Well, I'm not really sure. Fred called me and asked where I keep finding these fucking losers at."

"Fucking losers?" I questioned rhetorically.

Through a nervous laugh, Todd clarified, "I guess Billy's background check came back with a number of warrants out for his arrest for different felonies."

"WHAT!" I exclaimed as my stomach dropped.

"Yeah, I know right? But here's where it gets weirder- you're listed as his co-defendant," he said.

"There must be some kind of clerical error. I sure as shit haven't broken any laws!" I cried as I ran through every possible scenario that could have landed me a felony.

Unlike most accused felons, we were actually innocent (at least of these specific felonies). Because I was an organised, productive tweaker, I kept receipts from the random projects Billy and I completed around his mom's house. For example, replacing the windows throughout the house, which Billy's mom seemed to have forgotten about when her boyfriend asked her why she'd written so many checks out to me. Several thousand dollars later and an obnoxious defense attorney who made me feel like OJ Simpson, I stumbled through the process while somehow remaining clean and sober for another ninety day stint before I met my new chemical romance.

Thinking he was "just coming in to test drive", my latest appointment had arrived in the lobby. Somewhere between riding the pink cloud of early recovery and towing the thin line of drowning in anxiety, I dashed down the stairs from my corner executive office that should have belonged to anyone but myself, and overrode Tim's attempt at shaking my hand by going straight in for a hug. Making a bashful Jehovah's Witness blush, I pulled away and began to wave my KO magic spell-casting wand.

"It's soooooo nice to finally meet you, Tim! I feel like we're long lost cousins... or maybe high school friends with all of the emails we've sent back and forth!" I said thinking quickly on my heels knowing that my flirting may come off strange if he were envisioning us as cousins.

"Yeah. It's nice to meet you too. I don't think I've ever gotten a hug from a dealership before," he said quietly.

"Well, what can I say- there's no other dealership experience like this one, Tim," I said as I intentionally made a point to keep using his name as much as possible.

"As you can see I'm trying to butter you up so you buy a car! I've got three kids to feed and my husband is in prison, so I'm counting on you," I said while maintaining a stone cold face.

Looking like he might run out the front door, I gently grabbed his elbow and clarified.

"I'm only kidding, Tim. I have no kids and no husband. I only need to pay for back surgery since I jacked it up while helping a friend move," I said with my best seductive tone.

Laughing from relief, he shifted in his Levis 501 jeans and ran his fingers through his wavy, thick brown hair.

"I'm sorry to hear about your back, but I'm only here to test drive."

Nearly three hours later, Tim was heading off to the finance department to sign off on his new pre-owned powder blue BMW 6-Series. Before hugging him goodbye in the parking lot, I managed to get another ten pills off of him after he'd kindly shared two with me on one of our earlier test drives. I had legitimate pain, and besides, pills weren't 'my problem'. As I waved goodbye to another new happy customer and fan, I said hello to the comforting new feeling these magical pills were giving me.

Wearing a form-fitted pencil skirt the same color as Tim's new car, and a loose fitting spaghetti strap silky tank top, I locked eyes with the boy sitting shotgun in a new Ford Escape that was pulling into the lot. Unsure of whether it was the pills or his smile, I felt a wave of excitement as the bald-headed man gave me a taste of my own medicine.

Holy fuck... so that's how guys feel when I shoot them that sadistic, yet charming smile.

"Why hello there, Miss," he said as he stepped out of the Ford. With his crisp black slacks, slick polished shoes and perfectly pink Scottish kilt-patterned tied tie, he walked up to me with a look in his eyes that I'd never seen before.

"Ummmm, hi..... Bubba?" I said as I looked down at his name tag. "Putting in those hours, huh?" I said with a smirk.

"Hustling, girl. Always," he said behind the cutest grin I'd ever seen.

"Why are you on my lot?" I said with my hands on my waist, while trying to appear more like an hourglass than the box I was serving.

"Don't worry- if I end up selling something you had lined up for someone else, I'll take you on a date with the commission," he said before winking at me.

"Oh is that right?" I said laughing.

"Yeah," he replied as his customer walked up alongside him. "Jack, this is Kortney, my future wife. Kortney, this is Jack, my future customer."

Ignoring his attempt at being slick, I reached out my hand and gave Jack one of my signature handshakes.

"Future customer, it's a pleasure meeting you. I'm the internet sales manager for four dealerships in this auto-group, so feel free to drop this clown and find me in a few weeks," I said as I winked.On the same day, I found two new highs-- narcotics and a new boy who wasn't smoking meth.

It only took a few weeks before I replaced recovery meetings every day after work with the sweet high of Bubba. He was quietly confident, amazing at his job, had his shit together, and was thrilled to find a girl that wasn't out chasing the club life. Coincidently, and conveniently, we were both more than happy to replace "partying" with working out. Although unlike my situation, Bubba's partying was non life-threatening, so replacing bad influences and cocaine with weights was a perfect match. But for me, I replaced my nearly decade long non-stop party with pain pills.

It only took a few months before Bubba and I moved in together, and eventually bought a house in my name with my dad as a co-signer. Telling my dad and stepmom that one day in the future I'd turn the house into a sober living environment, they agreed to co-sign since I was clean and sober for over a year, minus the cunning pill addiction I was masterfully concealing. Much like meth, it was easy for me to hide the amount I was taking. My mom had just completed a round of surgeries from accidents she'd experienced on the job, and was a one-stop pill shop. On top of taking pills from her and with her, I found my own doctor to prescribe my own supply. Using the 'old college sports injury' excuse, I'd wear obnoxiously tight heels the day before an appointment and aggravate my foot to such a point that I could hardly walk.

During the first year, maintaining the addiction was easy. Then as expected, the benefit of the high got shorter and shorter, while my list of excuses got longer and longer.

I'd gotten to the point of barely being able to get myself out of bed as the thought of my meaningless job was making my skin crawl. It felt like my debt was slowly growing like a patch of black mold in a dark basement. Although there are no rules in recovery, it was highly suggested that as a new person, you spend your first year clean and sober with a plant. If the plant doesn't die, it's safe to move onto a pet. If the pet lasted, you'd be ready for a relationship. Additionally, avoid any major job changes if possible, never make another human being your higher power, get a sponsor, work the steps, and attend a meeting every day. All the things I wasn't doing and steps I wasn't following.

I kept referring to myself as clean and sober because, in my mind, I was. In most cases, my name was on the bottle, so I ticked all the boxes: I hadn't touched meth, and I hadn't (yet) touched a drink. Like Elvis Presley, I convinced myself that if it was prescribed, it wasn't an addiction. And we all know how that ended. In addition to my denial, I also hated being told what to do, even if the directions or suggestions protected my safety. So naturally, I ignored the instructions of the Big Book. However, without working the steps and getting a sponsor, I had zero chance of scratching the itch that my financial insecurities from childhood were causing me.

Blowing off calling my prospects so I could jump on Craigslist and start looking for paid implied nude modeling gigs, I felt the crushing weight of needing to make more money. I'd done enough dodgy shit in my past days while I was with Billy, that looking for something as tame as implied nude shouldn't cause Bubba too much unhappiness. All the bills were in my name, including the twenty two hundred square foot house we were living in. Plus, my pill habit was starting to cause a slight financial strain after it somehow went from one or two a day to five or six.

After minimal scrolling, one ad in particular seemed to jump off the screen and land right between my legs. The fact that I was to the point where I had to scrape myself out of bed with a spatula to get to work, made it that much more intriguing. Ever since I lost the passion of chasing the dream of becoming the POTUS, it seemed that every meaningless job I found chipped away at my soul. The more chips that flew off, the more shit I tried to put in my body to fix the dings, dents, divots and of course, cellulite.

Muscular calf video shoot.

$100/hour

Must have muscular calves.

Send submission photos via email.

All ballerinas & athletes must consider!

I re-read the ad about ten times to make sure I wasn't missing a sentence somewhere that mentioned I had to wear an adult diaper or something worse. I simply couldn't believe that I could make a hundred dollars to flex my calves.

Do I even have visible calf muscles?

I wonder if this is some kind of scam where they trick you into being a sex slave by getting you strung out on heroin or something?

Without a second thought, I immediately shut my office door and started taking pictures of my calves before emailing them off to the poster. In less than an hour, "Mick" was in my inbox scheduling a time to come up and meet me and my calves in person.

. . . .

Wearing a black skin-tight mini-skirt, I whistled the whole two mile drive to work with the prospect of this new and exciting opportunity. Although it was starting to constipate me, taking six pills a day was still managing to kill my appetite. (I mean, who cares about shitting properly if you're skinny?) Along with the two hour a day workouts, I was feeling slightly more satisfied with my body than usual. On a scale of one to ten, I was sitting at around a two and a half instead of my usual one.

The morning rolled into afternoon and Mick had arrived.

After making basic small talk about weather and cars, Mick got straight to the point.

"Ok- so basically I'm looking for an athlete, model- whatever you want to call it, to do a joint fifty-fifty venture with me," he said.

"I'm all ears!" I said while sitting at full attention.

"Looks like you're all calves, KO!" he said.

Hardly able to contain my joy, I smiled coyly and waited to get the dish.

"So it's pretty straight forward. There's a website that has a ton of adult content. I mean you can find everything on there from super weird white-people shit like pimple popping, to people dressed up in alien costumes doing anal."

Fuck- I knew there was going to be something fucked up. Why don't I ask more questions. When am I going to learn my lesson?

"Uh-huh," I said while still trying to not look disappointed.

"But there's a huge, and I mean HUGE population of guys who are into muscular women," he said. "The website takes thirty percent of the profit, and you and I split the other seventy percent. I film, edit and promote, and you just be you!"

"OK, that's interesting. But I'm not that muscular?" I replied. "I mean, I've worked in gyms for years and I've only seen a couple of really jacked women for comparison purposes."

"You've got muscles! But it's a bit of personality that goes a long way with this stuff as well. It's really about a woman in charge and winning that really sells the clips," he said.

"So, you mean to tell me that there are men out there who find muscular calves more attractive than a pair of giant, juicy, perky tits?"

"Like you wouldn't believe!" he said. "And it goes in all sorts of other directions from there."

"Well, if you think I have what it takes, I'm down!" I said excitedly. "What's next?"

"We just need to spend half a day filming some stuff, really," he replied.

"Ok, well how about tomorrow?" I said.

"Well, damn! Ok then, KO!" he whimsically replied as his bald head started to bead with sweat.

After setting a time, I walked Mick out to the front door and headed back to my office without a thought about all of the questions

I didn't bother to ask. When I got home, I told Bubba I was going to drive down to the Bay Area and meet a body building coach. It seemed that my lying about taking pain pills was turning into me lying about everything else.

Once I got down to Mick's apartment in Oakland, my nerves settled a bit. There was nothing unusual about his place, other than a tanning oil and a woman's posing suit on the living room coffee table. Noticing I was observing the contents, Mick explained.

"That's my wife's suit. Kalista is comp prepping right now and has a big NPC show in three months," he said.

"Ah makes sense," I said. Not wanting to have his wife roll up and find her husband filming me with a video camera, I asked, "Is she here?"

"No, but she'll be back in a few hours. I asked her if she could join us for a few clips," he said.

Wondering if he was going to try and pull some fast, threesome bullshit, I slyly pulled a pill out of my hidden stash spot I'd cut into my purse and shoved it in my mouth.

"Forgot to tell you-- I've got a business partner popping by in a few minutes. He wants to meet you and see if you're interested in shooting for his website."

"Ok, cool. I feel like some kind of big deal all the sudden. What's the website?" I asked, hoping it wasn't going to be some of that weird white-people shit he was referring to earlier.

Bubba would absolutely die. He's not even cool with me making out with another chick let alone do any nude modelling.

"It's a membership website of muscular girls flexing. He and another guy also have a webcam business for muscle girls," he said.

"Ah ha. Yeah, my boyfriend would lose his mind if he ever caught me on a webcam," I said.

"Yeah, it's not what you're thinking. The most risqué thing that goes on is being topless. Guys like to see women hulk-out of their clothes and rip them off!" he said excitedly.

"Seriously?" I asked in shock.

Taking my top off was something I was familiar with, and seeing that my tits were smaller than most dudes, I quickly changed my tune to, "Tell me more."

I truly had no idea what this was all about, or where it would take me.

London.

Paris.

New York.

Australia.

Several trips to the bank.

Hell and back.

"Yeah! They pay a lot of money too- I think it's like six dollars and ninety nine cents a minute for one on one chat."

Just as I started imaging the amount of money I could rake in trying to rip my clothes off, there was a knock on the door.

After the guys said hello, the new guy introduced himself.

"Hey! You must be KO!" he said as he stuck his hand out. "I'm Trevor, Mick's smarter and more attractive business partner."

"Haha! Yes, nice to meet you!" I said. "So you have a webcam and membership website Mick said?" I asked.

"I do! I'd love to photograph you today for the site if you're down. We pay two hundred dollars in cash for a photo set if you're down," he said.

"Yeah! What do I need to do?" I asked.

"Well, basically just flex! Did you bring any outfits with you other than what you have on?" he asked as he looked at my ripped jean shorts, flip flops and ribbed tank top.

"I brought a fitted bodycon dress, heels, and a bikini," I said.

"Ok perfect. We can walk down to Jack London Square and knock the pictures out before you guys film?" he suggested.

"Yeah, that's cool," said Mick.

"Why don't you go put your bikini on under your dress and we'll head down there?" he said.

After walking a few blocks, we were at a deserted town square by tena.m. As Trevor stood with his camera around his neck surveying the light, Mick took an exercise band out of his pocket.

"Get a little pump on!" he said, tossing it at me.

Standing in a slate grey bodycon dress, I stepped on the band with my black high heels and started repping out bicep curls.

"Ok, KO! Where you're standing is perfect. Now give me a front double bicep," Trevor shouted.

"A what?" I asked in total bewilderment.

"A front double bicep!" Mick replied while flexing both his

biceps in the air.

"Oh! Right!" I said as I shadowed Mick and flexed my biceps.

That morning in front of a circular water fountain full of mismatched rocks, I took in as much of the crash course of female bodybuilding poses as I could, and flexed whatever visible muscle I had. After an hour of pretending I knew what I was doing, we walked back to Mick's where Trevor handed me two, crisp hundred dollar bills before having me sign a release waiver.

"That was great, KO. The members are gonna love this. Are you on the XB website yet?" he asked.

Before I could ask what the XB was, Mick replied for me, "No, man. I only just met her yesterday!"

"What's the XB?" I asked as the guys looked at each other.

"It's just another schmoe website," Mick said.

"Schmoe?" I asked.

"Lots to learn!" Mick said laughing as Trevor joined in.

"A schmoe is the term used for guys in this muscle fetish world," Trevor said.

"Ah I see. Yeah, I have no clue about any of this stuff," I said.

"Before I leave, Mick said he mentioned the webcam site to you?" he asked.

"Yeah, he did! Sounds interesting. I'll give you my email and you can send me the details," I said. "What's it called again?"

"She Flex," he said.

After saying goodbye to Trevor, Mick got his camera set up on a tripod and instructed me to throw my jean shorts back on over the top of my school bus yellow string bikini.

"Ok, so I'm going to sit on the ground in front of the couch and you're gonna apply various scissor holds," he said.

"Scissor holds?" I asked. "The fuck is that!"

"Didn't you ever watch WWF growing up?"

"Yeah not really. I have an older brother who I idolised but we grew up without cable in the country! Plus he's eight years older than me. I used to try and fight back when he'd throw my baby blanket in places I couldn't reach, but he'd just sit on my chest and play Chinese torture by thumping on my chest and making me name ten of my mom's friends before he'd let me up," I said. "My mom didn't even have ten friends!"

As Mick laughed, he assured me he'd walk me through it after I got changed.

Sitting on the edge of the couch, Mick sat between my legs on the floor with his back against the couch.

"Ok- wrap your legs around my neck like a python, cross your ankles and squeeze," he said.

Getting his neck up against my crotch, I balanced myself with my hands and crossed my angles.

"Now squeeze!" he said.

Before I really put any power into it, he started coughing a little bit.

"God damn! I think I struck gold!" he said. "Ok now go hard,

150

and when I tap, let go."

Not holding back and striving to please, I started squeezing as if I was back in college spending an hour on the abductor/adductor machine. After a short five seconds, Mick was slapping the side of my right thigh. As soon as I let up, he started coughing again and laughing.

"Ok, KO! Now I want you to bend your right leg around my neck and lock the other one over the top of it like a vice and squeeze again."

After an hour of coaching me through various holds and hitting the record button on his video camera's remote control, we moved the operation down the hall and into his wife's closet.

"Alright- all you need to do is reach up on the top shelves and pull down some purses. Really flex your calves as you reach up, ok?"

As I reached up on my tippy toes and grabbed various bags off the shelf, Mick lay on the cream colored carpet with the video camera and filmed my calves. A rigid dichotomy between my outer appearance and my internal thoughts, I took to being the center of attention like a skinny white girl to a fat-free cheeto. After I pulled a bag down and pretended to inspect it, I slowly bent down and seductively ran my fingers over my cramping calf.

Shortly after the closet role play, Kalista walked through the front door. Standing as tall as my shoulders, she was a golden brown wall of pure muscle. With a matching set on, her veins bulge out from underneath the navy blue strappy sports bra and booty shorts she wore. I'd only seen a couple of other women this jacked a few times in my life. While working at 24-Hour Fitness, it seemed that every woman who sat down at my desk wanted to "just tone up" or "lose weight". Not a single one wanted to get ripped, jacked and tan, or buff as fuck.

The few magazines I'd thumbed through as a kid while visiting my Uncle's garage gym, only gave me a taste of what was possible for a woman to do with her physique. With women like Rachel McLish and Cory Everson appearing on covers, I hadn't yet heard of or seen machines such as Iris Kyle, or Kalista at this point. Although she was still feminine looking, she had a slight male energy about her. In a voice that was deeper than I was anticipating, she reached out to hug me.

"Hi KO! Lovely meeting you," she said as she leaned in.

Feeling slightly in awe and somewhat chuffed that she bypassed my hand for a hug, I followed suit and hugged her back. While my right hand landed on her shoulder, my left hand slid across her back and down her waist as I tried to push past my dumbfounded sense of reality and say something interesting.

"Jesus Christ! You are an absolute unit!" I squealed as I palpated her shoulder in my hand as if trying to squeeze a lemon. I had never felt a muscle so hard on a woman in my life.

"That's the best compliment I could hope for", she replied in her rough voice as she set her duffle bag down. "So Mick's had you doing all sorts of weird shit today?"

"It's all Greek to me!" I said laughing.

"How was training?" Mick asked.

"Yeah, just fine. I had an email from the guy I was telling you about yesterday- the one with the foot obsession that I saw a few months ago when he was in town," she said back to Mick.

"Yeah, and?" he said.

"Well- he's back in town and wants to see me again. As in tonight."

"Well he better pay a premium because he's cutting into my filming time!" Mick said.

"I can't shower before I go over there. He wants me wearing the shoes and socks I trained in!" she exclaimed. "I just wish I could get a foot-only guy. He wants half the time spent on lift and carry, so looks like I'm gonna have to work a bit for this one!"

"Well, let's get to it then," Mick said. "Speaking of lift and carry, I need some donkey raise clips."

"Am I fine wearing this or do you need me to put something else on?" she asked Mick.

"No that's fine."

"I think I know what donkey raises are, but I'm not sure what you guys are talking about with this lift and carry stuff," I said, feeling slightly lame.

With a laugh, Mick and Kalista looked at each other and smiled.

"Sorry KO, we forget that this is like a foreign language for people. After spending so many years doing it, it becomes your normal," Kalista said.

"Guys are really into demonstrations of strength through various ways, but lift and carry is probably one of the most popular categories," Mick said.

"Yeah, so the guy I'm seeing tonight is really into smelly feet, muscular women, and being picked up and carried around. There's everything from a fireman carry, a piggyback, a shoulder ride, or a cradle," she said.

"Show her a fireman carry, Kalista!" exclaimed Mick.

Without any kind of warning, after reaching up through between my legs, Kalista put one hand on my lower middle back, and stood up. Before I could blink, I was sideways in the air while resting on her rock hard shoulders.

"Oh shit!" I shrilled before she decided to take it up a notch and perform a squat, using me as her weight.

Setting me back down like I was a sack of air, I caught my balance while the blood rushed back out of my face, leaving me lightheaded.

"Yeah, KO. You're about to have your mind blown with the amount of shit you're about to learn," she said.

"So how much money do you make when you do this stuff?" I asked.

"Depends, but usually three hundred an hour is the norm."

"Three hundred dollars!!!!!!!!!" I exclaimed. "And you don't have to screw anyone?"

"Nope. I mean, there are a lot of bodybuilders and wrestlers who have "special" clients, but it's not expected," she said.

"Ok ladies, I hate to interrupt, but school's out of session!" said Mick.

"Yeah, yeah, yeah…," said Kalista as she rolled her mascara smudged eyes.

"Kal, why don't you start on KO's back and she can rep out some raises and then you can worship her calves, then switch."

"So what do I do?" I asked, feeling lame again.

"Just bend over and hold onto the side of the bookshelf for

support. I'm gonna hop up onto your low back as added weight. Then you just do calf raises while bent over for as many as you can handle," she said.

"Do you want me to use oil or anything?" Kalista asked Mick.

"Yeah, thanks for suggesting it!" said Mick.

As Kalista grabbed the bottle of baby oil off the coffee table, I wondered what she was going to do with it. Not wanting to look like a clueless ass again, I just went along with it. After she set the bottle down, I leaned over and braced for her impact. I felt my back twinge as she jumped on, but kept my mouth shut. There was no way I was going to look weak in front of this lady. As I started repping out raises, Kalista started talking.

"There you go, KO! You're so strong. I can feel all of your back muscles rippling underneath me. It's almost like a vibrator. Oh my god keep going!"

Like the teacher's pet I am, I kept going as I basked in her praise. After the fiftieth rep and nearly breaking wind, I stopped moving and stood up into a piggyback position while holding onto her brick-like legs. She slid down and touched the floor with her shoes as I let her go.

"Oh my gosh, that was impressive. I bet you need a little massage after all that hard work!" she said as she reached out and grabbed the bottle. Pouring oil into the palm of her hands before rubbing them together, Kalista valiantly tried to look turned on before she kneeled down in front of my calves.

Instinctually, I stuck my right leg out and came up on my toes to flex my calf. With both hands, Kalista massaged oil into my leg while she remarked about how hard they were. Although I knew her performance wasn't exactly Oscar-worthy, her words and her rubbing made me feel like royalty for a few minutes--that is until I felt a hunger pain and realised I needed another pill.

. . . .

My entire life, I thought that beauty was what was on the front of a magazine, in an ad, or what a celebrity looked like. Not once did it occur to me that maybe because I was attracted to 'non-traditional' handsome men or sexy women, that the rest of the world was in the same boat. For example, you would have never caught someone like Jepson on the cover of a magazine (at least not before 2018). Additionally, we are now living in a time where everything that used to be customary is no longer expected. Brands are using non-binary people in their marketing and ads, as well as taking steps to normalise traits such as gapped teeth and freckles. There's still a massive way to go, but it's certainly a step in the right direction. But the simple fact is, beauty truly is in the eye of the beholder. Beauty is not in the eye of advertisers.

Do the F*cking Work

Describe how you've made your happiness contingent on having an intimate partner?

Write about a time you "fell in love" with someone else to distract yourself from working on yourself.

Explain how you are a "fixer"?

Write about the last time you hangout with yourself, by yourself, willingly.

Write about a time you lied in a relationship because it was easier than hurting the other person's feelings.

In what ways (if any) do you flirt to get what you want?

Has it ever gotten you into trouble or a situation you comfortably couldn't get yourself out of?

Does lying make you low-key feel like a fraud, giving you low self-esteem?

Why do you think you're not worthy of having strong self-esteem at the expense of someone else's feelings? (p.s. screw that shit!)

Scan here for more good shit.

LESSON 8

A SCHMOE WOULD PAY FOR THAT

*B*etween being on the webcam and working with Mick, I fearlessly submerged myself into this new world of 'schmoes' with ease. After a few months, I was ready to do whatever it took to establish myself as the best of this unexplored Muscle Fetish terrain. A witty, feminine, bodybuilder with giant legs paired with a set of come-fuck-me eyes that trumped my tiny lopsided set of tits, I was lapping up this new level of attention like fresh water to a shriveled-up houseplant. What briefly started out as strange and weird, quickly became exactly what Kalista referred to as my new 'normal'.

Seeing the level of potential, I was ready to have my own website built. On top of blogging, I could offer men the ability to order custom video clips as well as launch a paid membership where men would get whatever exclusive photo and video content I posted for the month. I used to think that getting paid in one lump sum was an excellent compensation for exploiting my looks when it came to video and photo shoots. But after seeing what this clip store could offer, I quickly realised that the *real* payout was in residual income.

It seemed like there were two types of women in this new

industry. Those who were proper, hardcore bodybuilders and women who were more of the wrestling type. The wrestlers were athletic and usually had some kind of Jiu Jitsu background like me, but rarely had visible muscle. The bodybuilders were usually on some type of steroids and rarely wrestled as they didn't want to risk injury. All in all, a quick Google search reveals over *eighty three million* listings, so there is definitely potential for serious money.

As 'All Natural KO': No steroids, no fake tits, and no bullshit, I positioned myself to stand out in the marketplace by uniquely marketing myself to appeal to both the muscle-loving men as well as those who were into the wrestling type stuff. The more requests I received from fans to make these custom clips, the fewer cars I needed to sell. But selling myself in emails and causing men to fall in love with me was a breeze in comparison to the loveless relationship I had with myself.

I knew that focusing on my recovery should be my top priority, but my focus was about as good as staring at an eclipse with empty rimmed glasses on. I kept telling myself that I was legitimately in pain, and that pills weren't actually my problem. My *real* problem was being in debt and needing to make hay while the sun was still shining with what little youthfulness I had left in my late twenties. Making money was far more important than dicking around with the 12-step recovery bullshit.

Through working on the webcam and making clips with Mick, I spent the last few months of 2008 learning everything I could about the vast variety of what made a schmoe, a schmoe. As my name got out through all of their online forums, offers started coming in to film with other companies similar to Trevor's. From wrestling, to scissor holds, to rubbing oil, flexing and comparing muscle size with other female bodybuilders, it appeared that I was a breath of fresh air on the stale scene.

Raising two middle fingers high in the sky, I went from slanging metal to hustling the 'KO package' fulltime by late April. Somewhere between my untamed charisma and a growing pill addiction, a dynamite character was split between two personalities: Kortney Kay and All-Natural KO--both of which sat impatiently waiting to please anyone who posed slightly interested. Kortney kept scouring the earth for validation and purpose, feeling completely out of control with her inability to accept her body, while KO kept a white-knuckle death grip of control on every person, place and thing that surrounded her.

More glaring in differences than the Brittany Spears of 2001 and Brittany 07', the writings in my personal journal compared to what I was spewing on my public blog, had me questioning if I potentially had undiagnosed bipolar disorder.

04-05-2009

I know I need to stop taking pills. It's a total waste of money. Holding me back from obtaining my spiritual relationship. Makes me dumb. Not fun anymore. Just take a break? Think of your mom being scattered, it's sad. It won't be that bad getting off them because of how much I work out and sweat. Website was supposed to be done April 1st but still hasn't launched.

06-08-2009

Wow I haven't journaled in deep! Shits rollin' along fine. I'm getting big worldwide! No joke. I'm getting further away from working a 12-step program and instead wanting to do sessions though. Bubba is cool with it for the most part but if he could just roll with it completely, we'd be making a lot of money! All of my journal entries and thoughts always revolve around money. Too bad! Got denied for health insurance today too. Oh-almost forgot... Bubba proposed to me a couple of weeks ago too! I guess the important thing for me to realize is no matter what, DON'T DRINK.

CRUSHING IT

'Give that bitch a biscuit'

Hummmmmm….. the sun is out, and I don't feel like doin' shit other than blogging. My friend from Germany is stopping by in about an hour. On top of having him help me start planning my 'tour' over there, I'll have him teach me the metric system, lol. I know I only just started handing out these ass-whoopings in person a month ago, but I'm already ready to go international! It looks like there are a ton of you waiting for me in Europe!

I spent the past thirty minutes cutting three pairs of jeans into tiny micro shorts. Since my legs are getting so ripped, they aren't fitting in my pants. One pair didn't tear very well, so I thought I'd cut them into jeans-panties'! I'll be sure to use them in my next photo shoot.

I'm starting to become quite content with the fact that my job is to now motivate people to work out, as well as become a symbol of success and sex. I've made it my personal Mission to knock the skinny-ass supermodel types off the top. When fit girls with hard sexy muscles and some booty to spare make it to the spotlight, I'll be shouting from my soapbox, "GIVE THAT BITCH A BISCUIT!".

I read some alarming fact the other day in a shitty Cosmo magazine that something to the effect of 88% of 11-year-old girls in the United States believe they are overweight and want to start some type of diet. WHAT THE FUCK! There is something fundamentally wrong with that statistic. There are way more I could post, but I'll save those for another day. For now, let's just focus on having the women taking care of their body and working their fucking asses off training, be in the spotlight and hopefully motivating the youth out there. Like it or not, these 11-year-old girls who think they're "fat" are going to be running our country in the next decades. Of course, that is if we don't completely fuck the planet up before then. Which I'm pretty certain we are well on our way.

I swear to God, the next time I see a SUV driving down the road with only 1 person in it, I'm going to run it off the road. I don't care if you're going to pick your kids up from soccer! Ok, off to the dog park in my micro shorts to cause a scene. Love you all so much!

XOKO

Whether it was Germany, Egypt, London, Australia, Dubai, India or some podunk town in Missouri, these 'strange and weird' men came from all over the world. Knocking on my inbox with their fantasies and dollar bills, I was heavily distracted from accepting the fact that I was an addict. I had no problem admitting it, but acceptance on the other hand, was about as clear as the Thai alphabet.

There was no rhyme or reason as to how these men groped or drooled their way into the world of female strength and power. Thinking that one day I'd figure out some kind of characteristic profile pattern, the more men I encountered, the more I could see there were zero assumptions I could use to conclude as to who fit the bill as a schmoe. No part of the world, occupation, age group, race, religion, or look could help me figure out who was a typical, closet female-strength fanatic.

Once my website went live, I blogged nearly every day about my encounters throughout the journey. From the types of clip requests I received and experiences during sessions, all the way to how I was feeling about my body or how much or how little I hated Bubba that day. Minus the pill addiction, which stayed locked behind a secret diary that only my mom and a few fellow pill-popping friends had the master key to, I was an open book.

The easiest way for me to not look at my own shit, was by

looking at other people's; my fans to be precise. While trying to fumble my way through my own desire to be ripped up and strong, I wanted to understand how these fetishes developed for the rest of these schmoes as well as why this was all so hush-hush.

The only thing I thought men desired was what was plastered on the cover of a magazine. Although it became somewhat normal, I still couldn't wrap my head around how and why these men discovered these 'strange' desires of seeing a strong woman do the most random of things. But as long as I kept getting paid and wasn't expected to turn any kind of tricks, I was falsely content with trying to be the absolute best they'd ever experienced.

While trying to understand my own desire to be ripped up and muscular, I thought maybe I'd find answers by trying to understand their desire to be ripped up by a muscular woman.

Dear KO,

Thanks for asking questions on your blog regarding a subject that is not one I am able to voice often. I remember first being turned on by strong women very young. I can remember being 10 and looking at a playboy with friends. Everyone was salivating, and I said she has awesome calves. My friends ridiculed my comment, but that is what turned me on in the picture. The attraction never left me after that, and neither did the fact that I was ridiculed.

When I got older, I would secretly go to bodybuilding competitions on the weekend on my own. It was like taking drugs for me. I moved onto sessions, and even will hire female personal trainers to workout with. I've never had a male trainer. I date a lot, am straight, and love women. My fantasy has progressed to strap-on encounters with female bodybuilders; The ultimate role reversal. However, strap-on with a smaller woman is not appealing, nor is being with a guy.

I can't explain the desire I have to be completely in every way dominated by a strong woman, and a strong woman only. I do not want to be tied up and whipped. I want to feel unreal power and succumb to it. No restraints necessary.

It is a drug. I have no other vices. Women like you are my high.

By the way, yes- normally I am dominant in life, by day I am a federal agent.

KO, thanks for what you do, and who you are. More importantly thank you for asking and allowing me to divulge to someone.

My blog felt like a personal connection to these men who I was apparently helping. The more I helped them and felt validated in my work, the less I wanted to help myself. It seemed like I was the first woman in this industry that was truly curious to figure out how they got to where they were. Whether that be crushing tiny toy soldiers, losing to a strong woman in arm wrestling, being choked out between rock hard biceps, or getting dressed up in women's pantyhose and being called a little bitch unworthy of his mother's love, I was different and somehow special, and therefore, I would continue trying to get high off their compliments and praise. It didn't matter what their 'thing' was, so long as I continued to be the best. Unaware that compliments are like lines of coke and would never last long enough to make me feel whole, I kept pursuing this path paved with whey protein, pre-workouts and pills.

It all started with a few basic categories when Mick and I were making clips. From the scissoring fetish to slowly learning about an entire world that split my head apart.

"To be more specific than my previous email, I would want you in a black sports bra and black shorts. Start with a standing

shot of you doing hanging leg raises. After those you flex your abs while fingering your belly button, licking fingers and all that shit. Finger slowly and deeply. Rub oil into your abs and do some more leg raises. End video fingering your navel again. Your seven to ten minute for a hundred dollars is great. "

"Guess the main thing for a good tickling clip is, that you be stretched out lying on your back with bound hands above your head and bound feet, dressed in a small string-bikini. Another important thing is that you should try to stretch yourself out and suck in your tummy, because this makes you look more sensitive and sexier. Maybe it's hard to hold this position, when someone tickles you, but that's not bad. Just relax and try to enjoy it. It would be nice if a woman with long nails sensually tickles your tummy, (I have to admit, this is my favorite body part of you. Just gorgeous) hips, arms, legs and those adorable armpits. I'm not a fan of foot tickling, but I guess it would be good for the clip if she tickled your feet a little, too. I don't want you to be tickled in a hard and mean way. It should be a cute and erotic clip. It's all about your body being shown and touched in a tender and ticklish way. I want this to be bright and not a dark clip, where the viewer can admire your amazing body.

Also take some close-ups of armpits, tummy, hips, and legs if you can.

I won't be angry if it's not exactly like my wish. I'm happy if you just try. You don't need to hurry. I will be waiting until it's done. I like the anticipation. Best wishes and stay as beautiful as you are."

Like the phenomenon of getting bored only after a few months from the excitement of a brand new car, the requests started to feel so normal that getting offered four hundred dollars to grow my armpit hair out, sweat in a sports bra, and overnight the contents to the Kingdom of Bahrain started to lose their luster. Just like my addictions, I wanted more, and I wanted it yesterday. More opportunities, more money, more adventure, and more weird shit from these men.

Basically, more of anything that would keep me distracted from working a program and working on myself.

Fingering my belly button and getting tickled were just a spec in the universe of the different desires I'd encounter. Some guys were super basic with their asks, and some were basically asking me to assemble an entire production crew. But regardless of the effort needed to fulfill their fantasy, I had to ask:

Had I truly arrived?

I'm getting paid by some man in the Middle East so he can smell my sweat.

But also…

I'm getting paid to get sensually tickled by some hot chic of my choice for some dude in the Midwest, and yet I'm too busy scorning myself while standing in the aisle at Trader Joes, for nearly smashing through a bag of dry-roasted almonds while shopping for healthy food. Every Tom, Dick, and Harry was enjoying the benefits of me, but me.

So, I guess the answer was *not yet.* But meanwhile, I was prepared to try and repair whatever relationship I could with my mom because she had what I wanted-

"Hey mom, how was surgery?" I asked.

"They had to amputate a toe," she replied.

"Oh my GOD, mom!"

"April Fools, bitch!"

"Real funny! So, what's next?"

"Not much. I have to use crutches for the next few months, so I'm not sure how getting up and down three flights of stairs is going to work."

"Yeah, that sucks. I can come do some grocery shopping for you?"

"Yeah, that would be nice. I feel like I never hear from you anymore."

"I know, I know... I've just been so busy with my website and making clips."

"Yeah..."

"Yeah. Speaking of which, I talked Bubba into letting me do sessions so I should be bringing in a ton of money soon."

"So you're going to turn your new house into a whorehouse instead of a sober living house?"

"Ha-ha, real funny mom. And no--I travel to these men who are in town on business or I go on tour and they come to my hotel."

"And that's safe?"

"Yeah--all of these men are in this headspace of wanting to be inferior. It's crazy... "

"And they're just finding you on your website?"

"No, there's a public website called XB that lists all the women around the world who are bodybuilders and wrestlers. It gives their stats on size, and basically what their specialties are."

"Specialties, huh?"

"Yeah--I mean some women just stand around and flex so men can rub oil and worship their muscles. Like they find it more erotic than boobs, or sex. Or a nice ass, I guess. Some of them do the scissoring stuff where you choke guys with your legs, but a lot of them won't do anything else because they're prepping for a competition and don't want to risk injury."

"So what are you going to be doing?"

"Well, Bubba is only OK with me doing athletic stuff. So basically, arm wrestling, wrestling semi competitively, which means I can't do any of the 'fantasy' style wrestling because it's too sensual."

"What does that even mean?"

"Well, some men can't really wrestle. Whether they're not athletic or they're afraid of getting a bruise on their face type shit. So, they want you to just pin them in what's called a school-girl pin where you trap their arms alongside their body while you sit on their chest and they squirm around."

"And they pay you for that?"

"Yes! I know--it's crazy. Also, I can do scissor sessions and the lift and carry stuff I was telling you about."

"Wow. Seems like you hit the jackpot, my dear."

"No… I hit the jackpot having you as a mom!"

"Yeah, ok. So, what do you really want?"

"No, seriously! I'm sorry we have our ups and downs. I know I have a lot of anger to work through."

"It's ok. I'm to blame for most of that anger, probably."

"We'll figure it out. Anyway--I need to get back to work but I'll come by in a few hours. Oh, you think I can get a handful of pills from you? I can't get in to see my foot doctor for a week and I've already got my first session booked for tomorrow and it's semi-competitive wrestling."

"Jesus Christ, Kortney Kay. I knew you were calling for something other than to just check on me-"

. . . .

Most of the sessions that I had so far were pretty straight forward.

We wrestle. I win. I get four hundred dollars and he's left defeated, broke, but immeasurably happy.

But this day, however, was very different.

Very, *very* different.

I had given this one request a semi-decent amount of thought. But just like my 12-step work, I kept finding that a semi-decent effort was about as beneficial as attending a thirty thousand dollar rehab with crystal meth stashed in your bag.

This was the type of request that didn't fall into any category of services I offered, and the type I would normally turn down without even thinking about it. But as usual, I needed the money, and coming from a perceived place of scarcity, often resulted in me making relatively poor decisions—actually piss poor decisions, really.

There were supposed to be rules with boundaries that had black and white structures. Deep down Bubba was opposed to me doing them in the first place, claiming he was concerned for my safety. But really, we both knew it was because he didn't want to share his girlfriend, on-again, off-again, on-again fiancée with other men. Even though I assured him nothing sexual would happen in my sessions, we both knew that it was a 'sexual' experience for the men I met.

I sympathized with him, up until I'd get an email from a fan like Don, and I would once again continue justifying my actions. Every fucking bill was in my name and I was now the only one working. Maybe if we were still renting somewhere, but unfortunately it was my dad's name cosigned on our new mortgage. I had put my dad through enough shit in my earlier days and wasn't about to make his life any more stressful.

Dear KO,

I am also one of your fans who reads your blog daily and believe me, you are **WAY** more

than just a "sex symbol." You teach. You inspire. You make me laugh. You help me

spiritually. You care about your fans. You have and do it all. It is really strange that you are

able to write you blog in such a way that we readers begin to believe that we actually know

you. Then, when we watch your videos or look at your pictures, it is like seeing a friend.

Certainly, there is a sexual component to all this but, it is more than that. You do a lot of

good in this world and that is why I always say,

You go girl!

Don

After a couple of months under my belt, I got an email from a man living in what I considered the 'local' area. The long and the short of it was he wanted an 'enema' session. According to the dismal tone in his email, he'd been doing sessions for over ten years, but in his most recent ones, found himself addicted to the rush of pain.

He told me he'd love to be able to pay seven hundred dollars total for three hours of my time. Initially, I had replied that my 'donation' was three hundred and fifty to four hundred dollars an hour, but I could do something like seven hundred and fifty for two hours. Plus, I'd have to drive four hours round trip to get to him, so he'd need to meet me somewhere in the middle. For all of those years I spent hating my various sales jobs, I never realized these skills were transferrable and never a waste of time.

After I read the seven hundred dollars, the rest of the email turned into a blur.

Seeing that I wouldn't have to do much since it was more of an "instructional session", I guess I could justify the dip in pay for my rookie status. Although his last request of taking me to dinner in the last hour would have to be scrapped.

'How the fuck could any dominatrix, let alone any woman, be interested in a dinner date after administrating an enema?

I'm not a dominatrix. I hate seeing people in pain, I think?'

But the email couldn't have been sent at a more perfect time.

Bubba and I had just bought a brand-new mattress on credit. My credit. It had been a tight month, and after all, he did say I wouldn't be doing very much.

After going back and forth for several hours, I said 'fuck it', and emailed Doug back.

I quickly printed out the PDF attachment of his detailed step by step process, deleted all of our email correspondence, and folded up the papers to stash them in my purse until later that week.

The night before meeting him, I drove halfway down and spent the night at Mick and Kallista's house. Figuring I would kill two birds with one stone and get some filming out of the way for our clip store, I was pleased with my ability to maximise time.

With another bodybuilder in town crashing at their house, the three of them were

up drinking all night while we were filming. The next morning upon awakening, I sat and reflected on the fact that I was so utterly happy that I didn't drink, but somehow managed to gloss over the fact that I was now a pill addict.

With the clock ticking over to eight thirty a.m. and everyone still passed out, I got my stuff packed-up, and headed out without saying goodbye. I wasn't sure if I could actually share the details on what I was about to happen. Not because I didn't know if I could handle their reaction, but because I actually didn't know the details at that point. They had spent the last week collecting dust in my purse.

I knew Doug was a high-school history teacher, lived alone with his cat, and was in his mid to late fifties. What I didn't know was how bizarre and twisted this email really was. As soon as the amber light up ahead turned red, I pulled the papers out of my purse and started speed reading.

Dear K.O.

I'm very pleased you have decided to partake in my fantasy. I've been doing this now for quite some time, and have figured out the best, and most effective way to make the most out of

the session with the time permitted. I'm hoping to build a long-lasting friendship with someone local, who can do this fairly often. Being a high school history teacher has its pros & cons. My salary not being one of the pros.

Here is the outline for the session:

Mistress – you. Wearing some kind of black, dominating attire.

Step one – You will force feed me the following in this exact order:

1 - entree lunch from Panda Express (broccoli beef, kung-pao chicken, and fried rice)

2 - a cup of chocolate pudding

3 - a can of cold beef raviolis

4 - a can of Ensure chocolate meal replacement shake.

It's critical you make sure I eat every last bit. If I show any resistance apply a series of neck chokes to show me who's boss, and that you mean business. I'll have the food ready to go upon your arrival. Moving forward I'd request you bring this with you for our next session.

Step two- Upon completion of food, insert anal suppositories (again, I'll show you how this is done). While these are taking effect, you can talk some trash and flex those amazing muscles of yours. Then, I'll show you how to create the soap mixture used in the enema. Most enemas call for one eighth of a bar of soap, whereas mine uses an entire bar of soap. I specifically use a bar of Dove soap as it's the most concentrated, and easily can be broken up with a cheese-grater. It also dissolves the fastest and easiest in the hot water. The more soap used the more pain caused by the extreme cramping.

Step three: Hold me in your lap and make me kiss your biceps.

Step four: Make me go to the toilet. This will take about fifteen minutes. I usually will lose it out of both ends and will have you hold a bucket for me to puke in while I'm on the toilet.

Step five: Administer the deadly enema. Please disregard my crying and pleas to stop the flow of the soap. I'll administer the enema, again since this is your first-time, but have you hold the 'on-off' button, which is a clasp for the hose-valve. At any sign of resistance, or I'm non-compliant, use those chokes on me.

Ok, that about sums it up! Very much looking forward to seeing you. Lastly, you can park anywhere that's uncovered once you get to the apartment complex. The covered spots are for residents.

Thanks again,

Doug

The light turned green and I slammed on the accelerator of Bubba's brand-new Tacoma that was shockingly, in my name.

Fuck.

Oh my God ...

You've got to be fucking joking, right?

Fuck!

Why didn't I read this?

No way, this guy isn't for real.

He has to be kidding.

Ok, ok calm down Kortney, seriously.

After all, he isn't expecting you to do much except watch.

Fuck!

Pills ... take some pills.

As my thoughts were racing faster than my heart, I stuck my knee underneath the steering wheel and sped onto the freeway from the onramp. Hoping my polyurethane black leggings would grip the steering wheel, I leaned over and grabbed the bottle of pills from my purse. With my name on the bottle, I had no reason to hide these.

My back is killing me from wrestling Kallista last night.

After all, she is a blue belt, and sleeping on that stupid air mattress didn't help either.

With no hands on the wheel, I opened the childproof top, and dumped two pills in my hand.

No, don't swallow yet ... chew them up first you fucking idiot.

Two probably won't cut it, actually.

Better take another one.

No, two. Yeah, that should work.

Mistress? So annoying. I hope these pleather leggings are Dom enough.

Without slowing down, I screwed the lid back on the bottle and tossed the pills back into my purse as I added two more to my mouth.

As the bitter, chalky taste of narcotics spread across the back of my tongue, I started imagining my high school history teacher in Doug's place.

How could this be?

Could you imagine Mr. Smitt doing this type of stuff after school?

I can't believe this guy is a teacher!

I wonder if any of his students know how bizarre he is?'

I gritted my teeth as I swallowed the mouthful of chewed up pills and turned the radio up to try and drown out my thoughts. While Cyndi Lauper's "Girls Just Wanna Have Fun" blasted through the crisp Alpine speakers, I thought about Bubba.

God he would be so pissed off if he knew what I was doing right now.

But I know he loves sleeping on that new fucking mattress we had to have.

While I kept rationalizing in my head, I grabbed the bottle of pills and took two more.

Just two more pills, and I'll be done taking them for the day.

In fact, I'll stop after this bottle.

I gotta stop taking this shit anyway.

Shit. Shit?

Am I seriously on my way to administer an enema?

How do I get myself into these things? This can't be normal.

Why do people do these stupid things anyways?

Maybe it was inspired after Elvis's death?

Was he even alive when Elvis died?

Wish I wasn't so bad at math. I could maybe figure that one out.

I think Elvis had like seven pounds of undigested red meat in his intestine or something?

Actually, his intestine blew out while on the toilet from chronic constipation from opioids.

Fuck- what if I die like him?

I'm not drinking anymore though.

Just taking pills isn't going to kill you, idiot.

Calm down.

After driving for what seemed like hours, I pulled into Doug's apartment complex and found a place to park per his instructions. It seemed like that was the only part of his email I had previously taken onboard. After turning off the ignition, I grabbed my phone out of the cupholder and sent Bubba a text:

'Hey Love! Just wanted to let you know I arrived at Doug's house and will let you know after we're done wrestling and I'm on the way back. Have a great day.'

This was not only going to be my first "enema session", but the first time I was going to someone's house. At least when visiting a stranger's hotel room, I had the safety of being surrounded by other people as well as knowing it'd be relatively clean. However, realizing it was a little too late to back out, I started going through a list of questions inside my dangerously clouded mind.

Am I going to walk into a really clean and modern metrosexual man-cave with white sparkling freshly painted walls?

Would he have chartreuse as an accent color?

Will the pillows match the placemats, rugs, and the cat's food dish?

Or, am I about to walk into a dark, one-window, flea-infested giant litter box riddled with food-crusted dishes stacked a mile high?

With flashes of the food checklist contained in Doug's Step one outline, I pulled the bottle of pills back out of my purse to take an inventory and see if there was enough to spare for just one more.

Broccoli beef and pudding?

Maybe I can spare another two.

Knowing it was a brand-new bottle, it was easy to count. I had chewed up a total of eight Norcos during the drive down. I took a couple more pills out, leaving myself twenty pills to ration over the next week while I figured out how to get more. As I popped them in my mouth like Tic-Tacs and began to chew, I gave myself a once over in the rearview mirror.

You should be taking this seven hundred bucks and getting Botox, bitch.

You look like you haven't slept for a week.

Fearful of disappointing Doug, I leaned into the back of the cab and grabbed my makeup bag from my duffle bag. Black eyeliner would give me the finishing touch I was missing.

As I pulled my eyelid down, I could hear my aunt's voice in my head, "Make sure you use your ring finger anytime you touch your eyes or they're going to sag when you get to be my age".

I'm pretty sure I'd be her age right now.

Speaking of which, what the fuck am I going to do with my life in a few years?

CRUSHING IT

Will I make enough money to keep myself looking young forever?

Pushing my thoughts aside, I looked back at myself in the mirror. With my edgy transformation, I uttered, "It's showtime bitch" as I mentally slipped into the role of KO with the help of a pill-induced booster and thick black eyeliner.

Being on the outside of the door made me feel out of control. I didn't like being the one waiting for it to open. Blame spotted dick, I guess-- I liked being the one who opened the door. Doing this outcall shit wasn't sitting well, but at least once the door finally opened, the teacher was just like I imagined a single history teacher would look like.

There was nothing abnormal about him at all. Just your average fifty five year-old white balding male, standing five foot seven inches and weighing a mere hundred and forty pounds, Doug sheepishly said hello underneath his Great Clips combover and square, thick-rimmed glasses.

Once inside, I did a basic "glance around security sweep" for any immediate danger. Although probably not the best time to be evaluating red flags, I made a point to locate any additional exits, phones, kitchen knives, and cats. I hate cats. Potentially due to severe allergies as a child, and definitely due to cats being independent as fuck. Unlike dogs, they don't *actually* need you to survive unlike all the boys I attracted into my life.

Long turd short, I never did another enema session. If you want to know, paypal me a hundred bucks and I'll send you a seven minute clip explaining why.

Shit.

It's days like these that make you question *everything*.

In the true KO spirit of shit, shower, and semi-shine, I continued to experience things I didn't want, in order to better understand what I did want. And what I wanted was some kind of boundary that was more visible than just a faintly painted chalk line, hastily drawn on the pavement by city workers, right before a year-long construction job commenced.

Clear boundaries or not, after a few months of sessions, I had accumulated some stellar reviews and was well on my way to traveling the world, one hotel room at a time.

"KO"

Description

Stats: five foot seven inches, one hundred and sixty pounds, biceps: fifteen inches, quads: twenty eight inches, calves: eighteen inches

Location: Northern California, Bay Area

Specialties: semi-competitive wrestling, scissors, domination and role play

Additional Information:

"I've met **KO** and she is a stunningly pretty, outrageously strong, visibly athletic woman with a delightful giggle often heard when your position is utterly hopeless. She doesn't sneak up on you, she's just too built for her strength to be a surprise, but **KO** is nevertheless completely feminine in a sort of outrageous yet wholesome way. For all her muscle there is nothing androgynous about her at all. See **KO** if you ever get the chance" – **XB, Owner**

• 7/09: "I had an amazing session with KO. She is alarmingly strong, talented and absolutely the hottest wrestler you've ever laid eyes on. Her scissors are unreal - and her figure-four is already legendary - for very good reason. You will submit or pass out. But she's way more than just scissors - her BJJ training allows her to torment you with arm bars and chokes that are both painful and inescapable. Imagine a rear naked choke with her biceps. If you're fortunate enough to find yourself in her triangle choke - you'll have a tough decision - when to stop being captivated by her eight-pack abs and decide to tap before it's too late. You get the picture. What makes KO so different is that all of this is packaged in a vibrant, exciting, inspirational personality that makes time fly as she toys with you. She's not a clock-watcher, really seeks to understand what you want in a session - and delivers one hundred and ten percent. "

• 7/09: "Words cannot describe the best session experience I've had in twenty years. KO is the total package in beauty, brains and brawn. She captivates you with her looks and draws you in with her charm. She gave me everything I have ever wanted in a session and more. Beware her twenty eight inch quads as when she has her legs wrapped around you, you become her newest toy to play with. Add her BJJ training with arm bars and choke holds, and there is no weakness to her game – she is pure power and energy in a femme fatale form! I can't wait to meet up with her again!"

• 8/09: "I have been doing sessions for nearly twenty years and recently experienced my best ever session. The young lady in question was KO. KO is a beautiful, sexy, natural muscle girl. She has very impressive muscularity and incredible strength. The session was orientated around a number of competitive strength challenges including arm wrestling. I strive to session with the strongest female athletes and they have included world class powerlifters, strongwomen, bodybuilders and arm wrestlers. Overall, KO proved to be the strongest female I have experienced. For example, she gave me the best arm wrestling contest I have experienced with a female and provided a more formidable challenge than two international level female arm wrestlers I have previously wrestled of similar bodyweight. And arm wrestling is not a sport she has studied in depth!!!! The icing on the cake is her wonderful friendly, outgoing personality - she is great fun to be with. KO will be as competitive as you want her to be and was certainly up for all the challenges I set for her. If you want a competitive, semi or non-competitive session with an absolutely stunning, immensely strong, natural muscle-girl, KO should be at the top of your session list!!!! "

. . . .

I couldn't believe the number of "weird" requests I received the first six months in my new line of work. Concluding that nearly every single person in the world must be wearing some kind of mask, really took some getting used to. Again, people are wearing masks because of their fear of judgement. Imagine how you'd judge your history teacher if you found out they're addicted to pain and spent their savings on having someone give them a soapy enima!

Just like the excitement of owning a new car wears off after a couple of months, the weirdness became my new normal. Realising that there were men out there who would pay cold hard cash for things I absolutely hated about my body was simply shocking! The time spent exploring this new world, truly helped me understand that the world is not what we think it is.

Do the F*cking Work

Describe how you feel about men who are attracted to things that aren't mainstream or considered normal?

Speaking of which, define the term 'normal' in your own words.

Define the term 'patriarchy' in your own words. (Keeping in mind that women who wanted a business loan in many states (USA) were required to get a signature from a male relative. That ridiculous requirement might still be in place if it wasn't for the Women's Business Ownership Act of 1988.)

What would life be like if influencers, celebrities, media and ads celebrated/promoted things like stinky feet and hairy armpits as desirable?

In what ways have you judged someone for acting overtly outside of what's considered 'normal' for gender roles? (i.e. a man crying over having his feelings hurt, a woman scratching her crotch after finishing a heavy squat in the gym, or men being bisexual.)

In what ways do you struggle with gender roles?

How are you working to dismantle what behaviour is considered normal for so-called "real women" and "real men" set up by the patriarchy?

Sometimes we have to experience what we don't want, to figure out what we do want. Sometimes we also have to experience having our boundaries pushed in order to know where our actual boundary line is.

Write a list of your boundaries in work, friends, and romantic relationships.

Monkey see, monkey do. Reflecting back to lesson 1 where I watched my mom apply black eyeliner to make herself look "presentable"for her date, to earlier in this lesson to applying my own, what actions are present in your life that mimic things you picked up from childhood that are no longer serving you in a beneficial way?

Scan here for more good shit.

LESSON 9

EXPECT THE UNEXPECTED

• 8/09: "I have been doing sessions for about ten years. Not many, once or twice a year. Pretty much all of them have been scissor sessions with some pretty strong women and some not so strong women. KO is one of the strongest women, and if she continues to work her legs like she is talking about doing, holy crap. Watch out. Usually I don't tap much, I just like to see what limit the women can scissor. I tapped a lot more often with KO. She put me in a sideways figure-four with me sitting up and her laying sideways on the couch with her leg around my neck and I remember tapping, then she reapplied the pressure, and the next thing I remember is waking up on the floor. She put me out, I was snoring. After that I had some melons I bought for her to crush and she did it with no problem. I also have to say KO is one of the best-looking fitness/bodybuilders I have seen, her look reminded me of "Le Femme Nikita", she has a cute baby face with a killer attitude!!!! What a mix!! I am betting she has the ability to be one of the best out there. " -Clark

I owe a lot to Clark. If it weren't for Clark, I'm not sure where I'd be today. Sliding Honda car doors, I guess. I sure as shit wouldn't have a bunch of watermelon tattoos on my arm, and there's a fair chance I wouldn't have blue checks on my social media accounts.

Clark was a local fan. Pretty basic dude who worked as a graphic designer in the Bay Area. I'll never forget his email asking for a scissor session. He wanted to see if I "had what it takes" to knock him out. He'd seen maybe twenty bodybuilders over the last decade, with only one who could successfully knock him out. He ended the email asking if I'd be open to him bringing some watermelons for me to "try" and crush between my legs at the end of the session. Lastly, could I bring my video camera to film my "attempt"?

The words "try", "attempt" and "if you got what it takes" are a surefire way to get me onboard, dickhead. I don't see why not. After all, it doesn't involve an enema of any kind.

As usual, I wrote back with my cocky ass attitude, feeling the need to justify my rate, and make some kind of outlandish statement that would wind up having me stressed the fuck out until the session was over.

"Hi Clark-

In case you needed reminding, my name is KO for a reason. Be forewarned, I'm the best there is. Once you have a session with me, the rest will seem like a waste of money. When and where?".

KO always had to be the best.

KO had something to prove.

But Kortney felt like she had to justify herself, always.

We set the session up for the following week. Nothing out of the ordinary, I'd drive down to his office and I'd spend an hour living up to my email claim and name. The time came and I got dressed.

I slipped on my cute matching black Bebe thong and bralette, followed by tugging my way into the black, wet-looking pleather leggings that somehow one day appeared in my wardrobe. I pulled on one of my office 'dress shirts' which had the capability of sending me to the HR director back in the dealership days. Looking like a personal stewardess for Hugh Heffner on top and something out of the matrix on the bottom, I confidently bee-bopped my way towards takeoff and grabbed my video camera. With a slight pull of anxiety over whether or not I was going to come through and actually be 'the best he'd ever seen', I chewed up another few Norcos.

Guess I can leave my stun gun. I've had enough back and forth to feel comfortable with Clark. Because ya know... people are always who they say they are on the internet. Including myself. At least I don't feel fat today.

No longer a middle classer with a Honda, I painfully strutted my too-tight high heels straight out the front door and into my newly financed Acura. Adorned with a professional decal across the back window, I backed out of the driveway with zero fucks regarding the poor choice of personal branding. Underneath the enlarged words of HARD AS FUK! sat my website, as if some curious passer-by on the highway needed to know who I was.

Armed with an adequate stash of pills, I cranked the stereo up and lost myself in the music. After an hour and a half drive, I parked in Clark's office complex and walked into the building to anxiously find his suite. Feeling like I was in a scene out of Outbreak, I started walking the dimly lit hallway while feeling eerily alone and empty

Bit of a shitty rundown complex. I wonder if anyone else even occupies this building, and if so, could they hear me scream?

Just like most things that made me anxious when thinking about the 'what ifs', I was in front of Clark's door before I knew it, giving the rhythmic and happy sounding knock I learned from my dad, 'Bom, bom, bom-bom-bom. Bom. Bom.'.

Shit. I should have been a little more dominating on that knock. I sound like a girl scout trying to sell cookies as opposed to an FBI agent coming to fuck your life up. God I always fuck shit u....

Clark opened his office door and interrupted my train of thought as he stood there with an energy of intimidation and nervousness.

"Hey KO! Did you find the place ok?"

"Hi Clark! I did, thank you," I replied while reaching out to give him a hug.

Maybe that's what made me different. Maybe Rob programmed that hug when opening the door with strange men I've just met over the internet. Maybe I needed another pill. In the midst of our embrace, I looked around the five hundred-ish square foot office for any kind of sign he was a serial killer while my irrefutable inner voice butted in as usual.

Such a shame I took my real estate appraisal course while high on meth and drinking heavily. I really could have done something with that.

"So, what's with the tarp, Clark?" I said as it caught my eye. As I stared at the four foot by six foot crinkled, bright blue painters tarp, I immediately thought about all the late night interior paint jobs I'd done on Billy's mom's house while being high on meth.

"That's for the watermelon, KO! If you can actually break one."

"Oh, right! Guess it threw me off seeing that we're in your office!" I retorted as I looked around and noticed there were no windows.

"Yeah, it's my name on the lease and I only have one other guy who works with me part time, so why not?" Clark said with his cool guy attitude.

As usual, Clark was an average guy. Happily married but missing a piece of excitement in his life that I'm sure his wife could fulfill had they ever talked about 'it'.

After I set my purse down on the ground, I looked Clark up and down.

"So only one woman in over a decade, huh?" I said while noticing he didn't have a thick neck whatsoever. By my calculations, Clark would have only been one hundred and sixty pounds soaking wet.

As I sat on the floor and started peeling my skin tight leggings off over my high heels, Clark began rearranging some folding chairs.

"Yeah, I don't know what it is. I have this weird capability to withstand any woman's scissors with the exception of Yasmine. I've managed to really piss a few bodybuilders and wrestlers off!" he said with a little smirk. With his attitude and mannerisms, Clark reminded me of a stoned, hippy surfer bro from Manhattan Beach. But between his looks and the memorabilia sitting around his office, he screamed the NASCAR and Pabst Blue Ribbon type.

Feeling solidly high from my steady dose of daily narcotics, I stood up with just my thong, high heels and blouse on. All part of the KO tease, of course.

"Wow, KO!" Clark exclaimed from across the room. "Those legs are something else!"

I stood and looked down at my twenty seven inch legs and replied, "Yes, they're magnificent, aren't they?" while momentarily forgetting about how much I hated them when I was alone.

"Wait till you feel them around your neck, Clark. I'm not so sure you'll be saying the same words." I said seductively while tugging at the elastic sleeve around my arm. Pulling it up just enough to sit across the middle of my bicep, I flexed while Clark stood there with his mouth gaping open like some kind of cartoon character. Now completely in my KO headspace, I continued with my shit talking.

"In fact, I highly doubt you'll be able to speak at all by the time I'm done with you.".

. . . .

Now arranged in a straight row, I pulled my blouse off over the top of my head and instructed Clark to sit on the floor in front of the chairs.

Knowing that my 'figure four' had a decent amount of crushing force, I thought I'd start there. It wasn't my strongest scissor hold, but much like playing poker, I wanted to create some assumptions and illusions first. I liked to tease my boys and start out with about sixty percent of full-strength capacity before I started to really bring the pain.

On the same outdated low-pile carpet that was in my college dorm, Clark sat cross-legged with his back to the row of chairs as I laid across them on my side, facing towards the back of his head. Like a python, I slithered my bottom leg around the front of his body and gently put his neck in the fold of the back of my knee.

Similar to a 'rear naked choke', the figure-four was set up and executed in the same way but instead of using arms, I'd use my legs. I had a few years of Jiu Jitsu training under my belt, and was poorly experienced in the art of submissions. If applied effectively, the blood flow from the left and right carotid arteries which supply the head with oxygenated blood, are cut off and render the person unconscious.

After strategically placing my bottom leg around Clark's neck, I took my top leg and placed the back of my knee around the foot that was coming off the leg that was around his neck. I started to lightly apply some pressure by pulling my top leg down which was acting like a lever, and as anticipated, Clark immediately grabbed onto the leg wrapped around his neck with his hands.

I knew it took roughly seven seconds to knock someone unconscious once they were in my grip. If I were to keep applying force beyond those seven seconds, the likelihood of creating an increased chance of brain damage and/or death, would start ticking over quickly.

After a few seconds, I let up on the pressure for Clark, but never let my legs leave his neck. Like a spider pulling a live fly further into her web, I dragged Clark backwards with my leg to get him closer to the row of chairs. Now that I was warmed up and we were well on our way, I was ready to play ball. I needed to get his neck deeper in my leg grip so I could squeeze tighter.

As I felt the side of my crotch make contact with the ice-cold metal of the chair, I wondered who or what had previously been touching the surface. Laying and rolling around on disgusting, potentially disease-infested surfaces never stopped me before, and it certainly wasn't going to stop me now. The need to be the best, the need to win, and "I needed the money" always won whenever it came time for me to consider my actions or possible consequences.

So what?

I'm not sitting in the spotless Oval Office getting my dick sucked like Clinton had originally planned, but I'm pretty sure I'm making more money than Obama right now.

Not sure which one of us has a more stressful job, but whatever.

If I made it this far without my vagina falling off, I'm sure it'll be fine that my private parts are smashed up against some shitty folding chair right now.

I always used the extra sheet stashed in the closet of the hotel when I was wrestling. Whether it was arm wrestling or wrestling, body parts rarely touched the carpet. However, I can't say the same when it came to lying on airport floors when I was on tour and had to find a way to sneak a workout in. Looking good and getting attention was more of a priority than the possibility of what diseases could be entrenched in high foot-traffic carpets.

The fear of laying down on his own carpet without a sheet never crossed Clark's mind because he never saw it coming. Neither one of us did, actually. But that's how my life kept playing out. Even when I'm right in the middle of the shit, and there's a quiet whisper telling me, 'you're not a tree, move bitch!', I'd still stay stuck because I never saw it coming. I was always moving too fast, worrying about all the wrong things.

With the perfect amount of leverage and torque, I had him right where I wanted him. Intentionally blowing hot air, I leaned in and whispered in Clark's ear, "You ready to experience sheer, unfathomable fear little boy?". Before he could as much as nod his head, I went straight to eighty percent and started squeezing my vice grip around his neck while waiting for him to tap, signaling that he'd had enough.

I started counting in my head.

One.

Two.

Like someone with a megaphone in the bleachers, my mom's voice blasted through and into my thoughts,

Don't let me get to three, Kortney Kay!

Four.

Suddenly the sound of a loud "POP" cascaded through my ears.

Clark suddenly dropped his hands from my leg as his entire body went limp.

Impulsively, I extended my right leg to let all of the pressure off of my left leg which was still wrapped around his neck. Waiting for some kind of movement or sound, I lay on my side in paralysis contemplating if I had just snapped Clark's neck. Dropping my legs off of him completely, I quickly sat up and shifted them on either side of his back and waited for him to move or make a sound.

With no movement or sound coming from him, I felt that familiar feeling of my heart dropping down to my anus.

As I looked around the room in an absolute panic, I felt my fate cracking down like the federal judge's gavel whom I used to slap around.

Why the fuck was there a blue tarp on the floor again?

This can't be happening. Not right now. Not ever.

Semi standing up with both arms under Clark's armpits, I proceeded to gently lay him on his back before taking a knee.

Should I perform CPR?

Idiot- not on a fucking broken neck you moron!

Fuck what should I do?

Will I go to prison for unintentional manslaughter?

Should I call 9-1-1?

Roll him up in the blue tarp and dump the body?

This isn't Dexter you fucking fool!

As I sat there holding back tears, the panic had fully set in. Similar to emailing a friend intimate details about something your mutual friend had shared after you promised to not share, to only realise you'd emailed the friend you were writing about on accident, I was suffocating in terror. Then, in an instant and like the second coming of Jesus Christ, Clark let out the loudest, most earth shattering snore I'd ever heard in my life.

FUCK!

Then another one. By the second snore, Clark had rabid looking foam collecting at the corner of his mouth. A few more seconds passed when miraculously, he slowly opened his eyes, and let out a sound.

"Huuuuuuuuuuuuuuuuuuugh", he gasped. "Where, where am I?"

Unlike my response to Adriana when she woke up from her blackout after flying off the highway at sixty miles per hour, I replied to Clark with a different tone of voice while stroking his head.

"Hi there," I said sweetly while trying to play it cool. "How was your nap?".

"It... it was incredible!"

"Yeah, I told you everything about me is incredible, Clark."

As he looked up at me with glossy, dark brown eyes, I sat in a pool of brief gratitude before it was onto the next thing.

"Shall we get to crushing these watermelons?" I coyly asked.

I used to always find myself cursing whoever the hell this 'Murphy's law' person was. My life events have consistently shown me that there are unexpected twists and turns at every corner. Being a control freak and always feeling like I need 'a plan', it seems that my higher power has decided to award me all sorts of opportunities to experience what it feels like to lose control, light my plans on fire, thus giving me a chance to practice going with the flow. Such as when you think you may have just snapped someone's neck and potentially looking at twenty five to life for involuntary manslaughter.

Do the F*cking Work

Have you hated or currently hate parts of your body?

Where do you think the dislike (or hatred) for your body originated from?

Do you feel comfortable in your skin when you're interacting with others but when you're by yourself, the story changes? If so, what do you think started this?

In what ways do you identify with being a control freak?

Can you be sporadic and just whimsiclay decide to take a trip without having accommodations booked and gas stations planned out along the way?

What areas of your life are you constantly trying to control?

What would happen if you eased up on it?

Scan here for more good shit.

LESSON 10

SOMETIMES QUICKLY, SOMETIMES SLOWLY

*S*eeing that my domestic travels were going so well, I didn't even think twice about saying yes to this trip.

I was near feverish to be taking my first international trip and couldn't believe I'd gotten my passport in time. When I'd accepted the job in Canada to shoot with Scissor Foxes, it hadn't crossed my mind that I'd need a passport. All I saw was I'd be making fifteen hundred dollars for one day of work. I immediately opened the passport to the photo page and laughed.

As I looked at the Trump colored face smiling back at me, I started to question whether or not I looked like "the type".

Should've gotten my passport photo taken before getting my first spray tan.

At least I look lean.

I always do shit backwards.

I wonder if it's because I was born backwards.

Or because I was supposed to be a boy and came out a girl, my brain is mixed up.

I think I even write backwards.

Surprise mother fuckers!

That little thing you thought was a tiny dick was either my thumb or my asymmetrical vagina.

You know if I was born male, I would have come out with a giant dick anyway.

Seriously.

Putting my passport down, I started thinking back to Jeff warning me about making sure I ticked the box at immigration that indicated I was visiting Canada on holiday, and *not* to mention anything about paid work. He'd said some of the girls that had flown in from outside the country to work with them had been pulled aside by immigration. When questioned about their trip and seeing that they only had stripper-like outfits packed in their luggage, they buckled and were sent away. Even worse, some were even fined for the intent to work without an appropriate visa.

Could you imagine, my first trip outside of America, and I get arrested or fined.

I'm not even sure what the word "visa" or "immigration" even means.

I should sit down at the computer and google that shit.

I haven't even looked up the definition of those words in the Big Book I didn't understand from like two months ago.

I should probably find a sponsor I actually like and start making my program more of a priority over this muscle fetish career bullshit, but I'm not going to be young forever.

As I was packing my suitcase, I started thinking about what else I could pack to look normal and what kind of story I was going to tell. I'm good at telling stories. Especially to myself. Internet dating had only just become a thing, but I thought if I happened to get pulled aside, that I would simply say that I was visiting my boyfriend Jeff who I'd recently met online for a forty eight hour sex-fueled escapade. How hard could it be? I'd lied my way out of so many potential disasters that this shouldn't be an issue whatsoever.

Despite taking a couple of pain pills throughout the day, I had just surpassed one year of being "sober" and felt confident that I was capable of handling pretty much anything without drinking. With my suitcase sprawled out across our bed, I rolled up my black fishnet thigh-highs and caught sight of the Big Book on my nightstand. I knew it would be a good opportunity for me to work on my step-work during the six hour flight to Calgary, but the reality was I had far more important things to do that were going to generate money. I had a potential tour coming up in the U.K. along with what felt like a thousand emails to reply to.

I meticulously made sure all of my liquids and gels fit into the appropriate size zip-lock bag, folded my matching socks in the event I was able to get a couple of workouts in, and gently rolled my baby blanket up, tucking her into a zip-lock bag all of her own. Just before zipping up my carry-on suitcase, I decided to rearrange the stripper outfits and eight inch slip-on clear high heels, so they were underneath my baby blanket. If some official maple leaf went through my luggage, they'd have to dig underneath my twenty eight year-old dingy, precious blanket to find the only clue that might allude to the fact that I was a sex-worker who was entering the country without a visa, but who wasn't having sex. *"How crazy is my life!"* I thought, as I often pondered how I could be making so much money without having sex or sucking dick.

As I pulled the neatly rolled-up fishnets out from between the two stripper outfits I'd packed, I thought about whether or not I should bother bringing them. I despised them. Although they were "plus size", they weren't plus enough to stay put on my legs before they started rolling down after taking five steps. The silicone ring inside of the leg opening was a smidge too tight and made me feel like I was the last Jimmy Dean sausage hanging out in the old crusty package of a dingy refrigerator.

As I stood there filling up with anxiety while trying to make the most basic of decisions, Bubba walked into the bedroom.

"Heyyyyyyyy hey! How's the packing going?" he asked.

"Ah just dandy!" I replied, lying through my teeth. I didn't bother sharing the strife I was feeling thinking about the lie I was conjuring up in case this imaginary immigration person harassed me about my new online boyfriend Jeff, nor did I relay the travel tips Jeff had shared with me a week prior.

They say our dis-ease thrives on secrets.

That's how mold grows. In the dark. Lies grow in the dark. They fester and grow.

Shed some light on your concerns.

"Alright then. You want some tacos from down the street for dinner?" he asked.

"Yeah, that would be amazing, thanks." I said as I went back to considering sharing my worries with Bubba. As he was halfway back down the stairs, I shouted, "But just meat and salsa!"

"No… I'm going to ask for extra cheese and sour cream and tip them extra if they can deep fry them for you." Bubba replied in a semi annoyed tone from the bottom of the staircase. "Why are you acting like I just met you last week?" he shouted back.

"I know, sorry. Just have a lot on my mind right now," I yelled.

"Call your sponsor. You'll probably feel better. I'll be back in a bit," he shouted as he walked out the front door.

Why don't you call your Mother?

Or get a job?

Yeah, yeah… I know the agreement was I could do this work and we'd both quit selling cars and you could go back to school but fuck the stress of having to pay all of our bills.

As I sat there thinking about how much I hated being told what to do, I reflected on the incident we had a few weeks back over my issues with my body. The brief window of empowerment I'd felt about my legs didn't take long to wear off after leaving Clark's office nearly a month back. Then again, I'm not sure what I was expecting, since validation and nice words from others clearly weren't fixing me on inside.

Bubba and I were supposed to go to Costco to do our bi-weekly grocery shopping, when he walked into the bedroom looking for me.

"Hellooooooooooooooooo? Is anyone home?" he said in a goofy tone as he stepped into our bedroom. I was in-between sobs by the time he started walking through to the bathroom, "I thought we were leaving a half hour ago?" he asked as he placed his hands on the dual sink vanity while looking in the bathroom mirror before he heard me start crying again. Surprised to see me sitting on the floor in our walk-in closet, hugging my knees to my chest, "What happened?", he asked.

"Nothing. I just can't.", I replied with a face stained with mascara skid marks. As I wiped the snot from my nose with my forearm, I tried speaking again, but started sobbing instead. By the sounds of my crying, one would assume I'd just gotten off the phone with the hospital and learned that my Dad hadn't made it through his brain surgery. Bubba sat down on the carpet in front of me and tried again.

"Sweetie, why are you crying?" he asked as he gently placed his hands on my knees while looking in my tear-filled eyes with immense concern.

I'd spent the last thirty minutes trying on every single pair of pants I owned and couldn't find one pair that fit. After my third pair of jeans finally went all the way up and zipped, I stepped out of the closet and onto the linoleum bathroom floor. Looking in the chalkboard sized mirror, I wanted to vomit seeing my skin hanging over the sides of my jeans. I quickly unzipped the Rock Revival denim before practically ripping them off my body.

The last time Bubba had seen me earlier that day, I'd just gotten out of the shower and was happily applying eyeliner in the mirror. Although anxious about skipping the gym after talking myself into eating pizza with him the night before, I was excited to go out and spend the day with him. But now I was back in the mirror and my anxiety had catapulted into pure, unadulterated fear. As I stood there pinching my side between my thumb and pointer finger, I could feel the fat deposits shift around under my skin like tiny, impenetrable marbles. I looked back in the mirror and placed both palms on each thigh. Gently pulling my skin up, I saw what I wanted to look like, and what I thought I looked like yesterday.

I can't believe that pizza hit me that fast.

I knew those carb-blocking pills were a crock of shit.

I fucking knew I shouldn't have had any whatsoever.

It's the exact same with food as it is with alcohol or meth.

Once I pop, I can't stop.

I should take another pill, but I just had one like an hour ago.

At least that I can control.

Look at me.

I workout so hard, and I can't even eat five pieces of pizza without getting fat.

I dabbed off all of the oil with a napkin. Surely that would have spared me a hundred calories.

You can see it in my waist and my legs are literally riddled with cellulite today.

What's the fucking point of any of this?

Why am I working so hard to look a certain way, and I can't even eat pizza once a year?

I can't ever be happy.

Disgusting fat fucking pig with NO willpower.

You're weak.

Weak and in debt. Weak and no future. Weak and useless.

Why the FUCK am I even alive?

I can't stop thinking.

I can't stop obsessing.

I'm so lost.

I want out.

I'm fucking done.

I don't think I have enough pills to even overdose.

An hour later, he came back upstairs to find me in absolute pieces on the closet floor, contemplating suicide.

"NOTHING FUCKING FITS ME!" I screamed. "I can't leave the house looking like a fat cow. I'm sorry. Just fucking go without me!" I pleaded.

"Jesus Christ Kortney--are you fucking serious?" he shouted back in frustration. "You're telling me that every goddamn thing hanging in this massive closet doesn't fit you?"

I started sobbing again.

"I don't know how many times I can tell you how perfect, sexy, and attractive you are before you'll understand? In fact, I seriously can't take it anymore. This isn't how I want to spend my time. I feel like I'm talking to a brick wall!" he said as he angrily got off the floor.

Not thinking of anyone but myself, nor how frustrating it must have been to live with someone who was constantly saddened, disheartened, worried, anxious, concerned, and fearful over the way they looked, I just shouted back, "Yes, fucking leave, PLEASE!"

"You'll never understand!"

After calming down later that night, we decided that working a 12-step program was the most important thing I could do in my life right now. (Which I of course ignored again)

As soon as I opened my eyes the next morning, I felt anxious. My mental committee was in full-blown session, arguing in the land of "what if" scenarios.

I wonder if Canadian jails are clean?

Are these guys going to pay me if I don't make it across the border?

Wonder where Bubba is. Rare that his lazy ass is out of bed before me.

Am I taking his inventory and judging him?

Fuck it.

I hope I packed enough shit.

I wonder if I'll be bloated after flying.

I really should take my step-work on this trip.

Without a single thought of the 12-steps and asking for guidance from The Universe beyond "I really should", I let my Fred Flintstone feet hit the ground and went straight to the dresser to grab a pill from the secret stash space I created behind the zipper inside my purse. Ironically, next to my purse was one of my many journals. Deep down I knew what my soul needed to find serenity, peace and happiness, but my head kept me going around in circles like our bull terrier chasing its tail.

With a pill in one hand, and my journal in the other, I walked back over to my nightstand and pulled the top open on my South Fork Mountain water bottle and gave the plastic a squeeze, which immediately made me think of Jepson. Having just enough water to swallow my pill, I tossed it in my mouth, and headed towards the toilet, ignoring the subtle whispers encouraging me to focus on healing from the inside out.

With my journal still in my left hand, I pulled my boy shorts underwear down and sat on the cold seat to open up my journal. After a few seconds and realising I wasn't peeing yet, despite how bad I had to, I shut the cover.

Isn't that strange that when I'm on the balls of my feet, I can't pee?

Remember that one time a gynecologist said I had incredible control over my muscles?

I can't believe I saw a male gyno.

But if it weren't for Planned Parenthood who knows if I'd even have a vagina.

Could you imagine if I didn't have both abortions?

I guarantee those little souls would have come out addicted to meth.

I'm so glad I read "Many Lives, Many Masters".

I should read more.

Maybe if I read more, I'd be better in business and not be so stressed out about money.

Yeah bitch, try reading the fucking Big Book you idiot.

From all of the built-up pressure and velocity, I relaxed my feet on the floor and started peeing instantly, sounding like a man standing over a urinal. As I thought about Oprah and whether or not it was true that she had to put toilet paper inside a bowl when out in public, fearing that someone would hear her, I let the rush of relief wash over me momentarily before opening my journal back up.

You have so many journals.

CRUSHING IT

Just like everything in life, you start one and stop before you finish.

You never finish anything.

You get bored so easily.

Maybe you're addicted to drama.

I hadn't actually opened my journal in months. I just kept moving it around my room or taking it with me thinking I might actually write in it again one day. Forgetting I had plastered old photographs of myself into collages on both of the inside covers and the first couple of pages, I looked at the variety of pictures. The first picture that grabbed my attention was one with my head tilted back, eyes closed, and a massive plume of thick smoke coming out of my mouth that looked identical to a thunder-head cloud you could only find in the sky.

Ufffff gross.

I can't believe that was my life for like a decade.

I'm so glad the obsession to get high has left me.

Such a fucking gross drug.

The next picture that captured my attention was me laying on the carpet sideways, looking like I'd been shot. Completely unconscious in a blackout, I stared at myself laying on the floor in my oversized khaki cargo shorts, a form-fitting Adidas zip-up black jacket, and matching Adidas black samba tennis shoes sans socks.

After scanning the front pages, I flipped to the back and stared at the collage of my baby and childhood pictures. As I looked from picture to picture, I suddenly realized something I'd never noticed before. Similar to the brick wall I drove into when I got my DUI, it should have been so obvious to see, but somehow, I never managed to connect the dots.

Holy shit!

How many times have all of my friends and family laughed at my childhood pictures where I have my 'dump face' on and I never made the connection?

As I stared at the pictures ranging from the ages of two to seven I could hear my childhood friend's voice, "Oh! There's Kortney Kay and that face! Mom and I always used to laugh when we'd look at old pictures and come across the ones where you're squatting down with that look of concentration. Everyone knew you had to go to the bathroom when you had that look on your face!".

Wow.

I can't believe I totally forgot about that.

Like I loved holding onto a shit.

Have I been a control freak since I was that young?

I was toilet trained at like ten months old.

Toilet trained?

You sound like a dog you idiot it's called potty trained.

But I loved that feeling for so long.

I wonder when it stopped.

I think I even did it in high school.

Probably did it until I started smoking meth.

As I sat aimlessly on the toilet, Bubba walked in the bedroom.

"Good morning! I thought we agreed to shut the bathroom door when we were taking a shit, miss?" he said with a smirk.

"I'm not! I'm just peeing. What got you out of bed so early?" I replied.

"Am I not allowed to get out of bed before a certain hour now?" he asked.

"I was just curious, sorry for asking! Anyway-- I'll be ready to leave in thirty!" I said hastily as I reached out and pulled the door shut.

"He's such a smart ass sometimes", I thought as I set my journal on the floor and gathered toilet paper simultaneously. Noticing I had what looked like a head of cauliflower in my hand, I contemplated putting half of it back.

You can never have enough of anything, can you?

Wonder how much money you'd save if you only used what you actually needed?

. . . .

Before I knew it, Bubba was dropping me off at my terminal at the San Francisco Airport. I leaned over and gave him a quick peck, a short hug, and said, "Behave yourself" before winking and slamming the truck door shut. As I wheeled my carry-on behind me, I walked through the automatic sliding doors and assuaged my fears by popping another pill in my mouth.

. . . .

I'd been flying by myself since I was seven years old. Every summer, my two aunts would fly me down to Southern California for a couple of weeks to experience real city living and spoil me a bit. Flying never bothered me, or caused me to feel anxious, but today was different.

After the turbulence had finally settled down about forty five minutes into the flight, the cabin crew started to come through the aisles for the in-flight service. Assuming WiFi was available on all flights, I pulled my purse out from underneath the seat in front of me and grabbed mylaptop to start planning my tour and smashing through emails. Once powered on, I kept clicking on the universal symbol for WiFi and getting the same response. Just like a child asks their parents *"Are we there yet?"* every twenty minutes on a five-hour car journey, the response was one I didn't want to hear.

What the fuck am I going to do for the next five hours?

I hate watching TV.

I knew I should have packed my Big Book.

Fucking dick.

I can't believe I'm stuck in this seat with nothing to do for five hours.

Thanks Virgin America. You shouldn't give people the impression that all flights have WiFi.

Thanks, Bubba, for not working, causing me to stay stuck in my head constantly worrying about bills when I could have possibly thought to research this before leaving.

Sitting in the sixth row with my building resentments, the cart was nearly to my seat. With my skull candy headphones on, my sense of smell seemed to be heightened as I watched the row kitty-corner to me all order an alcoholic drink of some sort. Unable to see who was sitting by the window, I knew they were drinking some kind of red wine. The middle seat, which only revealed the top of a grey headed balding man, had ordered a jack and coke, while the middle-aged businessman in the aisle ordered a can of Heineken.

So unfair.

Seriously.

Why do they even offer alcohol on flights?

What if someone like me who hadn't quit got annihilated on a flight?

What would they do when I tried starting fights with everyone?

It's fine.

I'm way beyond that.

As I watched the woman collect payment from the guy in the aisle, I stared at her perfect body, in her perfect uniform, with her perfect face, as she finally smiled at the aisle guy with her perfect teeth before she took the brake off the cart and rolled down to me. Sliding my headphones off as she approached, I started to feel anxious wondering who was supposed to go first. I couldn't remember if it was the window seat out to the aisle, or the other way around.

How can you not remember what order they go in?

Every flight you have to sit in the aisle, or you get claustrophobic, and you somehow forgot?

Maybe it's different on every flight?

I don't want to speak out of turn and look like a pompous asshole.

Why do you care so much what you look like?

Looking at her name tag, I smiled at Jessica, opened my mouth slightly and started to order a diet coke, just as she reached past my face to hand a napkin and bag of pretzels to the older lady sitting in the window seat. Feeling my face get hot, I felt embarrassed for being inpatient and looking like an idiot. Of course, both women ordered wine. As the plastic glasses and miniature airplane wine bottles passed by my face, I started to feel more irritated.

Finally, Jessica was handing me a napkin and a bag of pretzels before asking me what I'd like to have. "Just a diet coke, thanks," I said sheepishly.

What the fuck has gotten into me?

I've normally befriended both people in my aisle by now and given Jessica some kind of compliment.

What is wrong with me?

I watched as Jessica poured half a can of diet coke over ice before safely stowing it back with the other open containers.

Why can't she just give me the whole can?

Why can't I just ask for the whole can?

What's the worst thing she's going to say?

Maybe charge me?

Before I knew it, Jessica had her back turned to me and was onto the row directly across from me. As I sat there with the springs digging into the back of my legs, I started thinking about how badly I suddenly had to pee. Knowing that I was now trapped in my seat behind the cart for the next forty minutes, I dared not look like a dick going to the front of the plane to use the first-class cabin. I started to feel yet another wave of anxiety wash over me.

Why couldn't you just ask for the other part of the diet coke?

For the cost of your flight, I'm sure it's justifiable.

If you were drinking, you'd have no problem asking.

Shifting around in my seat, I could feel the irritability, restlessness and discontent grow from a slow drip out of a coffee pot into a steady stream firing out of an espresso machine. As I sat trying to sip my diet coke, I slammed it back in one gulp. Unsurprised, I set the cup back down and looked at the bag of pretzels, contemplating if they were worth the calories.

I am getting a little hungry.

But what a waste.

Guess I have nothing else to do for the next four hours and forty five minutes.

No, just leave them.

You've got a shoot tomorrow and need to look lean.

One bag of pretzels isn't going to kill you, Kortney.

Yeah, but once I start, I can't stop.

Finally deciding to say screw it, I ripped open the tiny bag of pretzels and closed my eyes, while trying to methodically eat one at a time. Although the salty taste and smell of sodium from the pretzels was filling my presence, I couldn't stop getting whiffs of pungent red wine. I started to eat my pretzels faster and faster, ignoring the smell. For whatever reason, red wine was the only alcohol that could actually make my mouth start to salivate.

Look, one glass isn't going to kill you.

No one needs to know about it, anyway.

CRUSHING IT

Just think about it for an hour and see how you feel.

But it's just one glass.

Now fantasizing about what it would taste like in my mouth and how it would produce that warm, toasty feeling as it travelled from my tongue, down the back of my throat where my most excitable taste buds live, I sat with my eyes closed while leaning partially in the aisle.

After a few minutes of entertaining the thought, Jessica abruptly brushed by me with her shoulder as she pushed the cart back towards the plane.

Startled and irritated further as a result, I opened my eyes and nearly took my seatbelt off to finally have an opportunity to go to the bathroom until I realized the seatbelt light had been switched back on at some point.

Why do you care so much about following rules?

You never followed rules when you drank.

You've turned into a total panty waste, Kortney.

With my festering resentments growing and growing, and realizing we still had another three hours to fly, I switched on the TV and plugged in the headphones in an attempt to pass the time. While flipping through a number of shitty movies and TV series on offer, I started getting a number of knees in my back from the person behind me. Once again, unable to turn around and speak my truth, I reacted by pushing the recline button and jammed my back into the seat as hard as I possibly could. I pushed the silver button once again, bringing my seat back into its upright position, and quickly did it again.

Fuck that felt good.

Passive aggressive much, but I'm sure they got the point.

Suddenly the seatbelt sign switched off, and like a world class sprinter, with rapid reflex I undid my belt and jumped up into the aisle and headed down the long journey through the cabin to use the toilet in the back of the plane. Once inside, I discovered there were no seat covers for the toilet, piss on the floor, and no Kleenex available. With more resentment gushing into my gut, I sat hovering above the toilet and found that without relaxing my feet, I couldn't pee.

FUCK IT!

A six hundred dollar flight and there's no Kleenex to line the toilet, and I can only get half a can of diet coke?

I sat down on the toilet with my bare ass and took a couple of deep breaths before I started peeing. After washing my hands, still feeling full of rage, I started back down the aisle to my seat, and somewhere along the way made the decision that I too was going to order a glass of red wine. Before sitting in my seat, I stopped and made eye contact with the man behind me with the long legs and gave him the look of death to make certain that if I felt his knees again, I'd twist them into a pretzel.

Slamming back down into my seat, I re-buckled, and grabbed the in-flight menu.

I wonder if I should at least ask Jessica to make an announcement on the PA to find out if there are "Any friends of Bill W. traveling with us today? If so, could you please ring your call bell.". I've heard stories in meetings before where people got stuck on a long flight wanting a drink and needed to talk to another alcoholic and made a connection that way.

Then again, I only have a year to give up.

It's not that big of a deal.

I'll just have one glass of wine and everything will be fine.

Without a thought of trying to pray and ask for guidance from a power greater than myself, I clicked my call button. After what seemed like the longest two minutes of my life, Jessica appeared in front standing tall. "And what else can I get you today?" she asked. "Hi there again. Can I please get a glass of cabernet?" I replied in my sweetest voice possible, sensing I was an inconvenience based on the tone of her voice. Disappointed she didn't ask for my ID, she simply said, "Sure thing. We can only take credit or debit cards. All good to go, eh?" she said. "Yup!" I replied as she walked off and I reached for my purse under the seat.

I'll be fine.

Seriously, not a big deal.

It's been a year.

Just one glass.

Before I knew it, I was handing my debit card to Jessica, and once again, thinking of another resentment.

I've had this stupid Harley Davidson debit card with US Bank for six years and I haven't won shit. Probably some stupid ploy to get you to choose that type of debit card off the pipe dream that you might one day win a Harley.

What a fucking joke.

Fuck banks!

How much debt am I in now anyway?

Jess handed me back my card, followed by the same plastic glass and miniature bottle, and asked if I needed a receipt. "No thank you. I'll ring you for a second before we land though!" I said too enthusiastically. I immediately unscrewed the top and poured the entire bottle in the plastic cup and felt my stomach turn into a butterfly sanctuary. Filled with excitement that I'm sure normal people don't experience prior to imbibing, I sipped my first drink slowly, making sure to leave the wine on my tongue while I sucked in air to really get the flavor.

Idiot, you're only supposed to do that with a fine aged bottle of wine.

Not some shit like this Carlo Rossi comparative brand.

Without a second thought, I opened my mouth and drank back the entire glass and waited for the effects. The first few minutes were enchanting. I felt safe, warm, unstoppable, relaxed, at peace, and the voices, anger, resentment and fear all washed away. But as experience should have previously taught me, the feeling didn't last long. Doing my absolute best to wait another forty minutes, I hit my call button again. Like Groundhog Day, Jess was back and already had my wine, plastic glass and credit card terminal in her hand.

My second glass went down a little slower, as I knew I needed to try and make it last a little bit. Afterwards, I sat and listened to some music enjoying my little buzz and filling out my arrival card before I once again had to get up and pee. While in the toilet, I was unbothered by the lack of seat covers, the smell of piss, and happily sat down on the bare lid. Midway through my piss, the seatbelt sign illuminated, and the captain's voice boomed throughout the toilet informing the passengers that we'd be descending shortly and that the weather in Calgary was in clear conditions.

As I washed my hands, I quickly glanced myself over in the mirror and reminded myself of my story of Jeff and my forty eight hour sexcapade with my new internet lover if need be, and hustled back to my seat to prepare for landing.

It was time for my first bodybuilding event; The Olympia in Las Vegas 2009. It seemed like there was an endless buffet of opportunities ahead of me. The excitement buzzing around was almost palatable. I had several photoshoots lined up, with one in particular that was causing bouts of insomnia. The fantasy of hooking up with another muscle girl who was 'on my level', gave me all the motivation I needed to train with a newfound level of intensity. The similarity in physique, looks and attitude was unparalleled.

From the get-go, Bubba had made it clear that he was not comfortable with me hooking up with other chicks. Knowing that it was extremely rare for me to be attracted to another girl, he didn't think much of it when I told him that Trevor had organised a much requested and anticipated shoot with Muscle Queen. Seeing that the photographer was another girl, he had nothing to worry about, right? Almost the same size as me, Muscle Queen was sensual, feminine, and had a chest that drove me wild. Although I was slightly bigger, stronger, and a better wrestler, she was miles ahead of me in the definition department.

Aside from the photoshoots I'd lined up, I had booked out my session schedule to the point of having a wait list. Picking the Excalibur as my hub for the four days, I was told the rooms were bigger than most strip hotels, offering more space for entertaining schmoes. After declining a few session requests from both a pediatrician and a music producer, I had everyone lined up from eight a.m. to eight p.m. with back to back appointments at my hotel with the exception of one local man.

After considering my last experience of conducting an outbound visit with the high school history teacher, I decided that a local jewelry store owner with a burning desire to be held hostage between my thighs while I twisted and ripped at his nipples after shoving my dirty socks in his mouth to shut him up, was feasible (not to mention I never thought he'd be the catalyst to me getting married). In contrast, the request to command myself to fart in the pediatrician's face while wrestling, or step on mice to quench the thirst of the producer's craving for a crush fetish, was absolutely over my boundary line. I felt like Bubba would be proud of me for being clear on this particular boundary.

After getting dressed in a cobalt blue nylon cropped tank top and matching string thong to wear under my clothing, I slid my peacock feather earrings on and headed out to meet Muscle Queen and the rest of the crew after finishing my first day on the tour.

Needless to say, it was hard to not make out with her. But seeing that was all we did, I didn't think Bubba would get *too* mad when I reluctantly told him we kissed after he tricked me into thinking he didn't really care.

. . . .

Sometimes quickly, sometimes slowly, we eventually figure it out. For me, it can take damn near YEARS for me to learn a lesson. Especially when it comes to addiction. As kids, we learn lessons relatively fast when it comes to life and death things. If we touch a hot stove and burn ourselves, we generally don't touch a hot stove again because it hurts. But as adults, we can start to justify and rationalise why we do things. Children see things in black and white, and lack the grey area of thinking because we're not fully conscious yet. Again, hence why we can't rent a car until at least age twenty one. But as adults, we can start making up all kinds of bullshit in our heads as to why we should continue to do destructive things in our lives.

Whether we continue to stick our finger down our throat, drink too many drinks, or allow our partner to commit acts of violence against us, we will justify and rationalise until the cows come home. The most important thing to remember is that sometimes lessons can be learned incredibly fast, and then again, sometimes the most basic of shit can seemingly take forever to sink in. Don't give up on others in your life who seem to not be able to figure it out, and more importantly, do NOT give up on yourself. One of the cheapest, most effective ways to work on yourself, is by taking a regular inventory. So often we set goals, then never check back on our progress (unless of course they're weight loss goals for anything other than health reasons!). Think of it like this: If a pilot is one degree off on their flight path, they can end up in another country. So if you're not meticulously tracking your progress (on an emotional level), how are you going to know where you're going and if you're on path?

Do the F*cking Work

As you can see from my personal journal, I was able to write about a relapse while drunk. As an alcoholic (people who are not alcoholics or addicted to something can justify stuff in the same way) it's easy for me over time to forget how bad it got when I was drinking. I can start to think after several years of being clean and sober that it 'wasn't that bad' and I might be able to 'stop if I wanted to'. I also find it hilarious (now that I've recovered from alcoholism, of course) that my priorities were clearly screwed up by the way I wrote 'no hard body' would be had if I started drinking again. Keeping a journal is an excellent way to have 'ah-ha' moments as well as a cheap form of therapy.

Do you keep a regular journal, or have you ever tried to journal? If not, why?

List some of the New Year's resolutions that you've committed to in the past, but then fell off after a month of starting.

Why do you think that happens?

Write about a time where you worked yourself up into a shit storm for no reason at all by being in the "what if" mindset.

Describe a time where you had a friend stuck in a situation that was really bad, but they couldn't see it. Has that ever happened to you before? Why do you think that is?

How has your poor body image impacted your current or past relationship?

Do you think it's fair to your partner that they trudge the road with you?

A resentment is an unspoken expectation. Most often when we have resentment, we've played a part in creating it. A lot of which derives from poor communication on our part. (For example, thinking back to when I failed to communicate to the hairdresser what my expectations were for my hair cut. I specifically said "I don't care what you do", but ended up leaving resentful when in reality it was *my* responsibility to be more clear)

Women especially should take note on how often we don't speak our truth because we often feel bad for putting someone else out. That is the patriarchy working at its finest.

An example: I was so resentful of Bubba not working and micromanaging me, but I told him to quit his job and that I would support us, so I fully had a part in that decision.

Make a list of people, places, and things you are resentful about. Next to the list, write how you contributed to it. If you had absolutely nothing to do with it, pray for that person that they may stop being an asshole.

Scan here for more good shit.

07-28-2009

Boo! I'm drunk :(Told Bubba I kissed Muscle Queen and he broke up with me. It's just a girl riggggggght?.???? It was just for a photo shoot! so this is me drunk. NOT HOT I have everything to lose by being drunk, no hard body. @ least I know this now. @ least I'm grown up a bit As I sat here and waited, I ran across the street to get more; your perfect definition/description of an alcoholic. it's hard being in a relationship having this job. Honesty is the only way to go I can't seem to do that. But I've never fukt around on him holla! uh oh it's kickin innnnnnnnn

07-30-2009

So fuking irritated right now. Sitting at the meeting Bubba and I went to on Thursday night and just introduced myself as a newcomer. This was the meeting I got 'railroaded' into doing a 2 year commitment at. maybe I should have taken it Then maybe I wouldn't have drank. God before the meeting I really really, really didn't want to be here I feel better already. So weird how this disease works. I know I'll feel better for going, but my head/disease tells me I don't want to go and tries desperately to keep me from coming. any excuse in the book I got a grapevine for announcing myself as a newcomer. WOW... So wow. I can't believe I tossed 2 years of sobriety out the window for nothing. Not like my dog died, or a family member. . Maybe I needed to get it out of my system? Really not sure what the fuck happened. I cried the entire time after I drank. I didn't even really get drunk, drunk. I did call my old dealer and try to get some shit- unreal all day yesterday all I could think about was drinking a glass of wine, all day Since I have 1 day of sobriety under my belt, I thought fuck it!

I was just nominated as the second greeter, LOL! This higher power shit is really wild.

08 10-2009

So, I had a chat with Bubba last night Pretty crazy shit. When he got upset that I did a session, I was livid I had forgotten that I promised him that I wasn't going to. How dare him give me shit for taking an opportunity to make us money Yet this "make us money" is a joke because I resent him when I'm paying everything, I take advantage, or overlook the fact that he went from not allowing me to do sessions, to being ok with it. So, I could make extra money so he could quit his job and spend more time on us How hypocritical I am. If the script was flipped, I'd be livid. Even if he went out and drank in the same city (and he's not even an alcoholic!), state, country.

I'm so unthoughtful. I purposely left my phone at the motel, after fighting, and all he wanted to do was talk to me, as he was on the brink of death, contemplating suicide, his lover and best friend went out drinking and wasn't even there for him. He didn't want me to come to Canada to do this job in the first place. I was supposed to just work for scissor foxes, and I promised not to do a single session I came home and expected him to be happy to see me. wow such a bitch. I have so much growing to do. I have to think of others' feelings. I'm so stuck in the center of myself.

EARNING $1,666.66 AN HOUR STILL WASN'T ENOUGH

*I*couldn't work out what was more exhilarating; being my own boss, traveling to new places, making a shit ton of cash, or the high I was getting from taking prescription pain pills. The more pills I took, the less I thought about food, and the less I thought about food, the more ripped up I became. Making every effort to draw attention to my outsides to distract myself from the fact that I was destroying my insides, I decided to wear my shortest yoga shorts and skin-tight Hustler ribbed tank top before having my Grandmother drop me off at the San Francisco airport.

I stopped at the bottom of the stairs to alert her that I was ready to head out. Wearing a classy chartreuse duster with flowy black slacks, Pop stopped working on her crossword puzzle and peered over the top of her glasses while looking me up and down. Somehow maintaining a tone of sarcasm, and yet still sounding genuinely inquisitive, Pop asked, "Bitches get stitches, huh?", as she read the front of my tank top.

Staring at her sitting in my grandfather's chair where he used to aggressively try and teach me the rules of chess, I felt slightly embarrassed as I noticed she managed to match her bright red lipstick and vibrant green top with her glass-blown artisan necklace.

"Yup! I even paid to have my website screen printed on the back!" I enthusiastically replied as I turned around to show her. "It's great at grabbing attention," I said with a smile before I started walking towards the basement stairs. "Indeed, it does," she said through a semi-labored breath as she started to push herself out of the chair. As I reached the bottom of the stairs, my eyes caught the home-made printed sign my Grandfather taped to the wall next to the door leading out the garage. With my hand on the door handle, I read it for the hundredth time:

Please leave your golf shoes on and your attitude at the door. --The Management

Once again, I felt overwhelmed with embarrassment and regret.

He slowly died over the course of a year, and you were too busy getting annihilated, fucking random dudes, and skipping classes to drive an hour south and come visit, let alone help your Grandmother out. Wrecked his car and pawned his red-eye ping clubs. Fucking piece of shit. How's that for an attitude?

"You have everything you need?" Pop said from the top of the stairs.

Yes, except more pills if you have them.

"Sure do! Just a short trip. Don't need much," I replied as I opened the door into the garage.

I really don't have a problem. I'll stop in a few months.

Hating the quiet and stillness more than I hated slow songs, we drove in excruciating silence for most of the ten minute trip to the airport. Unlike the time I allowed her to thoroughly fill me with self-belief by meticulously pointing out how and why she was impressed by my first painting at seven years old, I had barely filled her with the details from my new lifestyle as an entrepreneur. In the silence, I reflected on what real feedback from Pop felt like all those years ago. Instead of glancing at my attempt of copying a watercolor painting in her house by telling me what a great job I did, she took the time to point out specifics. From my straight lines and steady hand, to the exact color match, I "had an eye for detail and was really going to go places."

While trying to be philosophical about it all, I gave her little sound bites about the past year including the webcam, paid photo shoots, clip store and my membership website, but always kept it relatively vague. Now that I had progressed to seeing these men in real life, I knew she wasn't going to give me the stamp of approval I was seeking, no matter how philosophical I got with her. I desperately wanted to tell her why I was catching a flight to Indiana. Not very many people can make five thousand dollars in three hours for simply standing around to have some old guy worship their calf muscles, but whatever.

Instead, as we sped down the freeway, all I could think about was what a failure I must have turned out to be in her eyes.

"Don't you have a sweatshirt or something?" she asked as she pulled her black Camry up to the curb. "It's in my bag, but no one will see my website if I wear it though!" I replied with another smile as I gave her a hug. "Thanks for the ride Pop! Be back soon!" I said casually as I pushed the car door. As soon as the door shut, I felt the brisk wind nip at every inch of my overexposed skin.

Approaching the check-in counter, I noticed there was only one person available and it happened to be a woman.

Damn.

The likeliness of getting a free upgrade is slim here.

I'm not even going to try and bother.

I'll just pay for it.

"Oh my gosh girl, look at your body!" she said as I approached the counter. "I would kill someone to look like you!"

"Well aren't you a diamond in a haystack!" I replied back while looking at her name tag. "They don't make em' like you anymore, Rebecca," I said as I noticed her eyes illuminate once her name came out of my mouth.

Feeling a strange new energy pulsate through my veins, I replied, "I usually feel like women look at me with disgust."

"No way! We're all looking at you wishin' we had what you got, girl! But maybe it's the tank top!" she said while laughing.

"Valid point!"

"Now where ya off to today with all that muscle, and can I see some ID for those guns you're packing?" she said with a grin.

Feeling like every cell in my body was having some kind of orgasm, I continued to make small talk with Rebecca.

"I'm heading to Indiana, Bec. Would you believe it if I told you some old man is going to pay me five grand to stand around and flex my calf muscles for three hours while he rubs baby oil on them and tells me how amazing I am?" I asked.

"Wait, whaaaaat! Is this real life, sis?" she replied.

"No sex. No wax on, wax off bullshit. Just straight up spend three hours being admired and worshiped while I stand around and flex," I said.

"Oh my LORD! Can I come work with you?" she said with

sheer joy.

"I know, right? I still can't believe it either. I usually only make four hundred dollars an hour to do it, but this guy is my biggest fan in the world," I said as I started to notice a line behind me.

Jumping up and down, she screamed, "*Four* hundred dollars an *hour*?"

Suddenly we both realized we were getting carried away in our own little time-space continuum as the entire surrounding area of passengers and other agents fell silent while looking our way.

Dropping my voice to a faint whisper, I leaned in and said, "Yeah! The bigger the better in this world. I've been in it a year, and still can't fully wrap my head around it!"

As she handed me my boarding pass and driver's license back she replied, "I was literally just thinking this morning that I needed to join a gym and lose some weight because my legs are too fat!"

"No, no, no! You got it all wrong. You just need to join the gym to get them stronger and defined!" I replied as I pulled out one of my business cards and slid it across the counter.

"I plan on writing a book about it all one day, so keep in touch and remember, the world is *not* what you think it is, girl!"

"Well Ms. Olson, all I can say is, you GO girl!" she said.

"Outstanding customer service Rebecca. Come to think of it, what's your boss' name and how do I lodge a statement of amazingness?" I said.

"Ah that's so sweet of you, but no need for all that," she said.

Feeling the biggest shit-eating grin on my face, "I always get what I want, Bec! Thanks again," I said as I walked off.

I felt like I had some vortex of electrifying energy flying around me as I passed by the row of other agents.

That was amazing.

But why?

I can't believe how different it felt to get a compliment from a stranger who doesn't have a penis.

It felt so good to hear her say all that!

I wish I grew up with Black girls.

What a trip!

God, I hope she goes to the gym and starts lifting.

Maybe I should start a business that teaches women how to do all this shit?

As I walked towards the security screening, I felt like I was floating on air.

All of my previous thoughts of regret and embarrassment had washed away as I started fantasizing about my new business plan on teaching women how to choke men out. Overwhelmed with a flood of thoughts stronger than the force of Niagara Falls, I decided to pull up to a row of chairs and start writing them down.

I'd need to teach them about all of the different types of categories.

I guess there's basically two different types of session girls; wrestlers and bodybuilders. Then you have the rare ones like me who do it all and haven't taken a bunch of steroids or growth hormone.

Well, do it all except suck dick.

I mean, I've pole vaulted over my boundary line a few times lately, but they were hot.

I'd need to teach them how to wrestle, arm wrestle, apply scissor holds.

Wait... First, I'd need to evaluate their strength levels and teach them how to work out.

What if I got every single woman in the world wanting to get strong and defined instead of skinnier?

Wow.

Then of course there's the booking process.

Always get a deposit.

What type of hotels to look for, and how to find the best online deals.

So much easier to get a hotel that doesn't need a key card for the elevator...

How to pack for tours.

Food prepping.

Maximize clothing for working out while on the road and sessions.

There's so much to teach!

Realizing I had far too much to contemplate, I decided to get myself through to my gate before I missed my five thousand dollar once in a lifetime opportunity. After I carefully tucked my notebook back into my duffle bag, I got in line at security and anticipated whether or not I was going to get the usual TSA treatment.

Disappointed that no one asked me for the second time in one day if I had a license for the guns I was packing, I quickly got through to my gate and decided to forfeit doing some kind of airport workout, and instead try and finish Eckhart Tolle's book, "A New Earth". I knew it wasn't a replacement for the Big Book, but seeing that it was written after the turn of the twenty first century and not during the nineteen thirties, I felt like Eckhart was speaking more of my language.

As soon as I got the book out, the boarding process had commenced.

. . . .

Since the day I launched my membership website a year ago, Don has sent me an email almost every single day. Generally, his emails were in response to my blog, but on the odd days I missed writing, he still emailed. Don loved to tell stories. He not only loved sharing his leg fetish with me, but also stories about his parents who'd passed away years back, what his sex drive was like when he was younger, stories about his cousin's sister's neighbor's drama, and even an occasional story from church. Although the theme and stories were always different, one thing always remained the same; Don had some kind of way of telling me how glorious, incredible, wonderful, generous, insightful, funny, intelligent, hard-working, loyal, and ambitious I was. Every single email ended the same as well.

You GO girl!

Don in Indiana.

As soon as the rubber hit the mat, I switched on my phone and sent Don a text message to let him know I'd landed. On top of paying for my flight and hotel, Don was going to pay me five grand to come all the way to see him in his Podunk tiny town. A retired trust fund kid who had a knack for gambling, Don was never married, had no kids, no real commitments, and simply loved my legs.

After making my way through the airport and finally out the exit doors to the baggage claim, Don was easy to spot. Standing a little over six feet tall and wearing a typical, retired older man outfit, he was holding a hand-written sign on printer paper that read, 'K fucking O!' From a good fifty feet away, Don shouted "Kortney!" as he started briskly walking towards me. Don had sent some random pictures of himself over the course of the year, so spotting him with or without his welcome sign would have been an easy task.

With a snow-white comb over, a neatly trimmed short beard, khaki trousers, plaid button up short sleeve shirt, black New Balance shoes, and gold rimmed square glasses, all Don was missing was a pocket protector.

"Hi Don!" I exclaimed back as I reached out to give him a hug. After a long embrace, Don stepped back and grabbed my shoulders whilst looking at my legs like he had just brought home a bag of magic beans, the golden goose, *and* the evil giant gagged and bound.

Without taking a single breath between statements, with his slight funny lisp he shouted,

"My GOD! You are fucking STUNNING! I never imagined you to be even more breathtakingly beautiful in person! I can't BELIEVE YOU ARE ACTUALLY HERE!" as spittle came flying out of his mouth. Feeling slightly concerned that people in the baggage claim were going to think I was a prostitute or a mail order bride, I laughed under my breath as I decided it was time to take control of the situation and get us the hell out of the airport.

"Yes Don, I *am* exquisite! Now let's get out of here and get this party started!" I said as I slipped my arm around his frail waist and pulled him off his feet. Unsure if he was hard of hearing or just overly excited that his dream-come-true was now dragging him with force towards a hotel, he went back to shouting. "FUCK! I can't believe your legs! I mean I could spot you a hundred yards behind the glass doors before you even walked out! I bet you turned every single person's head today in those shorts!"

"Yes, I generally turn heads, Don. You've read my blog every day for a year now, so you know the shenanigans I pull daily."

"I know! And now you're actually here! Kortney, how was your flight? Are you hungry?"

"It was fine, thanks! Why don't we get to the hotel and we can order room service?" I suggested.

As we stepped out of the airport and underneath the Indiana brisk night sky, my teeth started chattering as I started telling Don about my encounter with Rebecca at the airport. "Oh God! Let me give you my jacket! I can't believe I didn't tell you to pack something warm. But that would be a crime to hide those legs!" he said as he put his thin fisherman looking coat over my shoulders.

"What a gentleman, Don! So anyway, when I was walking away, she said 'You go girl!', which I found so ironic since you've signed off on your emails that way since the very first time you wrote to me," I said.

"Yes! That's just incredible, Kortney. I still can't believe you're here!" he said as he opened the door to his cherry red Cadillac CTS coupe.

"You like a little bit of speed, do ya?" I said.

"Why, yes. Yes, I do! And I know you used to sell these cars when you were all fucked up! Kortney, I've read every single blog you've written. I think you're just amazing, but I think you know that," he said as he slammed my door.

My God, he's eccentric! He might even cuss more than I do.

As we drove a short mile to the hotel Don booked for me, he went into detail about the 'schedule' and what he hoped to happen in our three hours together.

While Don checked in, I waited in the car and contemplated taking another pill. I had almost finished reading 'A New Earth' on the plane, and started feeling like I could hear Kortney Kay's voice coming through a little louder. But as I sat and started thinking about the three hours ahead and not wanting to order French fries for room service, I let the monkey take over and grabbed a pill before Don returned to the car.

Walking towards the room, I once again found myself hoping no one saw us together.

Why would I care what anyone might think of me anyway?

I have nude pictures all over the internet, and all the sudden I'm concerned someone might think I'm a prostitute?

Besides he could be my overly friendly Uncle for all anyone knows.

Without managing to shout this time, "Thanks again for making the trip out, Kortney. I can't tell you how much it means to me," Don said.

Once inside the room, my oxycodone kicked in and I instantly pepped up. Feeling inclined to share my recent learning from Eckhart, I passionately talked about the ego and how I was starting to understand my "KO" side.

"You know, Kortney. . . you've taught me so much this past year. I got a copy of the Four Agreements and felt like I had already read it. You are so wise, Kortney. Truly, truly wise."

Hearing Don repeatedly use my name, caused me to suddenly realize why Rebecca's eyes lit up when I went out of my way to say hers. Hearing my name made me feel recognized and important. As Don started rambling on about his cousin's brother's cat, my mind drifted to faintly recalling a training video on the topic of using people's names from my days of selling cars.

I wonder how much shit I could have learned had I stayed clean and sober the last decade?

It's OK, Kortney. These are just thoughts, and you are not your thoughts. Observe them, then without judgement, let them go just as easily as they came. Thoughts are not absolute truths.

Feeling elevated from my pill and my new-found sense of self-awareness thanks to Eckhart, I tuned back into Don's boring as fuck story just in time to hear him wrap it up.

"So, let's see these outfits you want to see me wear!" I said.

"Okay! THAT sounds like a GREAT idea, Kortney," Don said as he got up to grab the pink paper bag he had carried in from the trunk of the car. Assuming he had taken a little trip to his local adult only store from the non-branded bag, I sat in sheer anticipation while waiting to see what direction this big reveal was going to head in.

Envisioning Don methodically pulling out the items one by one, he instead tipped the bag upside down and dumped the contents on the bed.

With a cheesedick smile on his face, he looked over at me and said, "What can I say? I'm impatient!" as he chuckled in delight.

As he started separating the contents of the bag into what appeared to be outfits, as suspected, he explained that he visited an adult only store to pick up the thigh high stockings and the rest from a local 'cheapo Chinese' outlet store.

"I wasn't entirely sure what size shoe exactly. I know you have really wide feet, so there are a few pairs of shoes.".

As I looked at the hideous outfits, I smiled in relief seeing that he hadn't picked up some crotchless bullshit.

"You even got some jewelry I see," I said as I picked up what appeared to be a five dollar pearl necklace.

"Yes! I don't know why but thought it would be a nice touch," he said with another cheesy grin.

"Alright, I'll be back shortly," as I grabbed the first outfit and headed to the bathroom to change.

I fumbled around for the switch as I walked into the bathroom and started thinking about the fact that an hour had gone by already with us just talking. After getting my yoga shorts and tank top off, I examined the 'cheapo Chinese' attire and couldn't make sense of how five grand and a five dollar pearl necklace went together.

Instead of trying to figure everything and everyone else out, accept it for what it is.

Everyone has different taste and values.

Maybe fake pearls make his heart skip a beat.

Maybe fake pearls are a girl's best friend.

After spending close to what felt like an eternity getting the necklace to clasp, I moved onto the black sparkly tube top before slipping the bodycon black and white striped cotton skirt on and stepping into the glossy, closed-toe Wizard of Oz looking heels which ironically, fit perfectly.

I don't think I've ever seen someone wear such a hideous outfit in my entire life. Not a homeless person, not a character on TV or in a movie, or even a child playing dress up. Like this would absolutely have to win an award of the world's most revolting outfit ever assembled.

Showtime, bitch!

As I flung the bathroom door open and proceeded to strut across the carpet like a sultry vixen, Don grabbed his chest and dropped to his boney knees while exclaiming, "Kortney! You are FUCKING breathtaking!" Picking up that I'd noticed he was only wearing his boxers, he immediately asked if it was OK. "Yes, Don. You're fine," I replied as I fished a speaker out of my bag to help set the mood.

Playing "Hot With U" by Prince, despite wearing an outfit that resembled the toilet bowl after I had a purging session back in high school, I instantly fell into character and told Don to get the baby oil and stop fucking around. Faster than a tire-changer in a NASCAR pit-crew, Don was on his knees in front of my legs with both hands wrapped around my left calf.

"I can hardly fit both hands around one calf! You are just magnificent, Kortney."

As Don stayed perched on his knees, I stood doing some calf raises while he squeezed my muscles as hard as he could. "How can something be so hard yet be so soft? I just can't believe it."

The more Prince's voice filled the room, the more I turned it up. I walked over to the Ikea chipboard end table, and drug it back over with one hand to where Don was still on his knees. To the beat, I slammed my heel down on top of the table and firmly whispered, "Oil that" as I stuck my calf muscle out while assuming the mansplaining position.

"Oh, God! Oh my GOD your calves are just divine, Kortney," Don gleamed with excitement as "Darling Nikki" played in the background. After another thirty seconds of Prince wailing on the electric guitar and Don rubbing oil on my right calf, he looked up with tears in his eyes and said, "You know something, God really did break the mold when he made you." After a short pause, he bent forward and gave my calf a little peck with his lips before I switched which leg was on the table.

As Don joyously caressed, squeezed, and guided his hands all across my left calf, I started to stop being KO for a minute and actually paused long enough to realize what was happening. It felt like one of the many times I drove somewhere but didn't really realize I was in route and well on my way, until I actually arrived at my destination. I'd been driving through this world for nearly a year, telling people about what were once considered oddities but ultimately became my normal, yet hadn't yet really stopped to process the entirety or vastly deep scope of the experience.

Not once has Don stopped to point out what I considered an imperfection.

And why do I consider something an imperfection in the first place?

Why am I getting paid to have men worship my legs, but throughout my entire life I've visualized if it would be painful to take a dull butcher's knife and chop the inside fat off my legs every time I was in the kitchen?

He just had tears in his eyes over my perfection.

Yet how many times have I had tears stream out of my mine because I couldn't zip up a pair of fucking boots over my calves?

I took a pill to mute my appetite but am proud that I've managed to quit meth and blacking out from being hammered?

. . . .

The fog had lifted just in time and my flight took off on schedule for once. I had just wrapped up an insane tour; Indiana, Chicago, Washington D.C., Philadelphia, then finally Miami before heading home. Two weeks, five cities, and five flights resulted in over sixty one-on-one private sessions. Sixty hours of slamming guys into mats in hotel rooms across the country.

Three doctors.

A lawyer.

Two accountants.

A contractor.

A plumber.

The bass player from *the* eighties punk rock band.

Two teachers.

A psychologist.

Twenty eight thousand dollars.

I'd ticked over two hundred and eighty eight sessions in the past year, and I distinctly remember feeling like I'd had enough.

Two sixty-year-old ladies across from me ordered a jack and coke right after I had just ordered coffee with cream and sweetener. God forbid I have sugar instead of aspartame. Feelings of deep jealousy and envy washed over me as I started to question why I'd decided to compete in a bodybuilding show.

I definitely needed to find a new hobby other than bodybuilding.

Having body image issues and being a natural bodybuilder probably wasn't the greatest idea I've ever had. *I hate how I look, but please judge how I look.* I knew I was getting closer to wanting to get clean once and for all and thought that setting a goal of competing would help me get clean.

But when you wrestle strangers in five-star hotels all over the world who also pay for flights, rooms, and meals, coupled with wedding proposals in your inbox every day, yet look at your body in the mirror most mornings with hatred, you'd probably ask yourself what the meaning of life was more often than focusing on getting straight. I kept taking pills thinking that the leaner I got, the more I would be compelled to get clean. If I could just win this show, I'd feel accomplished and have purpose. I'd be somebody, besides just "KO". I was doing the deadly dance with "If I could just…" that I always did to rationalize my unhealthy behaviors.

Through all of the time I spent with these men, all of whom were from incredibly different walks of lives, it was just that: Men. Where were all the women? I was starting to realise that I was missing the Rebecca's in my life.

After retrieving my car from Pop's house, I started heading towards downtown San Francisco to meet my dad and stepmom. Trying to keep a brave face on while driving, I struggled. I was riding the high from having a giant bag of cold, hard cash on my person, all from earning through my own sweat, flirting, and flexing.

I was optimistic that my dad's surgery was going to be a success, but knew in the back of my mind that only death and taxes were guaranteed in life. And of course, relapse if I didn't start taking my recovery more seriously. Although technically, I was currently already relapsed.

Even though I had more than enough money to have my car valeted, I parked in the self-park garage. The fear of financial insecurity still had me by the ovaries. After a long walk and a short ride in the elevator, I was knocking on my parents' hotel room door.

"Hiiiiiiiiiiii!" I squealed as Barb opened the door.

"Hey, girl!"

After a brief hug, I dashed in to find my dad sitting at the table.

"Hi Daddy O!"

"Hey Kort!" he replied. "How was your trip?" he asked, seeming a little out of sorts.

"It was great! I made a shit ton of cash and met all sorts of interesting men, as usual!"

"I read your blog about the guy who got a little too aggressive for ya! Did you kick his ass?"

"Oh my gosh! Yesssssss, that guy almost got his head smashed through a wall!"

"Yeah it sure sounded like you kinda snapped!"

"Whenever someone manages to smother my face in a hold, I lose my mind. It's like I flip a switch and go ape shit!"

"Well, I guess he learned then?" he asked while laughing. "You messed with the wrong bitch," he said in his best Clint Eastwood voice.

"Yeah, you could say that! He apologised as soon as I took it up a notch and practically had him in tears."

"Damn Kort--and you're sure you're safe doing all of this?" Barb asked.

"I mean there's a risk that I'll get hit by a car on the drive back to Santa Rosa from here, but of course I do everything to minimise any risk. Besides, a majority of these guys are looking to be man-handled anyway," I replied, fumbling around my purse for the brown paper bag that once held my precious egg white muffin from Starbucks.

"Speaking of risk, what time is your appointment at UCSF tomorrow?" I asked.

"Ughhhhhh... I believe tena.m. Is that right Barb?"

"Yeah, ten a.m." Barb said from the edge of the couch.

"So other than knowing the tumor is benign, do they know anything else?" I asked as I sat on the floor.

"Well, it sounds like they're going to have to remove part of my skull to take the tumor out," my dad replied.

"Did we tell you that your dad had decided to downgrade our health insurance two days before going to his local doctor and finding out he had a tumor?" Barb asked.

"What!" I exclaimed. "You're fucking kiddinig me?"

"Nope! I call it the Olson luck!" she said.

"Well, how's THIS for luck!" I shouted excitedly as I tipped the brown paper bag upside down, pouring a mountain of twenty dollar bills on the floor.

As my dad let out a high-pitch whistle, "Oh my GOD, Kortney!" Barb replied.

"You *sure* you're not hookin?" she asked.

"No! I'm telling you--this is the most insane shit ever. This is an accumulation of back to back sessions across five cities, which is more than I've ever done on one trip."

"Great! Now you can pay me back for bailing you out of your tweaker check writing stunt you pulled up in Oregon!" my dad chimed in.

"I could, but probably best I keep paying that mortgage you cosigned on, dad!"

"You should really write a book one day, Kort," Barb said.

"I plan on it! Women need to know that the world is not what they think it is!" Reading their faces, I carried on. "The wildest thing about all of this, is how it seems like there are certain fetishes that pertain to certain races or regions of the world. Middle Eastern men love lift and carry, English men love biceps, Australians love wrestling, black men love feet... But the Middle Eastern one is the oddest because these men are coming from a country where women aren't allowed to be strong! Like I don't get it!"

"Yeah that is strange. So, was there anything weird on this trip? Well, weirder than before I should say," he asked.

I sat wondering if I should share this detail with them, before proceeding.

"I finally had someone with a mommy issue!" I laughed.

"A mommy issue, huh?"

"Yeah--I know I've told you how a lot of these guys like to be humiliated."

"Yes, I remember you telling me about the guy in Oakland who paid you to finish a session by making fun of him at the checkout in a Safeway."

"Oh yeah, that guy! Yeah, he had me act like I forgot the milk, then in front of the cashier said, 'That's ok, I can milk this fat fuck's tits later', while looking at him."

My parents erupted in laughter.

"I know, right? It was so hard for me to keep a straight face," I said laughing with them.

"But wait! This one's even better," I said as I waited for them to settle down.

"So, this guy wanted me to make fun of him for having a tiny dick and tell him that his mother would never love him, all while I smoked a cigarette."

"WHAT!", they both sang in unison.

"Yeah!" I said, laughing hysterically.

"But get this--I accidentally gave him the wrong hotel room and instead of texting 621, I texted 612 and he knocked on some poor woman's door with his dick hanging out of his zipper!"

"No way!" said Barb. "What the hell is wrong with these guys?"

"He said he was pretty sure she called the cops."

"Yeah, seriously?" my dad said looking baffled.

"Yeah, I've no idea. But they legitimately are all normal, nice guys."

"I can kind of understand the fascination with a strong woman, but the humiliation thing is just weird," my dad said.

Best I leave the enema story tucked inside a box forever.

"Yeah, you know the weirdest thing about all of this is realising that it's always men--like why are there no women out there with some kind of weird fetish?" I said. "I mean we might have daddy issues, but it's not like we seek out a way to spend our Friday nights pretending to be a coffee table while someone else puts a cigar out on our body."

With both parents looking relatively confused, I reassured them that this was not a part of my experience.... yet. There is always a 'yet'.

. . . .

To think that I made an average of $1,666.66 an hour on this trip to see Don (Five grand divided by three hours), and that wasn't enough to "make me happy", is baffling. Having a moment of clarity towards the end of our session was priceless, but it was fleeting. The next day when I flew back to California, I was sitting on the plane obsessing over how I could build more wealth and more muscle. In retrospect, I can see that no amount of money would bring me happiness. There's something else that guarantees happiness, but you'll have to keep reading to find out what it is.

Do the F*cking Work

How would you have grown up differently knowing that the entire world has different ideas on what is considered beautiful and desirable?

Guilt is a wasted emotion. It's like being in a rocking chair: It gives you something to do but it doesn't take you anywhere. What things are you continuing to beat yourself up over that you need to forgive yourself for and move on?

How can you make amends with people you've hurt in the past?

How do you view other women in general?

Have you ever complimented another woman who was a complete stranger?

What happened?

How did it feel?

Describe your feelings around financial security or insecurity.

Do you have any beliefs around money? (i.e. money is the root of all evil. If I could pay off my credit card debt I would be happy and feel free)

Scan here for more good shit.

LESSON 12

FIT AS A FIDDLE, BUT FLATLINING INSIDE

March 2010

3:02pm.

Denver.

Fuck he better show.

I don't get cancellations often, but still. I really need the money this time.

Jesus! How do you trample on someone's balls?

I'd better not suck at it...

I'd better look confident.

I've got KO tattooed on my shoulder- how could I not look confident?

My Diet Coke is flat.

This Cream O' Wheat is cold.

Wish I didn't use the hotel pen to stir it up. Now I don't have anything to write with.

Just like I don't have anything to scoop it into my mouth with.

I always get stuck in hotels without a spoon.

I'm not above eating it with my fingers.

The bananas I packed are brown and spotty.

Reminds me of Rob's disgusting penis.

Taking any kind of inventory is a fact finding and a fact-facing process.

It is an effort to discover the truth.

Why am I reciting lines from the Big Book right now?

What is the truth?

The truth is, I'm so fuckin frustrated right now.

I cook; never mind.

I have too much to write down and nothing to write with.

Yes, we just addressed this, Kortney...

I don't know where to start. I don't know where to end.

I should be on the webcam right now while I'm waiting, but I don't feel like it.

But I need the money.

Back to the truth, bitch...

The simple truth is that I'm a sick individual plagued by the disease of addiction.

Fuck that. Where is this mother fucker?

I'm so close to drinking.

So fuckin close.

Wonder if anyone else talks to themselves as much as I do?

What if I put lemon extract in my water?

Wonder if it'll give me a buzz unlike the last time I tried.

Lost, miserable, pathetic soul with no hope.

I have the world at my fingertips.

Can't fuckin' get my life together.

So together for everyone else.

With so much opportunity.

***Had** so much opportunity is more like it.*

How the fuck does that work?

I hate how I look when I wake up.

Yet I'm making thousands by the afternoon.

I stand in the mirror and am disgusted.

I don't see what they see.

One more day, noooo, no, no- one more week, then I'll stop taking pills.

How many fucking times have I said that? A thousand? Ten thousand?

I'll wean myself off. It can't be that hard.

It never turns out that way, give me a break you idiot.

I can't rely on how I look to support myself for much longer.

Should have paid to get your real estate appraisal license you fucking moron.

You were too busy getting high.

What the fuck am I going to do with my life?

I'm going to get old one day.

Older is more like it.

I'm supposed to pray for God's guidance and direction.

I think that's the third step.

Relying on "God" instead of myself?

Control seemed to work out just fine for Janet Jackson.

Forgive myself. Forgive yourself. Blah Blah Blah.

FUCK!

I'm so lost right now.

Who the fuck is God anyway?

I don't understand what's going on with me.

Why can't I be normal in my own skin?

I'm told I'm beautiful and amazing every fucking day...

Why every time I look in the mirror, do I feel disgusted?

I want to take so many pills I'll never wake up.

I don't think I'll ever learn to be happy.

Why do I have to LEARN to be happy? Why me? Why can't I just be happy?

Nothing and everything are ever enough for me.

I've never even thought about another man, let alone talked to one since being with him.

So why am I feeling guilty now?

Is it because I'm really unhappy?

I don't think I feel appreciated.

I'm looking for the easy way out, I think.

I think I think too much.

I'm probably pretty close to liver failure.

I guess I've become pretty tolerant of these pills lately.

Chew 'em up, two, three at a time, five times a day.

I pay the bills.

I do the laundry.

I pay the mortgage.

Fuck I want a drink.

I hate the laundry.

I have fifteen inch biceps.

I want sixteen inch biceps.

But seventeen inch biceps would be amazing.

No that would be borderline grotesque. I'd definitely get labeled as using steroids then.

I want twenty inch calves.

Those can never be too big according to them.

I pay for everything while Bubba goes back to school. How is that the "trade off"?

I'm stuck wrestling men in hotel rooms.

I'm stuck being a bodybuilder, constantly watching everything I eat.

I trample on men's testicles.

Well, I do now.

I turned down ten grand to trample mice! Ugh, what a fucked-up weirdo.

I majored in criminal law. Wait, still on the ten-year plan....

The only major right now is this major pain in the ass wasting my fucking time.

Where's Miguel at!!!

3:03pm

Outside the hotel, Miguel called me from his car.

Trying to sound enthusiastic but wavering with concern, Miguel exclaimed, "Hey KO!"

"Yeah man, what's up? You almost here or what?" I replied.

"I'm here, but remember how I told you I had this contraption thingy I made to bring to the session?" he said.

With a drawn-out questionable tone, I forced my words out,

"Yeahhh, what's the deal, babe?"

After a deep inhale, he sheepishly said, "Do you know if there's a side entrance somewhere so I can bring this up to the room?".

Miguel was my fourth session of the day, and god forbid I looked anything less than perfect for him or any of these other men. I had to be the best, because that's what I promised. I'm not sure if it was programming from my previous life as a salesperson, but I always remembered my ABCs: Always Be Closing. Once I got the booking, I shouldn't have cared so much about the client's desired outcome coming to fruition, but being a seemingly people pleaser committed for life, I cared more about their satisfaction than I cared about my own sanity.

Staring blankly in the ancient, outdated mirror, I quickly gave myself the once-over after reapplying my mineral makeup that had vanished during the previous wrestling session. Despite the mild situational depression some of these outdated, darker hotel rooms gave me, I'd somehow always forget that this 'good deal' was about to turn into my base where I'd spend ten hours a day, for two to three days straight... *Fuck me*.

"It's all good! Just come through the front, man--who cares?" I blurted back while setting down my compact case next to my cold Cream O' Wheat.

"Well, it's kinda big," he said.

I quickly ran through my head to see how I was feeling, even though I already knew what the answer was going to be; I was anxious, on edge, over-tired, under nourished, and completely twisted up.

Should have eaten that Cream O' Wheat while it was still warm.

Living out of hotel rooms taught me how to get really creative when it came to what I could pack and fly with in order to maintain my rock-hard physique.

One packet of Cream O' Wheat, a hotel coffee machine for boiling water, a disposable coffee cup, with a banana as a pseudo spoon, was usually my go-to meal. Diet soda was always readily available from the vending machines on site. Just like Oxy, the faint, shallow whispers echoing inside my head would gently tell me that diet soda was probably killing me, but I kept putting both in my mouth. I loved putting shit in my mouth to change the way I was feeling, though nothing ever changed.

I was beyond twisted up on this day.

How I responded to the twist in my head was *'better take another pill before this guy gets up here'*. How I responded to Miguel was, "Who cares dude! Just sack-up and walk past the front desk like you own the joint!"

Grow a pair. You're gonna need 'em.

Taking a razor blade and carefully slicing underneath the zipper inside my purse, I'd created a gorgeous stash space for the pills "I didn't have a problem with", because it's totally normal to have a sewn-in pill pocket in your bag. It never occurred to me that if I had to hide something, it was a sign that I shouldn't be doing it. But hiding pills or hiding the fact that I was about to break our agreement and do a ball busting session, never really felt like much of a problem. It wasn't like I was cutting up bodies and hiding them under my house.

Shit! Only four left? How the fuck did that happen?

I could feel the knot in my stomach twist even tauter. I felt like I was doing a decent job of managing my supply, but as time would repeatedly tell, despite all of my previous job experience and training, I still couldn't manage shit. Discovering I was down to only four pills left me with the most debilitating sense of fear and despair. Faster than the log falls off the top of the drop at Disneyland's Splash Mountain, the haunting and familiar feeling of my heart falling down towards my anus had greeted me once again.

The heart dropping was similar to the feeling of driving in the pouring rain down the highway at 2am right after getting my license back post DUI, then hitting a deer, but not realising it was a deer, all while being high on meth driving someone else's vehicle.

But at least it was an older vehicle that already had some dents.

Not to mention I potentially saved someone else from hitting the deer who might have been in a small car.

Just keep justifying, KO.

I had only spoken to Miguel on the phone once before agreeing to stand on his balls.

Technical name "ball-busting" I think. It was very, very rare for me to consider anything outside of an athletic style session, but now my habit had nearly tripled in price along with my inhibitions. Still thinking money would solve all of my problems, I tried ignoring the thought of how upset Bubba would be with me for not taking my safety more seriously. I always failed to conduct background checks. I'd build rapport via email and take these men's word for face value. I'm not sure which was more stressful; sessions, or the fact that the street value of Oxy was running a dollar a milligram at the time, which netted out to be about a hundred dollars a day. Not to mention I was almost out.

Out of time, out of money, and out of hope.

As I stood chewing up half of an 80mg pill, I heard a faint knock on the door.

As of late, I found myself craving the foul, chemical taste of chewed-up Oxy during the day.

My DOC (drug of choice) was always uppers. Although classified as a 'downer', Oxy seemed to do well in lifting my worries during the stressful session times. Back when I was a tweaker, just like the heroin addicts I'd laugh at who'd nod off face first into their bowl of cereal, I'd find myself with my thighs wrapped around some guys neck, squeezing him into oblivion, when suddenly I'd be regaining consciousness after a few seconds for a quick nap.

The potential that at any given moment I could get raped, stabbed, tortured, or robbed was overwhelming, however, getting clean off Oxy was way more stressful. Just the thought of it was unbearable.

I dissimulated everyone I knew. Even my mom didn't know how bad it'd gotten. On a surface level, I even had myself fooled. However, in the slower moments of my downtime, maybe while riding up an elevator to the twenty secondth floor of my hotel room, or sitting in the airport bathroom stall, I'd have a second to catch that inner voice, quietly whispering that I was fucking up, again. I was slowly killing myself with this pill addiction, beating up men, being their best real-life fantasy and making a shit ton of money doing it. I had no idea that objectifying myself wasn't going to fill that blackhole void that sat deep in my soul underneath a blue tarp.

I opened the door without a thought in my head other than, *Where the fuck am I going to find more Oxy?*

No thought of looking out the peephole to make sure Miguel

was alone.

No thought of getting prepared to potentially having to slam the door in his face if he gave off some weird ass vibes.

No thought of maybe I should find a different career path which wouldn't hurt my back, thus justifying the use of pain pills.

But just like most addicts, justification was my middle name.

It was *just* a ball-busting session. At least I never said yes to strap-on play.

I was *just* hiding some pills in my purse. At least I never hid bodies under my house.

I'm the one that has to wrestle and bring home the bacon. I'm just taking pills to get through it.

I'm not sticking my finger down my throat and puking; I'm *just* chewing food up and spitting it out so I can taste it.

I'm not a dirty junkie shooting heroin, I'm just taking pain pills and nodding off for a few seconds.

I didn't do any background checks, but I always packed a stun gun, just in case. I'd only ever had one guy that made me feel unsafe due to his mental instability. His shit was just not normal, even in comparison to all of this 'non-normal' activity. Shortly after the guy had arrived, I pretended that a local friend had called with an emergency and that I was going to have to give the guy back his money and cut. That fake phone call could have landed me an Emmy.

I flung open the hotel door and immediately my jaw dropped to the floor.

After taking a second to look Miguel up and down, including

the massive 'contraption' he held between both hands, I enthusiastically said, "What's up! Come in, come in! With arms opened wide; I couldn't help but notice how attractive he was. A late twenty-something year old Puerto Rican man, holding a mysterious wooden chest.

With a sheepish tone he stammered saying, "I told you it was kinda big."

Wonder if he's talking about his dick or this ridiculously large box he's holding?

"Damn dude! When you said you wanted to bring something you built, I was imagining something sized more along the lines of a shoebox!" I said as I was locking the door behind me.

In truth, I had zero fucking idea what it was, let alone how it worked. But I didn't care. I wanted my four hundred dollars and more pills.

Despite earlier memories of seeing a young man convulsing in a wheelchair in the hallway of St. Helena Hospital detoxing off of Oxy, I couldn't stop using. Not even close. That poor young man was a construction worker who'd never touched a drug in his life. The good ol' boy had fallen off of a roof while on a job, and under his doctor's care, was prescribed OxyContin. Last I'd heard, he'd sadly passed away, yet even his death didn't penetrate my drug addled brain.

That's the insidious thing about addiction; once a little bit of time passes, we forget how bad it really was. We forget everything and anything of value we'd previously learned.

Things like "don't fuck with Oxycontin or you'll die" or "stop booking cheap hotel rooms because you find them incredibly depressing". More often than not, I'd have to keep fucking up before I had an ah-ha moment—an overall pervasive theme in all aspects of my life.

I'd never done a ball-busting session before. Bubba wasn't OK with me stomping, kicking, or maliciously pulling on any guy's cock but his own. Not really sure I was either, but now probably wasn't the time to question that. Not only was I nervous because I wasn't supposed to be doing it, but I also didn't know if I'd be any good at it.

God forbid I not be 'the best' at something.

Let's go dawg! I thought in an attempt to psych myself up.

Safely inside my hotel room, I started to get past the anxiety and became curious.

"I thought you built this in your hotel room?"

"I did!" he replied.

"Well, set that shit down, I wanna have a look!" I said hoping for some kind of fucking clue.

What happened from there is a special-interest book all of its own. To summarize, however, for the next seventy minutes or so, I think I only thought about taking more Oxy about five times.

Not only was the contraption fascinating, it was also quite the stroke of genius.

This handsome twenty nine-year-old accountant (yes, he could have had your tax return in his bag), created a ball-torture device out of your basic Home Depot supplies while back in his hotel room. I wasn't going to do the session initially, but in my mind, Bubba and I needed the money. I was tired of having a mortgage, two car payments, utilities, insurance, and credit cards in my name, all with balances growing by the minute. Although I still counted on my fingers, I could work out that Miguel's testicles were worth the square root of two grand each.

Justifying what I was about to do, I reminded myself that I didn't even have to touch his balls. I was to simply just threaten them with my strong thick legs and fifteen inch biceps.

After some small talk, I told Miguel to get under his plywood contraption while I went and got changed.

Jesus, fuck, I thought as I walked off to the bathroom, still in disbelief over what was about to go down. Bubba kept crossing my mind.

Man, he'd be pissed if he knew what I was doing.

But it's not like I'm enjoying myself or finding this dude attractive.

It's strictly work.

What I would enjoy is finding a supply of Oxy out here.

I pushed the bathroom door open and attempted to put my game face on as I carefully walked towards Miguel in latex stiletto boots. He lay on the floor naked with his balls exposed under his contraption. I tried to imagine I was a panther stalking my prey, but the bunion on my right foot was screaming bloody murder beneath the painted-on shiny black latex.

Affixed to black plastic plant containers, two thin pieces of plywood stacked on top of another served as legs for his 'contraption'. With hinges and all, the top layer of wood was split down the middle and folded in and out like cupboard doors. The doors came together in the middle to seal tightly, minus a small square hole where his balls were supposed to fit through. Below the hole, there was a thin deadbolt that 'locked' the doors together.

CRUSHING IT

That deadbolt is smaller than most things I've kicked through.

I guess he forgot to get sandpaper because this wood looked pretty rough against his ball sack, so strike the genius comment.

Miguel patted me on my right calf from under his contraption. "Are you sure you're ok with this?" he said.

"Oh yea... I'm cool as a witch's tit in a cast iron bra! Sorry if I seem spacey, I didn't sleep much last night," I lied.

Ball busting.

How good could I be at it?

Bubba.

Mortgage.

In some kind of order, I guess.

It was time to go to work. With my inner thigh fat hanging over the top of my zipped up tight boots, I stomped around the sides of this guy's poor balls for the next hour. Letting him know who was in control, I'd stop to flex my biceps from time to time or strike my leg out straight in sync to the music. Causing my quadricep muscle to pop, I'd bend down and run my fingers across my skin, or squeeze my bicep, feeling my own muscles while Miguel stared up at me in total awe and amazement.

Oddly, these moves came naturally and without thought. I instinctively knew that this was part of the experience, because it was something I did naturally. I loved being muscular, and I loved showing it off.

Freaking the living shit out of this kid, I would stop mid flex, and suddenly rip my knee up towards my chest and hold it for a second before kicking it towards his balls. I'd pull the momentum and hover the heel of my boot an inch above his hairy, disgusting sack of fragility. As I peered down around the side of my leg with eyes that said 'your fucking pathetic ass belongs to me', I would catch his frozen face in a state of utter panic. Letting him savor the moment for a few seconds, I broke his state by winking before carrying on with the game.

In between gently pressing down with my boot and stomping around the sides of his balls, I kept bouncing between thoughts as Huey Lewis and The News played from my laptop.

This wooden piece of shit better not break. Damn... I don't even feel high.

Not the most dominating music, but I didn't care. I wasn't a dominatrix. I was a sexy, confident, muscular tomboy who also happened to be a lost, miserable, unrecovered drug addict and alcoholic.

I want a new drug, one that won't make me sick

One that won't make me crash my car

Or make me feel three feet thick

I want a new drug, one that won't hurt my head

One that won't make my mouth too dry

Or make my eyes too red

One that won't make me nervous

Wonderin' what to do

One that makes me feel like I feel when I'm with you

When I'm alone with you

Between craving more pills, reciting the lyrics to Huey Lewis, and justifying why I was doing this type of session behind Bubba's back, I kept my hustle on, and did what I do best--The ultimate people-pleasing, teachers-pet champion at making men's fantasies come alive.

After he got his clothes back on, I started in on my usual enquiry as to how in the hell he got into this type of fetish. Perplexed how all of these men were contradicting everything that society told me was beautiful and how gender roles worked, I stopped thinking about getting high as we talked.

While lacing up his mahogany dress shoes, Miguel shared his story.

"When I was five or six, I vividly recalled seeing a car drive over a soda can in the street, absolutely crushing it."

Truly fascinated, I listened with full intent and tried to keep a 'sexy edge' about myself while ignoring the increasing feelings of guilt due to dishonesty.

"But how did a can of coke, or whatever it was, suddenly turn into rocking up to a hotel room with wooden contraption you built to stick your balls in?"

"Honestly, I don't know. It just kind of grew from there. Seeing that can get crushed by something powerful was exciting."

I have another five fucking people to see today.

How in the hell amI gonna get through this on a limited supply of pills?

"You know that's interesting because a majority of the men I've seen have had a similar experience. Most of them started getting attracted to something when they were between seven and thirteen years old."

266

"Really?" asked Miguel.

"Yeah! I even had one of my clients who was in a Phd program create a bonafide University study so I could ask anyone who read my blog the same thing."

"What did you ask?"

"I asked if they could recall how and when their fetish started, if they were usually dominant in their everyday life, what they did for a living, and a few other questions but I can't remember."

"Did you find anyone else with a crushing fetish?"

"Darling, they've all found me. Seriously, I've heard of everything. But what I've come to discover is that you guys all seem to be fucked from the get-go," I said while unzipping my boots.

"Basically, men are born into a box. And if you step outside that box and 'act like a little bitch', you're going to be ridiculed. I mean think about it--you're supposed to be the breadwinner and the rock. If you came home from work and cried about how big of a dick your boss was that day, your wife would laugh you out of the house!"

"Yeah, I've never thought about it that way," he said.

"Look--at the end of the day, the conclusion I've come up with is that y'alls brains are hardwired to procreate, Miguel. As a result, you're all drawn to different things for arousal. If every man was drawn to full, thick wavy hair, big lips, giant boobs, a twenty five-inch waist, and a size zero, we'd have a bunch of Paris Hiltons populating the planet. But the reality is, you guys find everything arousing from hairy faces, wrinkly feet, tits flatter than a wall, giant Amazonian women, fat women, women with glasses and freckles. Basically, everything that is not on the cover of a magazine or on a billboard!"

Looking like Miguel had just discovered that his 401k was worth twice as much as he'd initially calculated and was now retiring twenty years early, he reached out to give me a hug.

"I thought I was the only weirdo out there," he said while burying his face in my chest.

"Not even close! So many of you were either drawn to powerful girls from either getting your ass handed to you during recess in elementary school, like before girls get a period, or from getting beat up by your much older babysitter. Or even watching WWF and Charlie's Angels! I've heard it all!" I said as I realised my next appointment was due in fourteen minutes.

After practically having to kick him out, I said goodbye to Miguel before stashing his contraption in the closet. With only ten minutes left to spare, I started sobbing uncontrollably over my current situation. I'd finally cracked.

How the fuck did I get here from Associated Student Body President and future first female POTUS?

Criminal law to accountant's testicles?

Law and disorder.

Fucking funny, Kortney.

What got me here?

Where next?

I kept sobbing. The kind of sobbing that renders you near hyperventilating.

I would have kept going for another hour, but the phone rang.

I quickly shoved a handful of dry almonds in my mouth to subside the hunger pains.

I couldn't help but think back to the days of when a small milligram of Oxy, or even Norco,

would...

Fuck it.

My thoughts trailed off.

How the fuck did I get here?

I played percussion in a gospel rock band for Christ's sakes.

Sorry Jesus...bad joke.

Unaware that the average person experiences self-talk at the rate of 850 words per minute, I let my inner dialogue control me as I sat waiting for my next appointment. Instead of observing my thoughts without judgement and letting them go like Eckhart taught me in his book, I allowed them to keep spewing like diarrhea, associating them as a part of my soul and my experience.

Continuing to fumble through life like a freshman second-string quarterback, taking the field for his first home game in front of a packed crowd, I lasted another few months before the day finally came. My life felt like I was carrying the weight of a team that was in the championship game, with 20 seconds on the clock in the fourth quarter, and constantly down by 1 point.

Isolated and alone by my own doing, I was the only one on the team with no coach, or backup, in sight.

. . . .

One of the biggest lessons in my life, has been learning that someone can be fit as a fiddle (you can thank Australia for that saying) on the outside, but on the inside they're knocking on death's door. From toxic habits or mental illnesses such as an eating disorder, depression or substance use disorder, we cannot conclude that someone is healthier than someone else just by looking at them. One of the biggest challenges you're showing up for in this lifetime is deconstructing body shaming. Fat shaming, fit shaming, thin shaming- all of it. There are people who society would describe as "fat" who can run circles around me.

Even now with this personal experience and higher level of self-awareness, my inner-asshole (self-talk/ego) will start judging people if they appear to not fit the conventional role of what is deemed fit. For example, take body positive influencer Meg Boggs. She constantly reminds me that any body type can be strong and powerful. I have to consistently deconstruct the programming which society has instilled in me from a young age.

It all starts with an awareness, my friend.

Scan here to watch the video:

Do the F*cking Work

What things are you trying to control on a surface level that are covering up things on a deeper level?

Are you aware of your negative self-talk?

Describe your self-talk: What's your script, and has it changed over the years?

How could you rewrite that more compassionately?

Thinking back to the opening section, you can see how fast our self-talk can spew (if you're old enough, you might recall the guy in the commercials for Micro Machines!). A big part of doing the work at the end of each lesson is to help you recognise how incessant and rapid your inner dialogue can be. It can jump from one thought to a completely unrelated thought, which *then* causes you to suddenly feel a certain kind of way.

Describe a time you experienced how your thoughts create emotions in your body?

Explain your struggle with being assertive.

Write a short list of times you said "yes" when you wish you would have said "no".

Play the entire scene out had you said "no". What's the worst thing that would have happened?

In what ways you ever engaged in disordered eating in some form to try and control your body?

What diets have you tried or currently trying?

271

Scan here for more good shit:

WHEN ONE HOTEL DOOR SHUTS, ANOTHER ONE OPENS

June 14, 2010 was one of the hottest days Sonoma County had seen in decades. Curled up on scratchy carpet like an infant, I dripped sweat profusely while shivering underneath a sheet on my bedroom floor. A fan pushed warm air across my body, while every joint seized and cramped as my thoughts raced incessantly. As every inch of my skin crawled with invisible stinging ants, I found myself pleading with God to keep me alive as I tried to stop the acid traveling up my throat from turning into a scene from The Exorcist.

After I made it through the first three days of detoxing, I drug myself to the gym in an effort to stave off the feeling of death. As a tear rolled down my cheek from behind the steering wheel, I took a picture of myself. I needed to let my fans know the truth; I was struggling. It was one of the first times in my life I felt like honesty was the best policy.

A few months had gone by and I managed to stay clean. Despite only sleeping a couple of hours a night, I managed to stay off narcotics and still do sessions without crawling out of my skin. One afternoon, I bulk emailed my lapsed website members in hopes of generating new revenue. I received a reply back from 'Dean' asking when I was going to book a tour in Australia. Not thinking much of it, I gave him my number and told him to call me sometime. The next thing I knew, we were on our way.

The handful of tours Bubba had previously tagged along for resulted in us fighting because I was too preoccupied on "making hay while the sun was shining". I'd book myself solid from 8am to 8pm and only leave a few breaks here and there to maybe think about eating. Previously stuck in my addiction, I couldn't see past my own dick to consider Bubba's feelings around what people should be doing in a relationship. I was purely focused on making more money. My name was on the mortgage. It was my name on the car and truck payment. It was my name on basically every bill, and it was my initials tattooed on my shoulder. I called the shots, and it was my way or the thigh-way.

We'd more or less been in therapy for the past year, trying to work through our "challenges" while I struggled to be rigorously honest. On-again off-again fiancés with trust issues were making me sicker than taking twenty multivitamins on an empty stomach. The fact that we'd been together for a little less than two years but managed to spend one of those arguing in front of a third party, wasn't filling me full of hope.

The only thing I wanted to be full of, however, was air. I'd tried everything to stay lean but after almost a decade of bouncing in and out of 12-step recovery, and realising that I had to face working a program or face death, I was slowly realising that nothing was making me happy. Making four hundred dollars an hour and having men obsess over me globally, wasn't doing it. And being my own boss and freely traveling wherever I wanted, whenever I wanted, wasn't doing it either.

Now at almost four months clean, I wanted to emphasize that I'd been paying attention during our last few therapy sessions. I was going to make a valiant effort to carve out time for us to reconnect in this far away land. After Pop's house burned down in the San Bruno fires a few months earlier, I had some kind of 'come to Jesus' moment in realising that nothing was guaranteed and all of this money I was trying to make and unsuccessfully save, wasn't fulfilling me.

Still being an insecure overachiever and a high-level perfectionist, I could hardly find an ounce of excitement for our upcoming trip. Booking my appointments meant hours of emails to find out every last detail to deliver the ultimate experience for my clients.

Searching for the perfect hotels to maximise our budget meant hours of guessing, second guessing, and reconsidering decisions ten times over.

With nearly a four-hour layover in Los Angeles, I had plenty of time to make sure Bubba was crystal clear on what my session schedule was for the next week ahead. I emphasized that I made sure to take two full days off, back to back, for him and me to spend quality time together. That's all he supposedly ever really wanted--to spend time with me and enjoy being the bosses of our own lives.

Acknowledging my schedule and seemingly appreciative that I took November 8th and 9th "off" so we could explore this new country while celebrating my birthday, we prepared for the next grueling fifteen plus hours of travel.

. . . .

"Hey, don't forget I have my first appointment in fifty minutes," I said after spitting out my toothpaste.

"Yeah, I know," Bubba replied. "I'm going to meet up with Phrase to go paint trains shortly." "What time can I come back?"

While sucking water off my toothbrush, I thought about how stupid the name 'Phrase' was.

"Six p.m.," I quickly replied.

I knew my schedule for this tour like the back of my hand and was rather proud that I'd considered Bubba's feelings for once instead of repeating my old behaviour based on "But we need the money". Giving up two full days of work on this trip meant foregoing thousands of dollars, and god forbid, severely disappointing some of my fans.

"OK, thanks for not booking anything too late," Bubba said as he tied his shoes.

"Oh, by the way," he went on.

Fuck- what's he going to say?

I can tell by the tone of his voice he's got something smart on deck.

After a pregnant pause, he started to finish his sentence.

"I made plans with another artist to go paint on the eighth and ninth. It totally slipped my mind when we were talking about the schedule at LAX."

I felt my face along with the tips of my ears instantly get hot, just like when I was coming down off of speed. Still unable to practice 'The Art of Pausing" my fellow addicts talked about in our intimate daily seven a.m. meeting, I fired back instantly, "What the fuck do you mean?"

In his semi-sarcastic, 'yeah I'm totally getting revenge on you' tone of voice, Bubba calmly said, "I'm sorry. I know it's your birthday and all, but I figured I might not ever have this opportunity again." Sadly, it wasn't the thought of spending my twenty ninth birthday alone that pushed me into an immediate rage. It also wasn't the feeling of betrayal from my off-again fiancé either. It was the plain and simple fact that I'd wasted the opportunity to make the equivalent of a mortgage payment.

The only words I could muster up between my burning ears was, "Wow... Just wow." Bubba was a lyrical ninja in comparison to me. He was a masterful salesperson who was the absolute best when it came to being assertive, something I longed for my entire life. Passive aggressive in its finest form, I immediately shut down and considered whether I had enough time to get into my email and try to book-out those two days before Dean was supposed to arrive.

Even clean and sober, it seemed I was still unable to express myself.

My mom while drunk.

The boys who called me Sasquatch.

The teachers who called me husky.

My stepsister after jacking my shit while I was in the shower.

Rob and his disgusting spotted dick.

The apprentice hairdresser.

To now Bubba completely fucking me around and playing childish games.

Unable to connect the dots that all of these ignored memories were stockpiling a river of resentment, I shouted at Bubba, "Why don't you just fucking leave and not come back?"

Calm as the sun rising over Martha's vineyards on a windless summer dawn, "Have a great day, KO," he replied as he let the hotel door slam behind him.

The fucking nerve! He never calls me KO!

With only thirty minutes left before 'Aussie Dean' was due, I reluctantly paid sixteen dollars for a day pass to access the internet and logged into my email. While there, I thought to re-read Dean's emails to make sure I didn't miss any important details or requests such as an enema or stepping on innocent, adorable mice.

Still in a haze from the journey, I started obsessing over when I was going to get a chance to workout. I'd already been taking a mental inventory of everything I'd eaten since the last time I was in the gym close to forty eight hours ago. *This is bad. This is good. This is OK.*

Suddenly my old Nokia vibrated.

I can't believe I just wasted all that money on an iPhone 3 and it's not smart enough to process an overseas sim card. Nothing is ever good enough!

I'm five minutes out. What's your room number?

'Shit! Where had the time gone? There's never enough fucking time do anything!' I thought as I hastily text him back with the room number.

I jumped up from the bar desk and grabbed a pair of clean underwear, ripped button-fly shorts, and a white tank top to change into after running a washcloth through my bits.

Before I knew it, there was a knock on the door and like Pavlov's dog, I instantly felt a wave of adrenaline from the familiar feeling of being in control.

With a beaming smile on my face, I lurched forward towards the door and flung it open.

Wow. Just wow, I thought for the second time that day. This was not what I was expecting.

Much taller than a troll, a man stood close to six feet tall with the world's most striking blue eyes I'd ever seen in my life was staring back at me.

"Good day, mate," he said.

Phonetically speaking, "good-eye-might".

Still trying to process my absolute inaccuracy, I quickly replied, "Well fucking hello there "D"!" I said while using my fingers to insinuate quotations around the "D" part of my response.

While I tried to catch my breath, unaware that detoxing off narcotics can result in a year-long process, I motioned for Dean to come in.

As he walked into the room with slight nervousness, I noticed I was drawn to his style.

Wearing an untucked crisp, white button-up short sleeved shirt and black slacks, I was impressed to see we shared a common interest in my favorite style of jewelry; Celtic sterling silver. With a matching bracelet and necklace dangling from his body, he stood with his messenger bag over his shoulder and looked at me for directions.

Following my usual procedure of delivering a hug, I instructed Dean to sit down in the only chair available in the dinky Best Western suite. Knowing that Dean had two hours with me, we sat and talked for quite a while as I did with most of my clients. Except this time was different. Very, very different.

Although his accent entertained me the two times I attempted to talk to him previously, now with him sitting in front of me, it was at an entirely new level of exotic. Upon opening the hotel door, he went from Steve Irwin to the entire cast of Thunder Down Under in two seconds flat. Unlike most of the men I saw, it was *me* doing a majority of the talking this time. As a master of "hustling" and similar to selling, I usually found myself asking men questions about their fetishes and life experiences, making them feel important and heard. In return, I'd semi listen with a highly intrigued look in my eyes while I thought about when my next pill was going to get demolished.

This time, however, it was Dean asking me the questions. But instead of talking back like a proper conversation, he sat and listened only to ask more questions. He listened harder than any therapist I'd ever spoken to, any cop I successfully talked out of giving me a ticket, or any best friend dealing with me carrying on about all the shit I'd gotten myself into.

"It's amazing that you've managed to stay clean while having to pay for everything," he said.

"Yeah, I know right? I often forget that people often die taking OxyContin."

"I don't even think we have that here in Australia."

"Let's hope I don't find out!".

"You know, the other thing that drives me nuts about Bubba is him putting conditions on me. Like I'm not allowed to make out with another girl."

"What about other men?" he said with a devilish gleam in his eyes.

"Yeah definitely not that! I'm rarely even attracted to other women, so I'm not entirely sure what the big deal is."

"Oh my gosh, I nearly forgot you were a member of my site! Why'd you cancel anyway?"

"I didn't cancel. I'd paid for a year just to support you but have never watched any of your videos or anything."

"Are you serious!" I said, now shocked.

Why the hell would someone pay for something and not expect anything in return?

"Yes, serious as Manchester City losing a match, Kortney Kay," he said as he gently smiled at me.

"Wait--how'd the fuck did you know my middle name?" I asked.

"Your passport."

Paying attention to detail or what? God his accent is going to make me come undone!

"Smart!" I replied as I felt more and more intrigued by this man. "So, why'd you not watch my videos? That doesn't sound like schmoe behavior."

"My office is one big open floor plan. Plus, I don't really think I'm a schmoe. I'm just highly curious about women with muscles, and you were something not of this world," he said with his cheeks blushing under his pale white skin.

It was like someone had just turned on a tap that wouldn't shut off. The words just fell out of my mouth like the twenty dollar bills I used to dump out of my purse after a tour. I told Dean about every issue I had with Bubba, from not having freedom to make-out with a woman, to paying for everything, and feeling the immense pressure of adulting while getting clean. I didn't just throw Bubba under the bus, however. I argued that we both had a part to play in the relationship, and I could have chosen to do things differently as well.

After realising the time, I immediately switched gears and told him to go get changed so we could actually wrestle.

"Holy shit! I had no idea what time it was, I'm so sorry! Did you bring something to change into, or am I kicking your ass while wearing underwear?"

As he stood up from the chair with a little smirk on his face and started walking to the bathroom, I realised how excited I was to have his body close to mine.

Stepping out of the bathroom wearing just black board shorts that made his pale skin even paler. Sitting on the corner of the bed furthest from the bathroom, I motioned for him to take his position across from me.

"Why don't we start out with an arm wrestle? Just try not to cry when I snatch your Manhood," I said with my signature KO sultry, confident eyes and smile.

As we both lay on our stomachs, we squared off in opposing corners of the bed.

Having had significant arm-wrestling technique training from one of my English clients when on tour in Las Vegas a year ago, I wasn't surprised whatsoever when I easily beat him on both the left and right side. "Maybe you'll have better luck wrestling," I said as I winked while grinning at him. "You're too pretty to wrestle." As usual, I was exactly where I wanted to be--in control.

Unable to get a clear read on whether he truly enjoyed himself, Dean thanked me for coming all the way out to see him and assured me that he had a great time. "I'm so sorry I have to go, but I'll be in touch. Promise you'll let me know if you need anything at all while you're here?" he said. Starting to feel slightly empty, "Yes of course, I promise!" I replied.

Unsure if I was overtired or really attracted to him, for the first time I was genuinely sad to see someone leave. Not wasting time trying to feel feelings, I jumped back on my email and got back to booking out my empty two-day slots. Not more than five minutes passed by before three-sentence-boy was sending me a paragraph via text. Thanking me for coming such a long way and telling me how I was such a remarkable person, he assured me that we'd see each other again someday soon and to please keep in touch.

I started replying back and quickly stopped due to frustration from having to revert back to the Stone Age and press the number seven button four times to get the letter "S" to appear on the screen. Then, the number six, three times to get the letter "O". After a minute I'd finally produced a, "So much fun. I really like you!"

. . . .

Over the course of the next few days, Aussie Dean had texted me more times than I could count. His emails went from one to two sentences, to two or three paragraphs. We couldn't stop talking. After three days in Melbourne, Bubba and I flew up to Sydney for the rest of my 'tour'. After spending my birthday wrestling five men back to back, I was excited to see him, and I asked about his day.

"Hey! It was good. Long, but good," he said. "I found you something cool for your birthday while I was out. I hope you like it."

After reaching into his pocket, he pulled out a matching necklace and ring that reminded me of something out of Clockwork Orange. Although it was a beautiful design, it wasn't anything I would ever wear. "Ah that was sweet of you, thanks!" I said as I gave him a hug while pretending to be somewhat excited about something I knew was going to sit on a shelf. "Where do you want to eat?" I asked, imagining he'd scouted somewhere romantic earlier in the day. "I'm sorry sweets. We must have walked ten miles today--I'm really tired and my feet hurt." "Oh, ok," I said while trying not to feel completely deflated.

I'm finally trying to be a couple, and he is completely fucking me.

"Why don't we get something delivered?"

"Yeah, my back is really messed up. I can hardly walk myself so probably best," I said as I started thinking about how he bought that jewelry with *my* money on a whim.

He couldn't even be bothered writing me a fucking birthday card.

Thinking he might offer to rub my back since it was my birthday and I'd just made twenty five hundred dollars for us, he sat down on the couch and asked what I was wanting to order. After a meaningless evening of eating flatbread pizza, followed by guilt and remorse for eating more than two pieces, we got into bed separately without more than a word to each other.

As I lay in the budget hotel's queen bed next to Bubba and stared at the ceiling, I saw the old trusty Nikon illuminate from inside my purse.

Sorry to message so late, Angel Baby.

I managed to leave Bali a day earlyand would do anything to see you again.

I really wish I could have spoiled you on your birthday. Speaking of which, what are your top five favourite songs?

Well that's fucking incredible. I bet he would have massaged more than my back.

. . . .

I spent the short flight from Sydney to Melbourne thumbing through the magazine shoved in the seatback pocket. As I neared the end of the publication, the words 'Eureka Tower' jumped off the page. An eighty four-floor skyscraper with an observation deck, I decided that it was a sign and something Dean and I could do. I told Bubba that Dean was just taking me to dinner, but that I was getting paid for my time. Under normal circumstances, Bubba would have vehemently declined me 'going to dinner' with a client. But it seemed we were both heading down the path of giving up.

After getting checked back into the same hotel we were at previously, I changed into a black sleeveless bodycon dress and quickly made sure I was semi-presentable. Although I was dog tired from jet lag, wrestling five hours a day for four days straight, and lingering narcotics still screwing with my sleep, I excitedly hobbled out the door and into the elevator. I felt like I had just started high school and was attending my first prom with someone I'd been lusting over all summer.

Exposing his matching dress socks, Dean was casually sitting with his right ankle balancing on his left knee.

How am I attracted to someone's socks?

With light grey slacks on, I immediately knew why Dean was sitting in that position. '*You aren't attracted to his socks, bitch.*

You're attracted to the mystery of how a man with such a massive cock can remain so quietly confident…

"Hiiiiiiii!" I wailed as our eyes locked.

"My Christ, Kortney Kay. You are breathtaking!" he exclaimed in his exotic accent. Still unable to take a compliment without feeling like a stuck-up bitch, I bashfully replied, "Ahhhhhh I'm OK, but thank you! So how was your trip?"

"No one got hurt and I wasn't accosted by any bag thieving monkeys, so all in all I'd say it was a success," he said. "Bag thieving monkeys?"

"Yes, monkeys that steal stuff out of your bag exist in Bali. I'll have to take you sometime."

"So where are we going and what's in the bag?" I asked inquisitively, still trying to get over the fact he called me by my full name. While gently grabbing my hand, he started toward the door and said, "You'll just have to find out!"

The few times I had tried to talk to Dean on the phone prior to reaching Australia were difficult, and come to find out, talking in person wasn't proving much easier, but I didn't care. For once in my life I was completely content without the need to fill the silence.

The warm evening spring breeze blew through my dress as we walked along the city street in silence while Dean pretended to not be lost in his own city. Before long, we were straining our necks staring up at a colossal skyscraper. With a gleam in his eyes, he pulled the glass door open.

"Does this look familiar?"

Still holding my hand since leaving the hotel, Dean walked me over to the VIP line to check-in.

VIP? I wonder if he's trying to impress me? He clearly doesn't have little dick syndrome. I felt that with my own body.

A woman with round cheeks and close to my age appeared from around the corner to greet us. "Right this way." she said as she started walking towards the elevator.

Once we passed the twenty second floor, I realised I had never been in a skyscraper.

What else haven't I done?

With the sun slipping behind the horizon, the crystal-clear sky started changing colors as we walked around the three hundred and sixty-degree observation deck. As Dean pointed in different directions, explaining where this and that was, all I could do was pretend to pay attention. Between trying to understand what he was saying and trying to understand what I was feeling, I couldn't make sense of either.

"Shall we sit down," Dean asked as everyone had pretty much filtered out.

"Yes! My feet are killing me! I hate wearing high heels for long," I said.

"Well, that's what happens when you kick walls barefoot drunk, miss," he said.

"You're *such* a smart ass!" I said.

Did I tell him that story in person or has he really read every blog I've ever written? Maybe I can write a book one day.

"Well, speaking of being smart, I got you some gifts for your birthday."

"I thought you were carrying around a turquoise bag just for fun!"

"It's nothing major, but it's your special day, and technically your birthday back home in the USA."

"That was so thoughtful of you!"

"But before I give them to you, I have to tell you something," he said as he took both of my hands in his.

As his eyes started to fill up with tears, he looked straight into mine and went on.

"Never in my life have I struggled for words. Never in my life have I met someone who left me speechless. Never in my life, have I met such an incredible human being. Your beauty is indescribable, but your spirit and character are beyond that."

What the fuck is actually happening right now?

"I've never believed in someone as much as I believe in you."

As a tear had rolled down his cheek, mine instantly welled up.

Squeezing both of my hands a little harder he continued on. "I don't know how else to say this other than you are a golden child, Kortney Kay. You have something magnificent to do in this world. I don't know what it is, and I don't know why we've been brought together, but I want you to know that I will support you in any way I possibly can. I want to fulfill the bottom part of your pyramid so you can focus on whatever it is you're meant to be doing. Whether that's emotionally, physically, spiritually, or financially, I will always be here for you."

Hardly able to speak, I let go of his hands, and placed mine on the sides of his face.

As I looked deep into his eyes, I slowly leaned in and kissed him for the first time.

After a couple of seconds, I let go and laughed between saying, "You made me ruin my mascara, prick!"

He picked the bag up off the floor and set it down next to me as he reached into his coat pocket and pulled out a card.

'He got me a card? You've got to be kidding me.'

"Here... I want you to read this first before I explain your gifts," he said.

As I looked down at my name written on the outside of the white envelope, I noticed how I was attracted to his handwriting.

Hey babygirl,   21/10/10

First up, thank-you for making me the happiest ♂ man in the known universe. I don't think I have ever had moments like ours, where just listening to your voice and your laugh, or just looking into your beautiful eyes - I'm taken to a completely different place. Thank-you, Thank-you, for being you and continuing to be the most amazing, wonderful, funny, smart, challenging, stimulating and downright brilliant person I have ever, ever met. You're the best Kortney Kay, don't ever forget that. ♡

Now, if you ever need me... Go to Station Ⓐ
Get the train line Ⓑ and call me! I'll be
there in ten. I'll always be (t)here for you
sweetness, and always around to make sure
you are happy, safe, warm and loved, just
like you should be. On your terms, like it
should be. Early in our journey together,
I told you I believe in you. I believe in you
more than any belief I have ever had. You
are a wonderful person, Kort, one I cherish,
adore, like and love. And I want to help make
you as happy as you can be. I love you, Kortney boy.
    Yours. Always. ▓▓▓ Xxxxxxxx Muse!

Pulling the card out, I gazed at three different clocks showing different train lines at the Flinders Street train station which happened to be down the road.

Around the frame of the picture, he wrote,

If you ever need me, you can take this line straight into my arms.

I opened the card to see the entire space was filled up with writing.

'What the fuck is wrong with me?'

I was physically turned on by this man's handwriting. How is that even possible?

More or less repeating what he had just said to me, I read his words in sheer disbelief.

Hey Baby girl,

First up, thank you for making me the happiest man in the known universe. I don't think I have ever had moments like ours, where just listening to your voice and your laugh, or just looking into your beautiful eyes, I'm taken to a completely different place. Thank-you, thank-you, for being you and continuing to be the most amazing, wonderful, funny, smart, challenging, stimulating, and downright brilliant person I have ever, ever met. You're the best Kortney Kay, don't ever forget that.

Now if you ever need me... Go to Station A, get the train line B, and call me! I'll be there in ten. I'll always be (t)here for your sweetness, and always around to make sure you are happy, safe, warm and loved, just like you should be. On your terms, like should be. Early in our journey together, I told you I believe

in you. I believe in your more than any belief I have ever had. You are a wonderful person, Kort, one I cherish, adore, like and love. And I want to help make you as happy as you can be. I love you, Kortney Kay.

Yours, Always.

Dean

"That was the nicest, most thoughtful thing I've ever received," I said.

"Since we both love dogs so much, I thought you'd love this iconic story from Australia," he said smiling as he pulled out a small book called "Red Dog". Unable to speak, he carried on.

"It's even based on a true story. I know you love documentaries and searching for true things in life," he said.

Doing everything in my power to keep myself from sobbing, I started thinking about my grandparents having sex.

"Your dogs are lucky to have such a great mum."

"Mum?" I said.

"Yes, darling. This is proper English," he said.

"Pffffffffff, anyway!" I replied back as he continued by pulling out an iPod shuffle.

"You know how I asked you what your top five favorite American songs are?" he said.

"Yes, how could I forget--I found that little exercise incredibly difficult! I have so many favorites!"

"Well, I wanted to give you something to listen to that would make you think about me in case you tried to forget!"

As I sat unwrapping the plastic off the little apple branded box, his eyes finally started drying up. "I found similar style songs from Australian bands," he said.

"Oh my God, you are SO sweet!", I said.

"I hope you don't think it's too shit!" he replied.

I noticed the word 'Tiffany's" embossed in silver on the side of the bag as he reached his hand in and pulled out a little box that matched the exact color of the bag. In an octave lower than I'd heard him speak before, Dean handed me the box and said, "This last one is so you never forget you have a piece of my heart, Kortney Kay."

I reached my hand out and took the box. Seeing what was sitting on the little white cloud of cotton padding after slowly peeling the lid back, I tried to ignore my hunger pains while being enchanted. The thick outline of a sterling silver heart attached to a dainty chain was staring back at me.

I pulled it out and handed it to him. Bushing his hands across my skin, he slowly put the chain around my neck and closed the clasp.

We sat for the next five minutes slowly kissing before we were informed it was closing time.

. . . . .

Bundled inside Dean's jacket and tucked underneath his arm, we walked around the city streets trying to find food before concluding our date. After finally landing at Subway, Dean sat and watched me eat something that, in the words of Huey Lewis, 'wouldn't keep me up all night, and make me feel three feet thick.'. Subway was the only thing open at that time of night in the city centre that I could fathom eating and not want to jump off a bridge as a result of too many calories.

"Are you sure you can't stay with me?" he said.

"I wish I could. If it weren't for my dogs and the tour I've already booked on the East Coast, I'd totally find a way!" I said while trying to keep my turkey, mustard and pickles in my mouth.

Holding hands, we walked back towards the hotel and stopped around the corner of the front door. With tears in his eyes, Dean took my other hand into his and reassured me that he'd always be here for me. With one more last kiss, we said good-bye and promised to keep in touch. As I walked away, I could feel my heart pounding in my chest. Unsure if I was more concerned about getting caught by Bubba, or if I was potentially walking away from the best thing that could have ever happened to me, I stopped before I turned the corner and blew Dean a kiss. Catching it with his hand, he mouthed something as I disappeared. 'Fuck, what did he just say? I love you, or Subway, eat fresh?' I thought as I walked through the automated sliding glass doors. I couldn't believe the last three hours of my life. Making sure I had concealed my gifts, I wondered what story I was going to tell Bubba about my 'date'.

The next day, as Bubba and I were sitting on the runway getting ready to take off, I found myself consumed with sadness. Fighting back tears, I blamed it on being over-tired. There was no possible way that I was this attached to a man I'd literally only spent a couple of hours with.

As I visualised running off the plane and leaving Bubba and my dogs, I felt paralyzed with fear.

That is the most ridiculous thought ever you fool.

You can hardly understand each other, and plus you have too many bills in your name.

Was it his sexy handwriting?

Was it his ability to listen intently and remember literally every word, I'd ever said?

Then again, how many words can you say in less than five hours?

Was it his quiet confidence?

Was it the thoughtfulness for all of the gifts he gave me on my special day?

Was it because he was an older man and I had fucking mommy issues?

"EARTH TO KORTNEY, HELLOOOOOO?" Bubba said as he reached over and touched my hand. "Sorry, I was spacing out," I replied, lying.

"You look like you're going to cry, what's up?"

"Nothing, I'm just tired", I said with a half ass smile. Lie number three thousand and one. As the engine kicked on and the Qantas airbus throttled forward, I slipped my headphones on playing the concealed iPod shuffle Dean had given me the night before.

What seemed like a week later, we made it back home.

. . . .

This concept of thinking we know what's best for us (better known as "running on self-will instead of God's will) is something most of us fall prey to. Because the word "God" is such a loaded word (people instantly assume the word pertains to religion) a lot of atheists and agnostics shudder at the sound of it. Not to mention people raised in a strict religious household will equate the word with the image of a demanding, revengeful and scornful old man up in the sky staring down at them, watching their every move.

What I've come to believe through working a program of recovery, is that I don't know what's best for me, but my Higher Power (call it God, The Universe, Mother Nature) does. When Bubba purposely made plans to be busy on my birthday, thus causing us that last huge fight, I wasn't able to take a step back at first and allow "God" to work his/her/their magic. Instead I felt hard done to and fucked over. But the fact is, The Universe had a completely different plan for me. Which you're about to read about!

Do the F*cking Work

When in your life have you felt screwed over by someone but ultimately it turned out to be a blessing?

Have you ever been in a situation that was incredibly painful but eventually came to realise you went through it for a reason?

If you have, did you ever stop to consider that you might not always know what's best for you? (i.e. the old saying, 'some of God's greatest gifts are unanswered prayers')

Have you ever been (or currently in) a situation where the fear of the unknown was more painful than making a change?

If so, where do you think this fear comes from?

Do you practice gratitude daily or do you find things never being good enough?

Scan here for more good shit.

THERE SHOULD ONLY BE TWO RULES IN A RELATIONSHIP

When my flight touched down, I felt an overpowering sense of anxiety like the spray in an automatic car wash. I couldn't believe I was about to spend the weekend at one of the most iconic hotels in downtown San Francisco with a man I hardly knew.

What if he had one nut?

What if it was the worst fuck in the history of fucks?

What if we ended up getting on each other's nerves?

I knew "what if" was a land that didn't exist, but I couldn't stop myself. Before I knew it, I was walking down the jet bridge and into the terminal. It only took a couple seconds to spot his bald white head standing above the others. With all the freedom and excitement in the world, we ran towards each other, dropped our bags, and hugged before he held me in a long, savory kiss.

Needless to say, we spent the next forty eight hours up against every wall in that hotel room. Just like most events I'd previously worked myself into a frenzy over prior to commencement, the weekend was over before I knew it and it was time to say goodbye.

"I've never been so sad before in my life, Kortney Kay."

"I know. I really don't want you to go."

"Can I ask you an important question?"

"Ummmmm, no?" I said sarcastically. "Yes of course!"

"Can I take your blanket with me?"

"You want to take my baby blanket with you?" I asked in sheer confusion.

"Yes."

"You mean the same blanket Bubba wouldn't let me bring in my bed?" I asked while Dean nodded his head.

"It's the best thing next to having you with me. At least I can still smell you."

"This blanket has been there for me through everything, so it would be a true testament to my liking you if I let you take it!"

As we sat on the edge of the bed and tried to figure out when we'd see each other again, I briefly imagined running off with him. Ignoring my daydream, I encouraged us to get checked out and on our way to the BART station so he could catch the train back to SFO.

After a painful goodbye, I went back to Santa Rosa and started working on booking out my next tour to New York. Now that I didn't have Bubba holding me back, I was determined to fly Muscle Queen out to the sub zero ice-cold city to help me warm up the internet by filming content specifically for my membership website.

Only a week had passed before Dean had another important question to ask me.

"I'm so, so very happy everything worked out, angel."

"Yeah, I cannot believe my dad. You don't really realise how short life is until someone you care about is potentially going to die."

"How's he healing?" Dean asked.

"My dad is such a clown. They rolled him out of the recovery room to meet us, and he literally acted like he didn't know who any of us were."

"Oh my God, you're kidding me?"

"No! He looked at my stepmom and deadpan turned to the charge nurse and said, 'I don't know who any of these people are though.'"

"How long did he play into it for?"

"Only a few seconds. I think he could see the look of utter despair in our faces."

"Dads are the best!"

"Yeah, it just blows me away that I've been so concerned with keeping my 6-pack abs and feeling stressed out over what I've been eating while hanging around the hospital. Meanwhile, my dad has brain surgery and manages to keep a cheerful attitude despite looking at the possibility of death in the face. And he's pulling practical jokes right after coming out of the ICU!"

"Well, I have some more good news on top of your dad being ok!"

"Hit me!"

"Are you sitting down?"

"No, I'm doing calf raises out front of the hospital."

"Ok, well try not to fall over."

"Ok! What is it already?"

"I managed to get two tickets for you to see Prince at Madison Square Garden!"

"WHAT?" I screamed.

"I know some people that know some people, baby girl."

"I totally thought you were talking out of your ass when you said you might be able to swing something! That show was sold out like 10 minutes after it went on sale!"

"It was pretty straight forward."

"Wow! So, when do you get in and what are you going to wear?"

"Well, you mentioned Jessica was going to come out from Vegas and film you and Muscle Queen, right?"

"Yea, that's the plan!"

"I thought you could take her and have a girls' night."

"Are you even real life?"

"Real life but out of this world, darling."

"Now are you sure you don't want to join us? Or even just sit and watch?"

"No, it just doesn't feel right, but I'm not about to stop you from doing what you want."

'What man would pass up the chance to mess around with two incredibly hot women?'

"Are you sure you don't care?"

"I promise--but you might want to double check with your brother that he isn't going to care that you're taking someone else to a Prince concert!"

"He won't mind."

Two weeks later, I had tickets booked for Muscle Queen to fly in, Jessica to fly out, and Dean to top it off. Jessica, the same photographer who'd initially worked with Muscle Queen and I a year prior in Las Vegas, was throttled to be my date for my first sober Prince concert. Not only that, she knew that the entire schmoe world was about to get shattered by the entanglement of the industry's two hottest fit bodies.

The plan was easy. Dean was landing first. Then the following day, Muscle Queen was arriving at noon, with Jessica a few short hours afterwards. That night, we'd film our steamy, highly anticipated content while Dean went out and entertained himself. The next day, Muscle Queen would go on her way, and Jessica and I would get ready to go see Prince.

I'd sent several texts to Jessica throughout the day with no reply.

"She must just be busy getting ready to leave," I said to Dean as we sat across from each other eating dinner. As I crunched on a shell-less taco salad void of sour cream and cheese, I couldn't help but notice my overwhelming concern that Jessica hadn't replied to my text messages.

After a two-hour session of ripping off the sheets later that night, I tried texting Jessica one last time while Dean lay next to me snoring.

As soon as I opened my eyes, I reached for my phone to see if she'd replied, but the only thing I had was a text from Bubba asking me if I had paid the electricity bill. I knew I had to accept the fact that Jessica flaked on me.

As I put my phone down, I heard Dean coming out of the bathroom.

"What's wrong sweetheart?" he asked.

"Ah just upset that Jess has just vanished. I'm not sure what I'm going to do about Muscle Queen."

"That is a bit shit," he said lovingly as he sat on the bed next to where I was lying.

As if I was buttering up my mom for pain pills, "Well--how do you feel about your videographer skills?" I asked.

"Really?" he asked.

Noticing that this was the first time I'd seen Dean not look enthusiastic about something, I hesitated to ask, but was left with no other option.

"Yeah! I mean, I kind of need you to take one for the team," I said.

"Well... if you really want me to, I guess I can give it a crack," he said.

"You're the best!" I said as I reached up and hugged him from the side of his waist.

"So, we're going to have to go find a camera to rent I guess?" he asked.

"Oh shit. I didn't even think of that! And you promise you don't

304

care?" I asked.

As he brushed my hair with his fingers, he looked deep into my eyes and said, "Listen, I only have two rules. One is that you are safe. And the other is that you are happy. Can you follow those two simple rules?"

After spending close to two hours trying to hail a taxi in the dead of winter while everyone in New York was last minute Christmas shopping, Dean and I were finally able to pick up the lights and camera equipment I had rented. Although I had been daydreaming about this opportunity for over a year, I was starting to have second thoughts. I knew Dean was truly not interested in some kind of threesome, and even less interested in filming his new girlfriend with another girl.

As the night approached and we were about to make schmoe-history, I couldn't help but feel like I wished I could cancel the whole thing. Something just wasn't right. Because Dean had given me the gift of allowing me to do whatever I wanted to do, I suddenly felt like I no longer wanted to do it.

With Dean holding the camera under a couple of bright lights, Muscle Queen and I made a series of videos according to my direction. Starting us out with muscle worship, we took turns rubbing baby oil over each other's muscles while we measured one another and giggled. After picking each other up in various holds and taking turns choking each other out with our legs, we decided to wrestle lightly.

Knowing that she could feel my awkwardness with Dean in the room, she went along with whatever I'd suggested. Just like I couldn't stand the thought of throwing away any scrap of food, I couldn't let the chance pass me by to finally hook up with her. Send me another hundred bucks via paypal if you want the details.

. . . .

With Muscle Queen back at her hotel, I laid in Dean's arms and listened while he questioned out loud what kind of world he'd entered himself into.

"I promise this isn't normal," I said.

"Yeah, this is just all really weird to me," he said.

"I feel bad for putting you in that situation."

"I'm a big boy. I think I'm just tired," he said.

While his orange arm hairs tickled my nose, I laid and listened to Dean snore for an hour. Unable to sleep, I ninja-crept out of bed and headed towards the bathroom. Doing my best thinking on the toilet, I had a revolutionary thought while wiping after expelling too many sugar-free energy drinks. printing across the carpet, I hurriedly made my way to a work notepad. Unknowing that this single thought would eventually shape the rest of my life, I wrote down what had come to me while peeing.

. . . .

Two days after Christmas, Dean came back to see me yet again. Instead of dealing with saying goodbye this time, I decided to go with him. I was moving too fast to process anything around me other than I knew this man made me feel safe and happy. Granted, doing a geographical and moving around hadn't made my problems go away previously, but at least this time I was moving towards something instead of away from it.

Elated with my decision, Dean started planning a surprise New Year's Eve together in Sydney after booking my flight.

Although I felt completely out of place sitting in business class, I was thrilled to have this new level of excitement in life. As we flew across the Pacific Ocean, Dean wrote me a love letter while I pondered what I was going to do with my life.

Dean had booked a suite at one of the most iconic hotels in Sydney. With a private view of the Sydney Harbour Bridge, we had a front row view from our balcony of one of the world's greatest firework displays. Sadly, I stayed awake until tenp.m.

After a private yoga session in Bondi Beach followed by high tea for lunch the next day, we flew to Melbourne to stay at a serviced apartment for a few weeks before I was due to fly back to the US for a photo and video shoot in Las Vegas. Excited to get my arms wrapped back around my blanket, we found Dean's car and headed towards the city with the planned pit stop.

"So why were you staying at a serviced apartment?" I asked.

"Well darling, my house is about an hour out of town and it was easier to be close to the airport."

"And why didn't you bring my blanket with you?"

"I didn't want to put any added stress on the poor thing, plus I kind of had a feeling you'd be coming back with me," he said, putting his hand on my knee as we cruised down the motorway. "I left it with the manager of the hotel for safe keeping."

After driving for a half hour and asking more questions than a four-year-old, we were pulling into the parking lot of the Quest Dean was last staying at.

"I'll be right back!" he said as he put the car into park, leaving the ignition on.

As I sat waiting for Dean to come back out with my blanket, I toiled with all of the different emotions I was feeling. Although he was fine with my continuing to roll around with strange men in hotel rooms around the world, I knew I wanted to tell women about this world I had stumbled upon. But how?

As I stared out the window in a hazy jet lag, Dean appeared from around the corner empty handed. While panic rose up through my legs, I watched him approach the car.

"Where's my blanket!"

"The main manager who I left it with is on holiday for two weeks and the wanker in charge wasn't sure where she'd put it," he said, frustrated.

"Oh."

"I'm sorry baby, I'll come back as soon as she's back."

The next few weeks I spent in the heart of the city hanging out in our serviced apartment while Dean worked a few blocks away. Planning my trip back to Las Vegas, I booked as many sessions that I could squeeze in between the long list of different models I was shooting with. Throughout the two weeks before heading back, Dean and I semi-sarcastically had long talks about getting married and even found a lab-made diamond ring.

After booking my flight back for a few weeks' stay, Dean promised that by the time I got back, he'd have a house for us to live in along with my blanket. The time came, and I left for Las Vegas. One night after being gone for a week, I had my nightly call with Dean.

"You sound hammered, hun," I said.

"Yeah I'm really sorry. I love you so much. Please don't be mad."

"I'm not mad. I just said I couldn't be around someone drinking."

"Ok, but still I feel like I let you down."

"You're not the one with an alcohol problem."

"Sometimes I wonder if I am though. I never want to stop once I start," he said.

"Yeah, that happens to a lot of people. The kicker is, how much do you obsess on it the next day?"

"Not much."

"That's the difference. I would be salivating thinking about my next drink in between."

"I have to tell you something," he said.

Ah fuck--he's slept with someone while I was gone. I'll fucking kill them both when I get back.

"Yeahhhhhhhhhh," I replied. "It's ok, I'm not going to be mad."

"Well- I think you will."

"No, it's OK. I'm just happy you want to be honest with me."

You can't get mad, Kortney. Also, you're the one rolling around with men in a bikini while they lust over you. Get a grip.

"I went back to Quest and the manager couldn't find your blanket."

I hadn't realised how much I truly valued you dingy, ragged, crusty baby blanket until I heard that sentence. After a long moment of silence, Dean came back with reassurance.

"But don't worry- I paid a private investigator a thousand dollars to find it. I've never felt so bad about something before in my life," he said.

Unsure if I was more upset that he lost my blanket or spent a grand on hiring someone to find it, I pushed past my distraught and reassured him that I was OK.

After clocking twenty two videos and four photo shoots, I was boarding my flight to head back down to Australia. Now approved to fly on staff travel as the partner of the fifth most senior person in the company, I awkwardly tried to blend in with posh people sitting in the business class cabin and started to write my book.

. . . .

With eight hours of writing, an hour of doing crunches in my flatbed seat, and a couple hours of napping in the books, the wheels of the Qantas airbus were slamming into the tarmac. I immediately switched airplane mode off and waited for my text messages to come dinging in. I watched and briefly read each one as they dropped down from the top of the screen in a preview format.

"What the fuck did Matt say?", I thought as I tried to process the text I'd just read from my friend.

Reading something about seeing me on TV, I opened up the messaging app and touched the text to expand the entire chat.

Matty J: You didn't tell me you were on Tosh.O- I just saw you on TV.

Unbeknownst to me, the comedian Daniel Tosh had taken the watermelon smashing clip and turned it into a comedy sketch.

Seeing myself plastered all over the internet was exhilarating. I didn't even care that my flat ass cheeks were hanging out the sides of my black thong--I now had bragging rights to say I was on TV. In fact, I was so elated about feeling important, I didn't really mind that my blanket hadn't yet been recovered. I almost saw it as a sign that Dean was my new form of security and that he could replace my baby blanket.

After weeks of lapping up the attention from being on TV, Dean had yet another surprise for me.

"We're going to fly around the world, Kortney Kay."

"You must feel really bad about losing my blanket!"

"I do, but I also want to show you my home and meet your family."

"What do you mean your home?" I asked.

"I know someone flew you to London previously, but I want to show you myself."

"Wait--you're from London? But you're Australian!"

"No darling, I'm an Australian citizen, but I'm from Britain."

"Seriously?"

"Yes! How did we not know this?".

"I'm not really sure."

"You couldn't tell from my accent?"

"Ummmmmm no!"

"I'm from where all your favourite bands and singers are from."

"Like who? I asked.

"Well, I can name off five I've heard you play so far this morning: Deaf Leppard, Pet Shop Boys, Billy Ocean, Rod Stewart, and the king of shit, Phil Collins."

"They're all American! What are you talking about?!"

Doubled over, Dean laughed hysterically.

"All of these people are English?" I asked, feeling more confused than when I found out that my brother and I had different moms.

"Well, from the UK," he said.

"What's the UK?"

With patience and curiosity, we made eager attempts at integrating into each other's worlds. I watched Ricky Gervais with subtitles on, while Dean pretended to laugh at Dave Chappelle's jokes until it was time to leave on our trip. We were flying staff-travel via first class from Melbourne to France, to London, and then onto San Francisco before heading back to Australia.

After twenty seven hours of flying, which included one stop in Hong Kong to refuel, we had arrived in Paris two days before Valentine's Day. In usual KO fashion, I spent our first day knocking out a handful of sessions at a premium price. Then came the day I would never forget. Well, kinda…

I woke to a sea of deep red rose petals covering the white linen. At the end of the bed sat a tray with a plate full of fresh fruit and coffee next to a perfectly laid out white robe. (One that I would definitely not be wiping my ass with) On the nightstand, a white envelope perched perfectly against the lamp. The only thing missing was Dean. Not waiting for him to return, I ripped open the envelope and read his card where he expressed his undying love for me on what used to be my least favourite holiday, Valentine's Day.

Figuring I could have fresh fruit and black coffee without feeling guilt or remorse, I slid on the robe and proceeded to tuck into the fruit after pouring a piping hot cup of coffee. Before getting halfway through the cup, the familiar sound of the deadbolt unlocking filled the air, and in walked Dean. Holding a giant bouquet of my favourite flowers, birds of paradise, he joyfully sauntered into the room with a massive smile on his face.

"HOW?!" I shouted.

"Because I listen to every word you say," Dean replied while his blue eyes sparkled in contrast to his white shirt.

"You are so not of this earth!"

"I'm afraid you have it backwards, sweetheart," he said, placing the flowers on the desk.

"Set that down," Dean commanded as I stood up with my coffee.

For the first time in my life I didn't mind being told what to do.

As soon as my cup connected with the table, he rushed me and pulled us close together.

As he bent down to whisper in my ear, I momentarily forgot about whether or not my body was looking tight enough for my satisfaction.

"I've got a fairytale day planned for you. Are you ready?"

"I think so!" I said, laughing like a little girl.

Breathing heavily in my ear and nudging his nose into my neck,

I felt goosebumps light up my freshly shaven arms.

After our couple's massage and steam bath in a private suite, we went searching for somewhere to eat that I considered 'healthy'. Finding egg whites and basic vegetables cooked without heavy oil was even challenging for Dean who spoke broken French. Throwing in the towel, I approved the sixth place we walked into despite the odds. Unable to refuse the freshly baked strawberry macarons we were gifted upon arriving at the spa, I mentally replayed the scene over and over again.

If I would have just had one instead of three, finding breakfast without too many calories wouldn't have been this difficult.

Throughout the entire meal, I bartered and rationalised with myself over how I could keep myself from losing any muscularity.

I wouldn't eat anything else for the rest of the day.

I would definitely do my ab routine once we got back to the hotel.

And I would certainly wake up early enough to do fasted cardio in the fitness corner of the hotel.

As Dean walked me around the streets of Paris, I tried to be present and not think about whether or not I was losing muscle and gaining fat by being away from the gym. After strolling in and out of several shops, we came across an alley where street artists were drawing portraits of passersby. After a pep-talk from Dean, I reluctantly sat in the director-style chair to see what the man wearing a fuzzy grey beret was going to come up with. Twenty minutes later, I was staring at a charcoal drawn image that almost looked like me, minus the sucked in cheeks.

Fuck this must be what he thinks I should look like?

The afternoon sky darkened as we made our way to the Eiffel Tower. As he walked with my rolled-up portrait under his right arm, Dean held me underneath his left while giving me a brief history of the tower. Closing in on a hundred-foot distance, Dean stopped walking and came up to hold me from behind as the chilly air nipped at my face.

"Look up, darling," he said.

As I looked up at the massive magnificence of the tower, I momentarily forgot about how imperfect I was. For a second, I was in Paris smelling the smells, hearing the sounds, and connecting with the sounds. Feeling a slight sense of vertigo, I looked back at Dean just in time to catch his expression change.

"I wonder if that is meant for us?"

"What's that?" I asked, turning around.

Rolling towards us, a shiny chestnut-brown beefy horse pulled a maroon carriage through the subzero temperature with ease. Lost in thought over how tight my new puffy jacket felt, I watched the horse's white shaggy legs gracefully continue to move in our direction.

In a matter of seconds, a wagon wheel was parked right in front of us.

"Bonjour comment vas-tu monsieur?"

"Très bien merci," Dean replied.

I can't believe I took four years of Spanish and all I can say is donde esta los banos. God, he drives me wild.

"Only the best for my baby," Dean said, squeezing my hand.

"I can't believe how romantic you are."

Dean and the driver made small talk while the man opened the carriage door for me. Once both inside, we posed for a few pictures, and began our tour around the tower. Shifting around trying to get comfortable, I couldn't shake the thought that my jeans were too tight, my jacket too small, and my butt too flat as the springs dug into the back of my thighs.

"You OK angel baby?"

"Yeah, I'm OK, hun. Think I'm just tired."

Although yes--I was factually dog-tired, the real reason behind my vibe of being irritable, restless and discontent was purely from severe body dysmorphia. Here I was with the most intelligent, charming, funny, and handsome person I'd ever met, in the most iconic, romantic setting known in any romance novel, and yet somehow, I couldn't see the royal flush I'd been dealt. All I could see were different suits that didn't match or fit.

The delicate skin above my lip burned as I held a Kleenex against my nose and blew. Tired, disgusting, and fighting off a cold, in the cold, I couldn't stop feeling sorry for myself. Even as Dean grabbed my hands in his, and started professing his love for me, I could hardly hear the words coming from his mouth.

"I have to tell you something," he said.

"Yesssssss?"

"I've never struggled with words. Ever," Dean said, as I watched his eyes become glassy with tears. Taking one hand and gently grabbing me behind the neck while he gazed deep in my eyes, he continued on while I did my best to stay present.

"All throughout University, I wrote plays, debated on a team, and charmed my way past any hurdle with words. Until I met you, I never experienced the inability to accurately articulate how I was feeling."

"Is this where I apologise?" I asked sarcastically.

"No, this is where you say yes, Kortney Kay."

My stomach immediately started fluttering as he got down on one knee and reached into his Ted Baker jacket to pull out a low sheen black box.

. . . .

I woke myself up with a violent fart. Jet lag had gotten the best of me, knocking me out cold in Dean's lap while he, Pop and myself sat in the living room talking about Paris before I fell asleep. My family knew everything; how long I had been clean, how we met, and how long we'd known each other before I'd said "yes". Needless to say, they weren't convinced that my 'third times a charm' engagement was a good idea. Especially my twelve-year-old niece.

The day before we had flown into the San Francisco International airport with the sole intention of Dean meeting and getting to know my family. But, as usual, something came up. After blaming Dean for the whoopie cushion blast, I checked my email before my longtime client turned friend, Chokepuppy, was due to pick us up. Ken was a rail-thin white boy from the South. As the only boy growing up under the command of five older female relatives, was there any doubt that he would manage to find himself as a trainee for a pro Dom in San Francisco after serving in the military?

Other than his obsession to be dominated and choked out by a strong, powerful woman, Ken was anything but odd. He loved sports more than any man I knew, and was a cheerful, "yes ma'am, no sir" polite, charismatic guy that wanted nothing but the best for his teenage daughter. Chokepuppy started out as a client, but quickly became the star in most of my video clips. He was also the first to volunteer whenever I needed anything.

Ken was graciously going to drive us from Foster City in his two-door silver Honda Civic up to Santa Rosa so I could collect some of my belongings at my house before we were due to meet all my family back in The Bay for dinner. After answering a few desperate fans wanting to see me while I was in town, I finally got to *the* email that changed everything.

Bob Bornstein was a name I couldn't forget. The first and last time I'd seen him for a session, was during the Olympia in Las Vegas. Bob had already asked me while I was in Paris if I had any plans to come back to the West coast. Remembering feeling like I needed to shower ten times over after our last session, I politely declined.

Although he was the one with my worn, sweaty socks in his mouth, he was one of the few men I'd ever encountered that just made me feel dirty. For an hour, this man endured me pulling and twisting his nipples while I repeatedly smashed his ribs in a body scissor between my legs. If anything, he should have been the one that felt dirty. But it was just something about his greasy hair, bad breath, and wirey, hairy body that made me feel nasty.

But this time, unlike the offers to crush mice for ten grand, I considered the revolting thought of being in this man's presence. Knowing that Ken would arrive soon, I instructed Bornstein to send me a text for further consideration.

Once in the car and out of earshot of Pop, I shared the news with Chokepuppy and Dean.

"Yea so how crazy is this--that guy in Vegas wants to give me ten grand for a session if we go tomorrow."

"Na na nahnoooo way th th this guy is pffff pfffff fucking serious?" Ken said in his predictable stutter.

"I know it sounds outlandish, but he said he'd send half the money in a deposit via Western Union," I said.

"We could always get married early in Vegas," Dean said, cramped in the backseat.

"Oh my GOD!" I exclaimed. "You are a genius!"

"Ye yeeeee yeah! Can I be your best man, man?" Ken asked.

"And Jessica is there! She can be my best woman!" I squealed as the adrenaline rushed my body.

"I don't know when we'd be back here, sooooo" said Dean.

"We might as well! Let's do it!" I touted.

As we coasted up the highway at the prescribed speed limit, the three of us discussed our great ideas as Dean pulled out his laptop and connected to his remote wireless internet. By the time we arrived at my house, Dean had stepped up by booking our flights on Virgin America, a wedding chapel, and our honeymoon stay at The Aria.

. . . .

I never knew what unconditional love meant. Even after being married for several years to the man who showed me the meaning, it still took a few more years to even realise that what I had was exactly that-- love without conditions.

I have a few friends that are swingers. Friends that I would have never imagined to live the lifestyle. One friend in particular is incredibly straight-laced. Well, minus the being cool with the orgis bit. But she doesn't drink, has never done drugs, and is relatively introverted. But start talking about sharing dicks and her eyes light up.

Talking to these friends, I have tried to imagine what it would be like to live that uninhibited while sober, as well as being that comfortable to share my partner with someone else. The closest I got to it was with Dean and Muscle Queen, but of course he declined so it never happened. The other time with Jepson and the elderly meth cook didn't count because I was high and drunk. But my point is that by being in a relationship where I didn't have any 'conditions' (such as hooking up with another woman being off limits) and only had two rules to follow (that I was safe and that I was happy), it made me want to be the best partner I possibly could be.

Because of my previous deceitful behavior in relationships, I was typically distrustful towards my partners, as I was untrustworthy myself. I was often suspicious and jealous of any female friends they'd have purely because I was acting wrong myself and insecure. I couldn't stand the thought of them being with someone else and could have never seen myself in an open relationship (I definitely would have ended up stabbing someone). But as I've gotten older, I can see the value in being completely honest with your partner from the very get-go in stating what your needs currently are and that they might one day change in the future. Putting rules or conditions on someone in a relationship when they're not completely in agreeance, is only going to cause future turmoil.

Do the F*cking Work

Define unconditional love in your own words.

Are you currently in a relationship where the other person has conditions in place? (ps if your partner has a condition that you have to be a certain weight or wear your hair a certain way, I have four words of advice: get the fuck out!)

If so, how do those make you feel?

Do *you* put conditions on your partner in a relationship, and if so, are they comfortable with those conditions?

Have you compromised together on these conditions?

What are your beliefs about waking up to the same person every single day for the rest of your life?

Where did those beliefs come from?

It was hardly a hundred years ago that Lysol was selling itself as a form of a feminine hygiene. (Don't believe me? Google it: https://bit.ly/3pBi43G) In their ad campaign, the first paragraph reads, "A man marries a woman because he loves her. So instead of blaming him if married love begins to cool, she should question herself. Is she truly trying to keep her husband and herself eager, happy married lovers? One most effective way to safeguard her dainty feminie allure is by practicing complete faminie hygiene as provided by vaginal douches with scientifically correct preparation like "Lysol". So this is presented as an easy way to banish the misgivings that often keep married lovers apart. Yet, women don't often hear that "a married woman can do whatever she pleases in a marriage".

So instead of asking yourself if your marriage is unhappy because your vagina doesn't smell like Lysol, ask yourself some basic questions--

Are you currently happy in your relationship or marriage?

If not, what would you want to change.

Have you done anything about it, and if not, why not?

If you are happy, have you shared that with the other person? (Remembering that whatever we focus on, we get more of.)

Scan here for more good shit.

THERE IS A GOD AND I AM NOT IT

Once the wall of hurriedness subsided, and I found moments alone in my new house as a married woman, I started to feel out of place and incredibly lonely. I had tried attending a few 12-step meetings, but I couldn't understand what anyone was saying. I couldn't even order a coffee without getting worked up. Still unwilling to learn how to drive on the wrong side of the road, in the wrong side of the car, I decided to walk to the local grocery store to try and find a few things for the kitchen. Dean was at work, and I needed a break from watching conspiracy theory videos on YouTube.

Walking to a local cafe in the small suburb's center, I nervously sat down and looked at what seemed like a foreign menu.

The Big Brekkie… uffff I hate baked beans. Reminds me of shitty childhood barbeques.

Ugh! And the word 'brekkie' is so horrific. It just sounds so dumb. About as dumb as having a separate, private gym inside a gym for women.

After pushing on the door that was clearly marked with a pull sticker, I walked in and immediately tripped on a little mat inside. With my face now on fire, an older woman caught my eye.

"Dining in or take-away?" she asked.

"Dining in, thanks!" I replied in my enthusiastic American spirit, looking to make new possible fans everywhere I could.

"That's ok. Go ahead and take the table by the wall," she said while pointing to the corner.

Why in the hell would she say 'that's ok', like I'd asked for an apology? Like I'm some kind of fucking inconvenience by needing a table?

As I sat scrolling Facebook and reading comments from fans, I couldn't help but wonder if I'd made a mistake by suddenly packing up my shit, abandoning my dogs, and moving to the opposite side of the world.

A girl looking no older than twelve came to take my order.

"Hi, sorry to keep you waiting. What would you like?" she said.

"Ahhh that's ok! I'll just get a cup of coffee for now, thanks," I said smiling.

"Right… what kind of coffee?"

"Just a regular coffee."

Looking somewhat annoyed, she asked again.

"Ok, but do you want a flat white, long black?"

"Ummmmmm…. You know--a black cup of coffee. Like a good old fashion 'cup of Joe'?" I said, feeling utterly stupid.

"Like an Americano?"

"Yeah sure, sounds about right!" I said, trying to laugh it off. "Haven't quite gotten used to the lingo around here."

"That's ok. I'll get that in straight away."

After drinking my jet fuel espresso, I walked down to the grocery store, dragging my resentment behind me. Dressed in jean shorts and a fitted tank top, I suddenly looked like a blind person who got themselves dressed in the middle of a tropical storm. Melbourne decided to show me how truly special the city could be by taking a crystal clear eighty-degree sky and magically producing a hailstorm in a matter of minutes.

Frustrated, embarrassed, tired, lonely, and pissed off, I trudged around the isles of the Coles supermarket searching for black beans.

What the fuck is wrong with this place?

Baked beans, that's it.

Except garbanzo beans.

Chickpeas? Why would they name it something so stupid?

There are jumbo size cans of baked beans.

Screw top plastic containers of baked beans.

Miniature pop-top cans of baked beans.

Reduce sodium baked beans.

But not a can of black beans in sight.

Instead of simply asking someone for help, I let my inner asshole take control and continued to drip drops of fear into my anxiety bucket.

After I sloshed to the end of the aisle, I stopped in my tracks and stared at the cold case full of cheese.

I haven't eaten cheese in years.

I don't even remember what it tastes like.

As I stood vacantly staring, a row of cheese jumped out at me.

COON cheese? What the actual fuck is going on here?

Irritated that I'd just moved to a country that had racist cheese and beans, I stormed out of the store flustered and headed back home to wait for Dean to arrive.

"Hi baby!" Dean shouted from the sliding glass door.

"Hi, hun!" I replied as I pushed my chair back from the table. I had spent the last few hours watching a documentary about September the eleventh. Excited to tell Dean about everything I'd just digested, I practically ran down the hallway into his arms.

"How was your day?" he asked joyously. "I'm sooooooo happy to see you."

Embracing in a hug, I spewed my newly learned knowledge.

"It was OK! I tried to go out and do adult things, but it was too hard," I said as I buried my face in his chest.

"Oh no! Adulting was too hard for you today, darling?"

"Yeah! Australian girls are mean and grocery stores are racist," I said in a pouty voice.

"Poor, poor baby," Dean said as he stroked my hair.

"But I did have fun on YouTube for four hours today."

"Four hours!" he exclaimed.

"Who do you think crashed the plane into the towers on nine eleven?" I asked.

"Terrorists," he said.

"Wrong! It was an inside job!" I proudly stated.

"Oh, really?"

"Yeah! And no one walked on the moon. Aliens built the pyramids. Bill Gates and Agenda 21 want to vaccinate and depopulate the earth. And the fluoride in the water supply is making everyone stupid by crystalising our pineal glands!"

"Wow! You sound like you've been very busy, sweetheart."

"I have. But really, it's so scary! The pedophile rings are the scariest though! There are satanic Hollywood cults that drink children's blood after torturing them!", I shrilled.

"Do you think maybe it's time to find a meeting out here?" he asked, smiling.

Feeling empty and sad that my daily NA meeting was no longer my homegroup because I had a new home, I reluctantly sat in a circle with other alcoholics and tried my best to participate. At least back home in Santa Rosa, California, I could understand what people were saying. I sat upright in my uncomfortable steel chair and waited for the main speaker to inspire me. I knew that I needed to change my attitude towards Australian 12-step recovery and that my disease was trying to hyper-focus on all of the differences instead of the one glaring similarity that had landed all of us in a room together.

After five minutes of intently listening to some random man with twenty five consecutive years of not having a drink, I immediately tuned-out as soon as he gave his opinion on whether or not cursing should be allowed amongst this group. What seemed like an eternity later, a sassy, gorgeous Latina rolled her eyes after someone called on her to share.

"Hi, my name's Alexandra and I'm an alcoholic," she said. "Look--I'm going through some shit right now and I don't know how to fucking tackle it. I mean, look at my life. It's seven p.m. and I'm sitting in the basement of a church drinking shitty instant coffee with a bunch of strangers. Not really my idea of glamour, but I'd much rather be here than out there dying. Since I moved here from San Francisco, I've had to deal with more shitty people in the not-for-profit sector than I'd care to think about."

I instantly felt like I was at home. She dropped more f-bombs than Eminem and was basically from my part of the world! I knew I had to ask her to be my sponsor. After the meeting was over, I quickly made my way over to Alexandra and introduced myself.

"Hi! It's Alexandra, right?" I said as I stuck my hand out to shake hers.

"Correct! And you are, again?"

"Kortney."

"Yes, that's right. I thought I heard your Yankee-ass introduce yourself at the start. So, what brings you all the way down here, girl?"

"Oh my God, I can't even. I'm from Northern Cali too, though!"

"Well no shit?" she said. "Yeah, look--I've gotta get going, but call me and let's set up a time to talk. How long ya got?"

"About fourteen months, but I've been at it for almost a decade!"

"Yeah, ok. Well, let me give you my number. Don't fuck it up and not call."

After a few weeks, it was time for Alexandra and I to get started on the fourth step. Once a week I'd come over to her apartment to read and talk. Every time we got together there was a new conspiracy I had to share with her.

"I don't know how to tell you this, but you cannot hula-hoop your way out of being an alcoholic, bitch! Stop reading books on paranormal activity and start reading the fucking Big Book!"

"I know, but this stuff is important! People are just stumbling through life not knowing they're in the matrix! It's like the world is full of sheep!" I exclaimed.

"It sounds to me like you're doing God's work by judging others," she replied.

"Yeah, yeah... I get it."

"Is there anything you can do to control whatever old white men bullshit you're bollucksing on about?" she asked as we sat on separate ends of her old navy couch.

"Probably not," I said.

"Right. Ok--so you were telling me about your husband. How long ago did you guys meet again?"

"Actually, about a year ago!"

"Wait--only a year ago? So, when did you get married?"

"We got married back in February. I can never remember the date though."

As Alexandra burst out laughing hysterically, I started feeling somewhat defensive.

"What!"

"So how long did you know each other before you got married?"

"Three months, give or take," I said.

"What in the fresh fuck! That is one of the most alcoholic moves I've heard in my entire life!"

Did she seriously just say that to me?

"I guess?"

"Well, let's hope this shit works out for the best!"

After I got back home, I joined Dean in the kitchen while he finished cooking us dinner, explaining that I think I had found a sponsor.

"She's lovely! And she's from San Francisco so I get her, ya know? She doesn't say weird shit like, "that's ok" instead of saying "no problem" or "you're welcome"!" I said, pulling out a chair.

"Well that's great news!"

"Yeah, I'm excited. Ya know, I've been thinking... "

"More than usual?" Dean asked.

"Ha ha, super funny! But yes, more than usual."

"And what have you been thinking about darling?"

"Well, I appreciate that you trust me to keep doing what I've been doing, but it's not really what married women do."

"Honey, married women can do whatever they want."

332

"True, but let me put it another way. I want to be talking to women, not men. I'm tired of being someone's fantasy."

"Fair play."

"I want women to know that the world is not what they think it is, and that someone would pay five thousand dollars to worship their calf muscles!"

"You need an overarching goal and a purpose for a platform," he said as he put the lid on top of the boiling water.

After turning around to face me, coyly leaning against the cupboards, he sat with his arms folded across his body for a minute before saying another word.

"Why not teach women about how to build confidence?"

"I like it!"

"Konfidence by Kortney, but with a K of course."

. . . .

As you can see, nearly a decade ago I was researching every single conspiracy under the sun. I became so paranoid at one point, I almost couldn't leave the house. I was unknowingly trying to control things outside of my control since I could no longer try and control a meth problem, a drinking problem, a cough syrup problem, and a pill problem. Although I seemingly still had a muscle and definition problem in my control, replacing the void that was in my life with conspiracies, was my unknowingly new obsession.

Once again I found myself struggling with balance, and ultimately trying to play God. I was directing my anger towards people who I would call 'sheep' because people wouldn't 'wake up' (sound familiar?). On one hand, watching all these various conspiracy theories helped me create awareness around a number of different topics and helped me learn to be more open-minded (such as the high toxicity of chemicals in our food, air, and water system along with if you follow the money, you'll understand why J.F.K. was assassinated the day after he gave his warning speech to the American people about a shadow government ruling behind the scene.). But on the other hand, I allowed this knowledge to turn into fear and ultimately felt like I could and should be stopping it all, without even knowing if it was true or not.

Do the F*cking Work

Have you ever looked into any "conspiracy theories" (i.e. the September eleventh incident, Coronavirus being grown in a lab and released by the Chinese, the 2020 election, etc.)? Do you think they're all bullshit, or just some of them?

Have they helped you question your beliefs at all?

In what ways would you consider yourself to be open-minded?

Are you able to take in a thought different than your own without dismissing it out of hand?

Make a list of things that you wish you could change in the world that keep you up at night. Have you questioned how you balance your ability to make change versus playing God and risk losing your sanity?

If you have discovered conspiracy theories, have you applied them to all communities and not just certain groups? (For example, seeing a rise of awareness from white women around child trafficking and satanic rituals has been interesting. While a lot have started acknowledging that this is a real issue, a lot have also failed to see how that intersects with BIPOC (Black, Indigenous, and People of Color) communities in everyday real life such as having racist neighbors call CPS and have children taken away without a shroud of proof that there has been actual neglect.

Scan here for more good shit.

"NO" IS UNIVERSAL PROTECTION

*J*ust as I was starting to feel somewhat more at home in Australia, the biggest drama of a lifetime was lurking up ahead. We'd just moved from Melbourne, Victoria to The Gold Coast in Queensland so Dean could take over as the CEO of a national rugby team. Not only was Dean the new King in town (the city literally has nothing else to talk about other than their rugby team), but I was going to be an assistant strength training coach for the junior team. It felt like I was finally going to find my calling, but the impending newspaper headlines would say otherwise.

I found a couple of AA meetings and finally started to embrace recovery. Since we'd been back from our three-week holiday in hell, I knew that attending as many meetings as possible would be the only thing to help me push through the hideous amount of body hatred and resentment I was experiencing. We'd spent three weeks in Rome, Italy and the South of France, and just like when he took me to Paris, I was miserable. This 'trip of a lifetime' was supposed to be an opportunity for us to enjoy ourselves before moving to a new state and Dean starting a relentless, stressful job.

Unable to joyfully eat gelato in Rome, pizza in Italy, and crepes in France, I had reverted back to chewing up food and quietly spitting it out when no one was looking.

Not only had we spent the entire three weeks with me being utterly miserable over how fat I felt, but Dean was stressed beyond words over his new role at the rugby club. The level of stress tied to the wreckage caused by the previous CEO, led to us spending most of the time fighting.

To top it off, the day we arrived in Florence, I learned that Ken (Chokepuppy) had died suddenly from AIDS.

See my wonderful friend here:

His soul signed up for this shit before he came down.

We are all where we're meant to be in our journey, and there was nothing I could have done to save him.

I mean, I guess it makes sense that it's just our ego that suffers when someone dies.

First universal law of energy is that it cannot be created nor destroyed, or some shit?

Ken is not really gone, it's just his body.

His energy has passed onto something else, so I need to sack-up and stop being sad about it.

I wonder if me spending three weeks obsessing on every single thing I could hardly put in my mouth was a way to distract me from feeling guilty over Ken dying?

Or maybe it was all from me feeling like I'm a fraud thinking I can make a career as a strength training coach in a sport I know nothing about?

I just said 'sack up' as if men's ball sacks are something sturdy and strong.

God I'm so glad I watched Jean Kilbourn's documentary.'

The week prior I kept hearing a recurring theme in meetings. It seemed like every other person kept talking about the topic of service, and how through it, they were able to escape self-pity and self-obsession. I was exhausted from the incessant stream of negative thoughts sloshing around in my head as I glanced over at the clock. Realizing that I still had several hours before I needed to report for training, I decided to head down to the volunteer center I had spotted when we'd first moved to our new city.

Still feeling awkward driving on the wrong side of the road while sitting on the wrong side of my Mini Cooper S, I threw the car into park. Smashed with a wall of humidity as soon as I opened the door, I couldn't believe tomorrow was the thirtieth of November. It was hotter than the hottest day I'd ever experienced in the dead of summer back home in the USA. As I walked up to the front door of Volunteer Gold Coast, I read the festive piece of paper taped to the glass door, stating that the office would be closed from December fourteenth to January fourteenth.

I can't believe this country closes down for like a month during the holidays.

So weird that Christmas is even celebrated out here.

CRUSHING IT

Most people don't even know that St Nicholas' outfit was red and green.

I bet if they knew it morphed into red and white because Coke-a-Cola hijacked the holiday, they'd stop buying so much shit and putting themselves into debt for a year.

Jesus wasn't even born in December.

It was like August, I think?

I mean, I still believe Jesus was an amazing guy, but this holiday shit is out of control.

Santa Claus should not have ball sweat and be riding a surfboard.

A gust of chilled air slapped me in the face as I pushed the door open. Noticing an overwhelming sense of gratitude for once, I smiled at the person behind the front desk.

"Hi, how ya goin?"

"Hello! I'm good, thank you for asking. Yourself?"

"Ah look, my shift just started but it's Friday so happy to get on with it."

Still struggling to understand what the fuck anyone was saying, I felt anxious as I tried to pretend I understood what she'd just said.

"Do you have an appointment?"

"No, just want to inquire about volunteer opportunities. My husband and I just moved here from Melbourne!"

"Ah yeah? Cool. Well I can give you a list of what's available and we can go from there."

"Sure! Sounds good."

As Lindsay reached underneath the counter and pulled out a clipboard, I thought about how dumb I sounded trying to feel important by pointing out Dean's new role. Dean had spent the last three weeks waking up at three a.m. from a dead sleep to look at the breaking news from his phone. Every other day the media was writing about the changes and drama happening around the rugby club, so I just assumed everyone knew about it.

"Do you have a Queensland driver's license?"

"No, I don't. We just got here a week ago."

"Ah OK. Well, I don't think there's going to be much available until you have a state ID."

Feeling defeated and irritated that I drove all the way down here for no reason, the lady told me she'd return after talking to a volunteer coordinator.

"The only position you can apply for using another form of ID is with Big Brother, Big Sister as they're the only international organization we're working with right now."

As soon as she said "Big Brother" I felt a tingle in my toes.

"Ahhhhhhh, yes. That's the Christian based mentoring program, right?"

"Right as rain."

"I'm sorry, what was that?"

"Yes, that's correct."

"Ok, great! I'd love to apply."

"Sweet. Before you fill out their application, we require an application on file here first." she said as she set down what looked like a mortgage application.

"You can take a seat and start working on this while I go get their application."".

As I sat filling out the general application, I couldn't believe I imagined I was going to be signing up to feed homeless people or picking up garbage off the freeway. I was amazed I'd hadn't thought of exploring the option of mentoring a younger girl.

I guess this is something I wanted to do ever since I thought I was going to be a world champion boxer and share my story to younger girls about meth and creepy ass older men. How could I not have thought about this?

I really need to start being nicer to myself.

Probably because you're finally praying for guidance and working a 12-step program now, you stubborn dickhead.

After spending over an hour filling out paperwork, I made it back home and ripped off my sweat-soaked tank top and sat on the bed. Seeing that I still had an hour before I needed to leave, I grabbed one of my main journals off the nightstand to start writing. As I started flipping through the pages, a stack of papers fell out from the back of the emerald green A4 book and onto the carpet. As I sat contemplating picking them up, my eyes locked onto the top piece.

Recovery vs. My Job —
don't identify w/ your job.
follow your dreams. But what if my
dream is to mentor young kids as well as
be a naughty ~~sexxy~~ muscle goddess?
12-21-10

LOL

So I'm up @ 6:03a on Tuesday morning
in NYC. I'm with my new 'mate' David.
He's asleep. We've averaged 2-4 hrs of sleep
per night. I did exactly what I said. I
wasn't gonna ~~do start~~ seeing someone
again. But ~~I can't~~ stop my feelings.
Amazing person. Let alone 25 new members
in one week, masters degree, and delightful
conversations .... I can finally work more on
relaxing. Thinking about moving 1/2 way
across the world is crazy! Part of me feels
I ought to help ███ financially bcuz
he's been a part of my life for so long.
I love him. But I become more resentful
the longer I see how much time + energy
have been wasted in our past relationship.
Anyway my reason for starting to write:
I wrote a note to start tagging
'Kortney Olson' in videos, + realized
earlier I contacted a group called
'Radical Reality' that mentors kids. So these
videos of me hooking up w/ a chic under
my name... what kind of msg does that
send? Part of me says 'fuck off!'
Religious bodies making up rules such as

marriage, etc. who's to say it's
wrong or right. But then again
kids are unpredictable. So do I use
a different name, not try + get involved
@ all, or totally change paths?
Beautiful contradiction —

Also - on programming:
I was suppost to be a boy!
Born breech like 'fuk you' world!

I felt torn for many reasons. Not only had I failed to connect the dots over where this void was coming from, but I was also suddenly embarrassed I expected Dean to film Muscle Queen and I when he clearly wasn't into it.

This is it!

This is why I went through everything I've gone through!

I wasn't supposed to be the first woman POTUS.

I wasn't supposed to be a world champion boxer.

I wasn't supposed to go into the FBI or the CHP.

I was raped, became an addict and alcoholic, and discovered the muscle fetish world so I could pass all this shit onto young girls so they don't make the same mistakes that I did!

God, I hope they get my application before everyone disappears for the month!

Jumping up to change for training, I felt like I'd just won the lottery. It was as if a dump truck had been hoisted off my chest. This wasn't the same feeling of winning fifty dollars off a 7-11 scratcher when I was down to my last dollar, hit of meth, or pill. This was the feeling of what I imagined winning the PowerBall Mega-Millions would be.

. . . .

As I sat at the kitchen table thinking about the 12-step meeting I'd just left, my phone rang. Thinking that it might be Big Brothers, Big Sisters calling, I was a little disappointed to see Dean's name appear on my screen.

"Helloooooooo?" I answered.

After a long pause, Dean finally spoke, "Hi hun."

In less than a second I could sense that something was wrong.

"Ummmmmmmmm, hi!" I replied. "What's up?"

"I think you should come to Melbourne with me tonight," he said.

"When and why are you going to Melbourne?" I asked.

After a pregnant pause of what felt like twenty two full terms, I asked, "What's wrong?" as I could feel my body go limp.

"They're going to write a story about you. I'm so sorry, honey. I don't know what to say," he said.

"Okayyyyyyyyy, and what exact story are we talking about?" I asked.

"It's the muscle fetish stuff."

"Are you serious?"

"I'm afraid so. Please don't go down to the center. There's a handful of journalists outside with cameras."

"What the hell are you talking about?" I said as I could feel my heart throbbing through the side of my neck.

"Just pack a bag and I'll tell you about it on the way to the airport," he said.

"I don't understand," I said as I felt my eyes fill up with tears.

"It's going to be ok, but just stay in the house and I'll pick you up in a few hours. I love you," he said.

"I love you too," I choked out as I hung up the phone.

Not having a clue as to what was going on, I sat at the table thinking about all of the different scenarios in my head before finally getting up to pack some shit in a bag.

After several hours crept by at snail speed, Dean walked in the door and dropped his bag.

"Come here angel baby," he said as I started walking towards him holding back tears.

As we embraced in a hug, the tears poured down like rain on a stormy day in London. Crying into the lapel of his slate grey suit, I stood on top of his shoes with my bare feet while breathing in my favourite scent; hot chocolate, amber and red peppercorn. As we gently swayed back and forth, he stroked my neck while resting his chin on my head.

"This won't last long, I promise. They just needed something to write about," he said.

"I'm so sorry this turned sideways on you. Should have pursued publishing a book about all this fetish stuff six months ago."

"We're flying to Melbourne at ninep.m. I booked it a little later just in case there were any journalists at the airport."

"There's an arm-wrestling competition down there tomorrow. Can I compete?" I asked.

"Why are you asking me!"

"I don't know. You might have plans for us already."

"You don't think I wouldn't love to watch you arm wrestle? It's only bodybuilding shows and Jiu Jitsu matches I can't watch," he said sarcastically.

"It'll be a good distraction," I said.

"Let me get out of this suit and get a bag packed," he said as he kissed the top of my head.

. . . .

The next few weeks proved to be incredibly challenging, but at least I had a new title of 'Australia's first female arm-wrestling champion' to flaunt around. With little technique training, my strength allowed me to smash the only three international competitors who flew in to try their hand.

It seemed like every day there was a new headline in a different paper around the country, or somewhere in the world.

"Mom, I just can't believe all of this shit!" I said as I sat staring at the cover of the local newspaper that started the drama. Finding a raunchy picture off my Facebook page from years ago, along with a picture of Dean and I from a charity gala, the headline read, 'EXXXCLUSIVE: Mrs. Titan's Porn Past'.

"I'm still flying out next week though, right?" she asked.

"Yes, don't be crazy. Just because my tits are on the front page of the Sydney Morning Herald behind a tiny black rectangle doesn't mean your flight got cancelled or you've been banned from coming to visit!"

"And you're sure you're ok?" she asked.

"Yes, Mom. Look--I've done enough work on myself to know who I am, where I've been, where I'm going, and who's going with me. The media could call me a sheepfucker for all I care. I know I haven't fucked any sheep."

"So, what *exactly* happened? Like how did this all get started?"

"Some bored journalist ran out of shit to gossip about and started searching for things. A quick Google search of my name, and he found my clip store I guess."

"Yeah, but you don't have anything up there that I should know about, right?"

"No! It's the same old clips of me beating men arm wrestling then laughing at them, the watermelon smashing clips, some scissoring and lift and carry stuff. I just left them up because I thought they were harmless."

"Not even anything topless?"

"No! I mean, you can find the one or two photoshoots I did topless if you look back far enough but not on that clip store. It was purely a guilty by association type situation."

"Wow--I'm so sorry hun. What's Dean have to say about all of this?"

"He's been nothing but supportive."

"Well that's at least a positive!"

"Yea… journalists have even mentioned I've had two past abortions. As if being a drug addict and rape survivor wasn't enough to talk about."

"What assholes!"

"I even just had a fan in Denmark send me a picture of the newspaper via email. You can't read anything in whatever the hell language they speak, but the word 'pornstar' you can sure make out.

349

A hideous headline with me doing a front double bicep flex-"

"Denmark?"

"Denmark, the U.K., India, New Zealand. It's floating around all over the world!"

"So, you're infamous now huh?"

"You know what mom?" I asked.

"What?"

"I watched this woman's documentary called "Killing Us Softly" like the week before this all popped off. She mentioned something that I'd come across in all my conspiracy research that made this all make sense."

"Ok…."

"Syndication!" I said. "All of the media is owned by like six corporations. So, when something is deemed 'newsworthy' it gets sent around to all these stations to say the same shit!"

"Yes, ok. That makes sense."

"It really helped me see how insidious the media and advertising are. I mean, someone pointed out in a tweet that an All Blacks rugby player…"

"Wait, is that the team Dean coaches?"

"No, mom!" I said laughing.

'I guess I didn't know what the fuck rugby was before getting out here. Be patient Kortney.'

"The All Blacks are a team that are a part of rugby union. And

Dean is the CEO, not a coach, of a team in rugby league. They're two different federations with different rules. Anyway, one of their star players married an actual pornstar a year ago, and the entire country was high fiving him!"

"Right!"

"Yeah… it's crazy. The media talks about me like I was taking a bunch of dicks in the ass, when I was only being a strong, powerful woman. Pisses me the fuck off."

"Wow, Kort."

"We'll watch this documentary when you come out. But seriously, women are always talked about in politics and sport for what we fucking wear. And anytime you turn on the TV out here, there's a commercial on with women cleaning the floor, changing a diaper, or picking kids up from school. But men? They're changing tires, barbequing, or drinking fucking beer on 4X island!"

"What's 4X island?" she asked.

"It's a stupid brand of beer."

. . . .

Over a month had passed since the so-called porn scandal broke. My mom had made it out for her first visit, and everything seemed to be ok. Back at the kitchen table writing a blog, the phone rang. Having completely forgotten about Big Brothers, Big Sisters, I nearly forwarded the unknown number calling. After it rang a few times, I answered with anticipation, hoping it wasn't a journalist.

"Hello?"

"G'day! Is this Kortney?"

"Yes it is."

"Hi Kortney, this is Kyle from Big Brother, Big Sister. How ya going?"

As relief washed over me, I responded joyfully.

"Hi Kyle! I'm great, thanks for asking. How about you?"

"I'm great, Kortney. Thanks for asking."

"Awesome."

"Kortney, I'm calling today to let you know we received and reviewed your application here."

"Yes! I almost completely forgot about it Kyle! In America, we're used to one, maybeeeeee two days off during the holidays!" I sarcastically replied.

"I know, hey! We're super blessed out here!"

"Yes, indeed."

"Well, we had a look at everything you're doing with your website and think it's great that you're working on a book from what we could gather from your blogging?"

"Yes, I sure am!"

"Outstanding. Well, we hope that all goes incredibly well. Now as far as the application goes, it looks like it got turned down because of the recent media coverage that's been happening." he said.

Feeling like the time I got bucked off the back of a sheep at the rodeo, I froze in shock.

"You still on the line, Kortney?"

And for the one thousandth time in my life, my heart dropped straight down through my anus.

"Yup."

"Right. Look, Kortney…", Kyle said before taking a long pause before carrying on. "You know, these aren't my rules, and we all think you'd be great here, but unfortunately thanks to Google, a student's parents could potentially get the wrong impression and that could reflect poorly upon the agency. It's just silly policy and procedure," he said.

"Yeah, OK. No worries, Kyle. I totally get it. But thank you so much for letting me know," I said holding back tears.

"Yeah, sweet. Thanks Kortney! Keep working on that book and thanks again for applying!"

"Cheers, mate," I said as I let my hand fall from my ear.

I sat staring at the phone while I watched the screen disconnect the call, and immediately started sobbing. Every broken inhale I took, my shoulders lurched up and down in sync with my sobs. As steaming hot tears rolled down my face and snot dropped down over my top lip, my thoughts started racing.

I can't believe this. I'm a horrible fucking person.

What am I going to do with the rest of my life now?

All of those moms calling me a slutty piece of rotting rubbish were right.

What was I thinking?

Everyone was so concerned I was going to drink through all of this.

But now that's all I'm actually qualified to do.

I can't work with kids.

I didn't take my real estate appraisal test.

I can't train the rugby team.

I can't make training videos for Konfidence By Kortney because I don't have a videographer.

I can't publish my book.

Why the fuck am I even alive?

I sat there sobbing into the dish towel, hard enough to cause my dogs to come and sit at my feet.

While the sobs uncontrollably rolled on, I murmured out, "*God?*" while I tried to catch my breath. "*Whyyyyyyy?*" I whispered while biting my lower lip to try and stop it from quivering as my hands kept trembling.

"*Why me?*"

Hearing me wail from downstairs, my mom appeared at the top of the landing.

"What's wrong toots?" she asked in a concerned tone as she headed towards me.

Between sobs, I managed to get some words out.

"They denied me," I said as I cried into her shoulder.

After several minutes of crying into the safety of my mom's shoulder, I suddenly stopped. As if someone took my tear and snot-stained wet towel had slapped me across the face with it, I was instantly catapulted into a feeling of rage. Like a giant neon sign illuminating the street in front of Madison Square Garden, the word

354

"NO" flashed in front of my mind.

No.

No, no, no!

Fuck this shit.

Similar to when I used to drink, I flashed from feeling grief to grit, and suddenly the words just bubbled up like a hot spring.

I'm not going to let some organization, some random fucking bloke, or some journalist dictate what the FUCK I'm going to do with the rest of my life!

"Fuck you, you fucking fucks!"

ALL OF YOU CAN FUCK STRAIGHT OFF!

I'm going to start my own shit!

A program ran by people who've been there and done that.

Not just talk the talk, but walk the walk.

Kids respect the truth and they can smell bullshit from a mile away.

. . . .

I picked up the phone and called Dean.

"Hey Hun, what's up? Everything OK?" he whispered.

"Yeah, everything's fine. You sound like you're in the middle of something, so I'll tell you about it when you get home but want you to know that I'm going to create a program for teenage girls."

"Oh yeah?"

"Yeah. Fuck this shit. Watch me."

"Ok Hun. I'll watch you do anything."

"See you tonight," I said as I hung up the phone.

And just like that, the Konfidence tattoo on my lower back now needed the word Kamp added to the top left-hand corner. My concept of helping young women learn the truth about the trials of this world for our gender, had instantly turned from Konfidence by Kortney into Kamp Konfidence.

. . . .

Being in sales positions for most of my twenties, I was always told that "no" just means "not yet", and you've gotta hear nine no's before you get a yes. So when I heard "no" from Big Brother, Big Sister- I was initially crushed. But what I've come to believe, is that 'no' means The Universe has another plan. As long as I continue to remember that I'm not running the show and that I'm exactly where I'm meant to be on my journey, every second of the day, things always go as planned (God's plan, not my plan). The whole "Let Go & Let God" bullshit used to drive me nuts. I truly struggled with the concept of religion and spirituality in early days. But eventually, the more I remained open-minded, the more I allowed in. In the coming chapters I'll explain how this one single concept of turning my will over to a higher power truly set me free.

Do the F*cking Work

Recall a time you got triggered by a headline and reposted content on social media without looking up the source of the content.

Thinking about how I was portrayed in the media as a sinful, irresponsible slut with a former drug problem, versus how a male footballer was treated for marrying a proper porn star (remember we all have different opinions as to what that means), in what ways have you noticed how women are portrayed in the media and advertising?

What are some ways you can be of service to others without having to start a not-for-profit? (i.e. Use someone's name at the checkout after looking at their nametag and watch what happens. Or, smile at a complete stranger in a car passing by and notice the exchange in energy.)

What are some random acts of kindness you have found yourself doing as of late? (Remember that all of these little acts build up similar to the drops that fall into an empty coffee pot in the morning-- before you know it you have a full pot. To build self-esteem, do more esteemable acts)

Scan to watch the trailer for "Killing Us Softly" by Jean Kilbourne:

Scan here for more good shit.

BELIEFS CONTROL EVERYTHING

Tony and I met at CrossFit. And just like Clark, I didn't see it coming. He would become such an important player in my life, and it all started with me throwing him around the room like the queen I am.

I found it incredibly ironic that our first workout together was a partner WOD (workout of the day) which involved burpees and fireman carries. Being that I'd only been a part of the CrossFit scene for less than a year, I was a relative rookie to every movement. But the fireman carry, of course, was a movement I owned. Having practiced this with men in hotel rooms all over the world—and getting paid bank for doing it, gave me that little boost of confidence I needed. Sadly though, the only thing I got paid that day was one compliment to myself, from myself, that lasted for a total of half a second.

Come to find out, that half a second of time is worth more than any four hundred dollars I made in a session.

Tony stood close to six foot four and weighed roughly around one hundred and twenty kilos. We took turns carrying each other as a fireman would drape a passed out human body over their shoulders, while running two hundred meters out of a burning building before coming back inside to set the partner down and proceed to complete ten burpee-jump-overs before switching.

With all two hundred and sixty four pounds of this gargantuan man riding across my back, I made it through all three rounds without dropping him once. For a split second I thought fondly of myself,

You sexy fucking beast!

The thought of kindness towards myself hit and ran faster than Lindsay Lohan. Before I knew it, I was back to the consistent, nagging, thought of being a fuck-up.

What am I going to do with my life now that I was exiled from being one of the first female strength and conditioning trainers in the NRL?

As we laid on the ground creating the illusion of a crime scene with our sweating bodies,

Tony explained how he'd gotten into what he called "subconscious psychology". Recently retired from playing "footy" (rugby), Tony started the first conversation of our friendship with ease.

"Which form of footy?" I asked inquisitively.

"The NRL. I used to play for St. George down in Sydney," he casually replied in his North

Queensland accent.

That's funny… if it were me, I would have walked into the box and let that be the first thing out of my mouth so everyone knew who I was.

As soon as Tony confirmed he was referring to the NRL, my

heart skipped a beat. Wondering whether or not he "knew my story", I figured he was living under a rock between CrossFit classes if he didn't.

In usual fashion, I instantly had to say something about my tragic, recent stint in the national media.

"Ah the good ol' fucking N-R-L!... I'm sure you recognized me at the beginning of class then, huh?" I said in a matter of fact tone.

"Yup, I sure did. But I wasn't going to bring it up!" he replied with a cute little smirk on his giant face.

Making sure to use my fingers to put quotes around the pornstar bit, I replied,

"Ok, well let's hear more about this subconscious psychology blah-blah you were talking about, because my 'Ex Fetish Pornstar' story is going to need more time than we've both got to give at this precise moment!"

As soon as Tony started talking again, my mind started drifting. I was back in my head thinking about the last two months that had more or less been one of the worst experiences of my life. Because I was too busy trying not to die in class, I hadn't thought about having a broken heart and feeling worthless for the first time in a long time. Similar to grappling some bloke twice your size in Brazilian Jiu Jitsu, intense training seemed to be the only time I could shut my thoughts off.

While explaining how it was a part of the process with this new 'subconscious psychology' my ears pricked up as soon as I heard him mention the word "meditation". I'd been consecutively clean and sober for about a year and a half and had yet to actually incorporate some kind of regular daily meditation practice. I knew how important it was, because I'd been hearing about it over and over throughout the last decade whenever I'd attend a 12-step meeting.

Over the years I always heard the phrase 'mind, body and soul', but as usual, I never connected the dots as to what that actually meant. I simply just regurgitated the words.

But what did the whole 'mind, body and soul' shtick actually add up to?

I had some kind of grasp on the 'soul' bit through exploring spirituality, kinda. I'd found Jesus for a bit when I was attending Catholic high school and playing in a Christian rock band, but of course, once I started smoking, snorting and eating speed, he kind of became like most of the boys I dated—boring.

I certainly had a grip on training my body physically. I was a master at this juncture of the buzzwords. After all, I'd been at that since I was in elementary school—acutely aware of my body twenty hours a day, seven days a week from the age of seven.

Unknowingly, when it came to the 'mind' part, similar to my self-esteem, I had absolutely nothing when it came to tools in my toolbox with understanding the power of the mind. Other than skimming the tip of the iceberg by reading books by Eckhart Tolle and Stuart Wild, I was completely empty handed other than knowing that I needed to meditate.

I wasn't really sure why I needed to though. I was just regurgitating what others were saying over the years of bouncing in and out of recovery and counselling sessions. Having seen plenty of therapists in my past, I somehow never linked psychology to mind training. It was more of a "I'm fucked up, please fix me by listening to my problems" outlook.

Still laying on the ground, Tony recommended we do a session sometime. Before he could even finish his sentence, I started to invite him over. Being in my usual over-stimulated state from just finishing a ferocious workout coupled with the large scoop of pre-workout I had skulled before class, I told Tony to jump in my car.

"Let's go bask in the glory of my A/C and discuss this further," I said between recovery breaths.

After getting settled inside my Mini Cooper, Tony started to explain subconscious beliefs. With his knees practically pushed through the glovebox, he broke it down for me in paint-by-numbers style.

"You know how when it's time for New Year's resolutions people commit to getting healthy or losing weight and they go out and buy workout gear, throw away all the crap food in their house, join a gym, and start out the first few weeks of January in beast mode?" he asked.

"Yup!" I replied.

"Then after a month or so, they find themselves sitting on the couch with a bowl of ice cream, completely off the idea, and wondering how they got derailed."

"Yeah... it happens all the time. And?" I said.

"Well, it's simple. It's because subconsciously they have a belief that they're not worthy of health or weight loss, and belief controls everything," he said.

Noticing the wheels turning behind my eyes, Tony went on.

"Imagine you have a younger sibling, right?"

"Ok," I said.

"You're five years old, and your little sister is two. You're on the floor trying to tie your shoe. Your Mum is in the kitchen cutting up an apple, and your little sister is in her highchair standing up, mucking about, and is close to falling face first onto the ground," he said as he started painting a clearer picture for me.

"At the same time, you call out to your Mum, "Mum help! I can't tie my shoe!" Your Mum stops cutting the apple and looks over at your sister flailing about, then looks over at you and abruptly says, "Just a second, I'll be right there Kortney!"

"That's hard to imagine because I was usually fed fast food and raised by wolves!" I exclaimed.

Completely ignoring me, Tony went on without skipping a beat, "Your Mum quickly puts the knife down and runs over to your sister to position her back down in the highchair right before she nearly falls out of it."

"She should have let that little shit fall out!" I said.

"Now, what's the belief you potentially created right then and there?" Tony asked.

Looking for my 'good girl' reward, desperate to get the answer right, I sat for a second while critically thinking for the first time since waking up.

"That she's better than me?" I replied.

With a slight flash of excitement in his eyes, Tony exclaimed, "Yes, that's exactly right!"

The excitement brought me straight back to rehab.

I loved being the teacher's pet.

I loved answering correctly.

I loved finishing first.

I loved the validation and the attention.

And I fucking *loved* being the best.

Tony went on.

"And is that the truth?" he asked.

As if I'd just solved the Jeopardy puzzle and Alex was about to wine and dine me, I proudly stated, "No!"

"Exactly right. It's not the truth. The truth is, your Mum was just being a good parent and making certain your sister didn't crack her head open by falling out of her highchair. But herein lies the challenge," Tony said as he started to lower his tone, insinuating something important was to come.

"You have no awareness that you've just created this belief, and nor does your Mum. So now you've taken this belief that you're Mum loves your sister more, or that your sister is better and more worthy of her attention, and you've bloody stored it in your subconscious mind along with all of the other programs or limiting self-beliefs that aren't true."

I tried to imagine what it was like being five years old, but couldn't conjure up anything before the age of seven. It seemed like my childhood memories started when being blissfully unaware of my body came to a screeching halt. Other than feeling like I was a disgusting fat shit, my earliest memories were few and far between-- all of which were highly disappointing.

"Then you wonder why every time you see your sister at family gatherings as an adult, you want to punch her in the face!" Tony exclaimed as I was sifting back through memories.

"Your subconscious mind is *forty million* times more powerful than your conscious mind, which is what you're hopefully listening to me with right now," he said, making sure he really emphasized the forty million part.

Fuck, how did Tony know I was potentially thinking about other shit right now? Like what the fuck am I going to do with the rest of my life?

"Yup- go on..." I said.

"Have you ever heard the saying that humans only use three to four percent of our brains?"

"Yeah. I've heard varying numbers ranging from five to seven percent, but yeah, I'm picking up what you're laying down," I replied.

"Well, that's because that's just our conscious mind. All of that other percentage is the subconscious mind, and that's where we spend eighty five percent to ninety percent of our day. Our subconscious mind subsequently holds all of our autonomic programming, like how and when to blink our eyes and beat our hearts," he said.

"What's autonomic?" I asked.

"Do you have to think about blinking your eyes before you blink, or tell your heart to beat?" he asked.

"Obviously not," I replied.

"Imagine if we had to think about everything before doing it. Like, imagine having to brief yourself every time you went to take a step or stand up! Tighten core, squeeze ass, now... right foot forward, left foot forward, right foot forward," he said, simulating some kind of robotic walk.

"So, whilst it's overwhelming to think that we have hundreds of thousands of limiting self-beliefs in our subconscious mind, causing us to make certain decisions and actions without being aware of them, it's also good because we don't have to think about other stuff like breathing!".

"OK, so when are you going to come over? I want to do a session!" I exclaimed noticing the time as well as the hunger pain that had just knocked on my abdominal wall.

"How about next week--like Wednesday after class?"

"Yeah perfect!" I said.

"And you can tell me about your pornstar story," he said.

Sideways hugging across the car and congratulating each other on finishing our massive workout together, we agreed to meet at my house next week.

. . . .

Throughout the following week, I began having little ah-ha moments around what some of my limiting beliefs were. As I was heading to the cashier in the grocery store, a little whisper spoke loud enough for me to hear, "don't pick that line- it's going to go slowly". Like dominos falling, I observed an internal battle of the mind around second guessing which line to stand in. After finally picking one, sure as shit, the other one started moving.

As I stood there in line, I felt a sense of accomplishment from catching my limiting belief in action., Although it clashed with the annoyance of making the wrong decision and slowing down my speedy schedule, I was proud of my ability to create a new level of awareness. I just wish Tony was there to tell me what a good girl I was.

Before I knew it, Wednesday had arrived, and it was time for Tony to visit.

I always imagined a mind coach to resemble the hippies I grew up around in Garberville and nothing like a normal run-of-the-mill retired professional athlete like Tony. Following me home from CrossFit, I had little time to anticipate what the session might be like. After pulling in the driveway, Tony followed me inside and up the stairs to the sweltering, open-level third story of the townhouse Dean and I were renting.

After a brief chat about my run at being a pornstar sans the porn, Tony excitedly clapped his giant, dry Michael Jordan sized hands together.

"Right! Shall we get straight into it then?"

I nodded, not knowing I was about to be nodding a fair bit more.

"OK--I want you to take a couple of deep breaths with me," he said, sitting on the edge of my black leather office chair.

"Let your belly hang out, let your palms rest on your knees, and just relax your shoulders."

As I followed suit, I could feel myself start to relax in every inch of my body.

This is so idiotic. How can two intentional deep breaths feel like biscuits and gravy? The simplest, free of charge stuff are the things I always forget are there.

It was like magic.

To get me into a meditative state, Tony proceeded to guide me through what he called 'the clearing process'. Between repeating some mantras and moving some imagined ball of energy between my hands around my body, I could sense that I was completely and totally relaxed after just a few minutes. For once in my adult life, I didn't have a rush of thoughts coming in or flooding out. Unsure if I was everywhere or nowhere, I realised that I was just... present.

Somewhere I rarely felt.

There was no worrying about "what if" and no self-pity in mulling over the tabloids, comments, fury and tears. I was just sitting on my black pleather couch, breathing.

Suddenly I heard Tony's voice fill the air.

"Ok. What I want you to do now is in your mind, ask to connect to your subconscious through conscious connection. After you've asked, nod your head."

I nodded.

"Now, I want you to ask your subconscious what your number one limiting belief is," he said softly. "The first thing that comes up is the answer. When you get it, speak it out loud."

In a matter of seconds, my mouth opened, and I uttered the words,

"I am fat."

"Ok," Tony murmured. "Tell me a little bit more about that."

Still feeling relaxed and completely aware that I wasn't in my usual state of mental diarrhea, I sat and waited for something to happen. Then, out of nowhere, the word came.

"Pedophile."

After several moments of deafening silence, Tony's familiar

response came, "Ok... tell me a little bit more about that."

I sat in utter bewilderment while wondering why this word, which had so much disgusting baggage attached to it, arose from the depths of my grey matter. Still in some kind of meditative state, I found it difficult to try and start thinking. Instead I observed that I truly had no answer.

So, we sat.

I could feel the warm breath coming out of my nose, as I listened to Tony shift around in his chair. Then like an avalanche that suddenly snaps without any kind of warning, my mouth draped open and the words started flowing.

"When I was seven, my best friend's older brother Gary took me off into the woods and touched me in some inappropriate places."

More silence.

Tony exhaled a long, drawn out breath.

"Ok, please start to bring your awareness back to the room by feeling the couch underneath your legs, then move your feet around gently."

As I began to slightly move around, I could slowly feel my thoughts start to come rushing back. I scratched my arm, cracked my neck, and opened my eyes.

"What in the hell! I can't believe what just came out of my mouth!" I exclaimed as I opened my heavy eyelids. Bringing my gaze up to slowly meet Tony's from across the couch, I noticed a mixed bag of energy that ranged from feeling accomplished yet concerned.

"Let's debrief then, shall we?" he said.

Hanging onto the lingering, savory bits of a quiet mind, I continued to sit in silence while Tony filled in the gaps.

"The human mind is wildly fascinating. You'd be amazed at the number of people who have blocked traumatic events from their memory similar to this."

After a few minutes of processing my original response of being fat, my inner asshole started chiming in until Tony began to lead me back through the clearing process.

"Now we're going to connect to your higher self so you can find out what the message is behind the word pedophile."

Whatever the fuck that means.

I hated having the thoughts back.

Once again, I effortlessly found myself in this state of calm and peacefulness, despite the obvious.

"In your mind say, 'please consciously connect to my higher self', and nod when you've done so."

I nodded in a matter of seconds.

"In your mind, ask your higher self if she has any messages for you at this exact moment in regard to this experience, and again nod when you've done so."

Another nod.

Just like before, I sat quietly and waited. I could have sat there all day in that state of mind.

But ask a question, and you'll typically get an answer. And in this case, the answer blew my mind. In an unusual monotone voice, I started speaking.

"My higher self says that this is the first time I ignored her. She told me not to go off into the woods with Gary. I heard her, but I ignored her. As a result, I was violated. I knew what he was doing, that it wasn't right, but I wasn't entirely sure why. Immediately following this experience, I created a vision of myself being ripped up and strong in order to feel safe, protected and worthy."

I had plenty of psychologists in the past give me a similar conclusion.

"Kortney, it sounds like when you were young, someone you looked up to and relied on, told you that you were fat. You need to stop carrying around this anchor and cut it out."

Like the children's movie "Frozen", just let that shit go, huh?

Great advice!

But fucking how exactly?

Also, sorry mom for thinking it was you.

Now armed with the facts about who, what, where, when and why I was obsessed with being muscular and strong for as long as I could remember, I felt hopeful that I could potentially stop spending every waking second thinking about how much I was dissatisfied with my body. As Alexandra had once said to me during one of our step-work sessions, "Without awareness of a problem, there is no fucking problem to solve. Capiche?"

Over the next nine months, I sat at my kitchen table and took Kamp Konfidence from a concept of conviction to a tangible framework for teaching teenage girls everything I wish I'd been taught in school.

And so, it began.

I couldn't believe it took me until my early thirties to discover how powerful our minds are. Understanding where, when, how and why we create beliefs, along with how powerful our subconscious mind is, can truly elevate your life. The other day I was reading a book about remote viewing (developed by the military- think MK Ultra and the hit show "Stranger Things" on Netflix). The author mentioned something that Ingo Swann, the original developer of remove viewing, had paraphrased during a presentation. He revealed that "only one millionth of what our eyes see, our ears hear, and our other senses inform us about, appears in our consciousness."

When I stopped to think about it, I was reminded of another correlation between consciousness and something one of my favourite authors had talked about in my most cherished book, "The Infinite Self", by Stuart Wild. Stuart talked about how the technology of electricity has been around since before the beginning of man. So when the Egyptians were lugging stuff up the pyramids by candlelight, the power of electricity was right there in front of them, they just couldn't see it.

I truly believe we are all capable of bending spoons with just our minds like in the movie 'The Matrix'. There is so much information that is withheld from us in our education. When you start to make connections between events in your life that aren't actually 'coincidences', you'll start to see how powerful your mind is. The next time you think of someone that you haven't spoken to in years, then they 'coincidentally' text you the next day, may you start to acknowledge that you are more powerful than you previously considered.

My favorite quote in the world:

"Whether you think you can or think you can't, either way you're right." - *Henry Ford*

Do the F*cking Work

One time I unknowingly grappled with a transgendered woman at a tournament who was similar in skill and experience, and the exact same size as me. We rolled for a five minute round, and were unable to tap one another out. After learning she was trans later that day, I questioned whether or not I would have moved differently while grappling. This experience further slated my personal belief that 'beliefs control everything'.

Thinking back to the story of Tony and I talking in the car, what are some of your personal subconscious beliefs you hold? (such as you always hit red lights or pick the wrong line)

After reading "The Psychology of Belief" by Dr Bruce Lipton, I started questioning whether or not my parent's belief that I was supposed to be born a male contributed to me having more masculine traits both physically and psychologically. According to Lipton, we start creating beliefs as early as in the womb.

What are some societal beliefs you hold? (such as certain religious groups are more prone to violence than others, Christopher Columbus was a good guy, or that women are the weaker sex)

When I think back to the first lesson where I was asking my mom questions while she got ready in the mirror, I imagine that I created the belief that I wasn't worthy of my mom's attention because she was preoccupied with her own shit. When I look around at parent's on their cell phone while their kid tries to get their attention, I think about how many of them are subconsciously creating the belief that they're not worthy of their parent's attention. While it seems like a silly little thing, not being fully present for kids can cause all sorts of problems.

What are some incidents that happened to you as a kid that you could have potentially created untrue beliefs about yourself? (Like your parent's divorce was your fault, etc.)

Scan to watch Darren Brown's subliminal advertising experiment:

Scan for more good shit.

FAKE IT TILL YOU MAKE IT, BUT BE AUTHENTIC AS FUCK

*K*amp number five was upon us. As I put the last Tupperware container in the fridge, I ran through a quick checklist to see if I'd forgotten anything. Although it was our fifth Kamp, it always felt like the first. I still had no clue how to structure or run a company, but I was rock solid on the content. As each Kamp grew in size, so did my resentment. My pride was so thick that I was expecting a letter from President Obama asking me to bring the KK (Kamp Konfidence) format back to the United States.

As I pulled my phone out to check the time, I ran face first into a brick wall of panic. Forgetting that I'd be without cell reception for the next forty eight hours, I tried to remember what it was like back in the day before having the answer to everything at the tip of fingers. Like clockwork, my two partners pulled up the gravel driveway, following one another.

After getting their bags out of the car, I ran out to meet them.

"Bisssssssssches! Always so good to see you!"

"I can't believe it's our fifth Kamp!" Soraya said joyfully.

"Oh my GOD I can never get used to not having my phone, but…!" Emily chimed in.

"Tell me about it! Put your shit down and I'll run you through the list of girls again to refresh," I said.

Emily, a twenty five-year-old CrossFit coach and HR professional, had the perfect attitude to relate to teenage girls. The youngest of the trio, she was great at twerking off the walls with the girls and able to relate to current shit I knew nothing about. Soraya, a twenty nine-year-old primary school teacher working on her master's degree, loved working with teenage girls, and although a total square, was way down to earth and super hip. She commanded respect from the teens and was best able to play the authoritarian role between the three of us.

We made the ideal team. We balanced each other out perfectly with our diverse backgrounds and personalities. Without having any kind of institutional oversight, we could do, be, and say anything we wanted. After Soraya and Emily put their stuff down, they joined me at the big wooden table outside to go over our roster.

"I still can't believe it's coming up to winter at the beginning of May!" I said.

I'm so excited it's time for Kamp again! I think I get more out of it than the girls do sometimes!" Emily said.

"I know! I'm the same. I love that we're in a dead zone out here. I think that's why this works so well," Soraya said.

"Sorry to be a Debbie downer, but what the FUCK are we going to do if another carpet python slides into the shack like last camp? Lisa isn't here this weekend, and I know the three of us aren't qualified to handle snakes," I asked.

"Oh my GOD!" Emily yelped as she jumped up and danced

around like a ten-year-old. "I HATE snakes!"

"We'll be fine! We just need to make sure we keep the back door shut," said Soraya.

"I'm so glad we decided to not use the tents. Sleeping inside the shack together is so much easier to keep an eye on all of them," I said, changing the subject.

"Ughhhhhh! Imagine all the shit that could creep in if we were using the tents!" squealed Emily.

Noticing we were running out of time before the girls started getting dropped off, I pushed us along.

"Ok, ok. Let me run you through the list really quickly. So, we have ten girls this weekend. Everyone is relatively low-risk with the exception of Katie. According to her Mom, she could potentially do a runner and is actively using drugs. Apparently, she has an older dope-selling boyfriend who she might try to call to pick her up."

"Yeah, good luck with your phone little girl!" Emily said with a chuckle.

"Everyone else is our classic profile. Marissa is actively cutting, Geneva has been severely bullied and at her third school, Jessica, Rebecca, Jill and Sarah have incredibly low, poor body image with Sarah potentially purging. Her Mom said she's been going to the bathroom a lot more after meals lately and has lost a significant amount of weight. Betsy is close to dropping out of school because of bullying, Vanessa is sleeping with every boy she goes out with, and finally we have Courtney who seems the most mentally sound of the lot," I said as I put my pen down.

"Do you know what area Marissa is cutting on?" Soraya asked.

"I believe the upper thigh and stomach." I replied.

"Damn. So clearly she's past the stage of wanting attention."

"Yeah, her Mom told me she found her in the shower with the razor she uses to scrape the calluses off her hand from CrossFit."

"Well team, let's make some magic happen!" Emily said.

"Yup! Same drill--Em you get the girls comfy while Soraya and I will do intake down at the bottom of the driveway," I said.

Like clockwork, the girls and their guardians all showed up at their allotted time over the half hour registration window. No one tried to run away or swing on their parents, but all nine girls were visibly not excited to be getting dropped off. After Vanessa was checked in and heading up the driveway towards the main tin-wall cabin where we'd be spending a majority of the weekend, I told Soraya she could head up and help Em while I waited for Courtney and Donna to show up.

Not more than five minutes later, Donna and her two daughters arrived.

"So lovely to put a face to the name, Donna and Courtney!" I said as I reached out to give them both a hug. "And who do we have here?" II asked in my best, cute little baby voice, while sticking my index finger in the hand of the little two-year-old.

"This is Martina!" said Courtney as she pinched her little sister's cheek.

"Babies are like horses. They can sense when you're nervous and usually start crying around me!" I exclaimed.

"Yea, nah!" said Courtney as she and Donna both giggled.

"Yea, nah?" I asked. "Is this some new, hip teen talk I'm unaware of?"

"Yea, nah!" Courtney said again while laughing. "It's Straya, mate!"

"Ok, looks like I'll be the one learning some stuff this weekend, hey!" I said enthusiastically.

"Speaking of which, let's get your paperwork and head up!" I said as I looked over to Donna.

While Donna was reaching into her purse, she started to tear up.

"I can't tell you how much it means to us that you were able to make this happen," she said as she handed me the paperwork. With her bottom lip starting to slightly quiver, I knew I was screwed.

"I would do anything to protect my baby girl. She's been through so much and has everything in the world in front of her." Before she completely lost it, she managed to get out one last sentence, "I wish I had something like this when I was growing up."

Just as the sun slipped behind the horizon, the baby was the only one not crying.

"Oh my goodness! What happens at Kamp, stays at Kamp!" I said as we all wiped our faces.

"Beat it woman!" I said to Donna. "We'll see you Sunday at three p.m.!"

"Bye Mum. Bye poopskie!" Courtney said as she gave her Mom and sister one last hug before we headed up the driveway.

. . . .

As Courtney and I walked through the door of the main building, we could hear Emily screaming over the top of the music.

Sure as a shit, Emily had her feet on the wall, with her hands on the floor as she showed off her twerking skills. Per protocol, Soraya and Emily had done an exceptional job of getting all the girls familiar with each other and not a single one was sitting on her own.

"Oh, sweet Jesus!" I shouted. "Emily stop poisoning these young girls' minds!" I said laughing.

"OKAYYYYYYYYYYYYYYY GIRLS! LISTEN UP!" I belted out with my hands cupped around my mouth. Stopping to give Soraya the head nod to turn down the music, I waited patiently for the quiet to fill the room.

"Circle up over here on the floor. We're going to play a little game called the name game!" I said with my hands in a circle, tapping my fingertips together like Doctor Evil.

"Here are the rules. You have to think of a positive adjective that starts with the same letter of your first name. Now if you don't know what an adjective is, don't worry about it. I sucked at English too. Soraya why don't you tell us what that is."

"An adjective is a word or a phrase used to describe a noun," said Soraya.

"OK, so basically that means a word to describe something," I said. "I'll give you an example. You all know my name is Kortney with a K. So, something positive that starts with a K, I could say I'm Kinky Kortney, but the truth is, I'm super vanilla. I can't even talk about sex!"

"Oh my GOD, Kortney!" Emily screeched. "It's so true girls. You'll see on Sunday when Darlene comes to talk about sexual health, Kort will literally turn bright red and run out of the room!"

"Yup, it's true. Rather funny because when I was eighteen, I think I slept with like thirty three guys. Surprised my vagina didn't

382

fall off." As I looked around the circle of girls to gauge their reactions. Making eye contact with Soraya, I winked just as she crossed her eyes.

"I'll give you the backstory on that in a wee bit when I tell you all my story and explain why we're all here this weekend. But first, we must play the name game, followed by the judgement game. Ok, so I'll start, then Soraya will have to say my name, then introduce herself, then Emily says my name, Soraya's name, then introduces herself."

As I looked at Courtney, who was sitting on my right-hand side, I concluded, "You, my friend, have the shittiest spot! You get to remember everyone's name!" I said, reading that she was excited about the challenge.

As the room's energy quickly shifted, I started.

"Kind Kortney," I said.

"Kind Kortney. Sweet Soraya," said Soraya.

"Kind Kortney. Sweet Soraya. Electric Emily!" said Emily.

"Kind Kortney. Sweet Soraya," said Jill, before pausing.

"I forgot to tell you girls; the person next to you is always the hardest to remember. I don't know why, it's just a fact!" I said. "But we're all a team, and if you get stuck, we're here to help."

"Electric," Marissa whispered to Jill.

Electric Emily. Ummmmmmmmm," Jill bashfully replied as her eyes dropped to the floor. "Come on! SO many positives in the J department!" I exclaimed.

"Joyful!" shouted Courtney.

"Jolly?" questioned Rebecca.

"Joyful!" said Jessica and Sarah in unison.

"Joyful Jill?" said Jill.

"Great job! OK! Keep at it," I commanded.

Finally, after a labored ten minutes, Courtney nailed everyone's name before stating, she was "Cheerful Court! And that's Courtney with a C," she said as she looked at me.

Faster than the instant in instant rice, I immediately recognized the look in Courtney's eyes. Looking for the "great job" from someone outside of herself, I smiled and said, "Great job!" straight at her before addressing the group, "You all killed it!"

To give myself a taller appearance, I deliberately went from sitting cross-legged to sitting on my haunches.

. . . .

As the girls all gathered back in the room, I got them back into a circle.

"OK, time for storytelling little ones! Gather around."

After telling them to fasten their seatbelts and tighten their helmets, I carefully maneuvered through my life story, making sure I weaved in and out of the bits that their Mom's might lose their minds over.

"Alright… so where to start? I'm going to get really raw with you girls. I don't always encourage people to share as much of their life as I do, but once you've been on the front page of a national newspaper with a little black box over your tits, you tend to build up a strong sense of resilience. Sometimes people can take your vulnerability and try and throw it back in your face or use it against you, but remember, that's their shit and not yours."

"But in my experience, authenticity is freeing. As long as I know my shit inside and out, and I'm the one telling it, no one can take it away from me, or talk behind my back because I'm the one saying it. I know where I've been. It wasn't always that way for a good decade because I was usually so drunk or high, I couldn't remember. Also, I've spent so much of my life hating my body and being stuck in my own head obsessing over what I ate and how I was going to work it off, that I don't really have a lot of fun memories. How many of you can relate to that?"

As I looked around the room, I wasn't the least bit surprised to see every girl's hand raised.

"I figured as much. You'll learn tomorrow that it's not wise to make assumptions, but this was one assumption I could pretty much consider fact."

"Everyone in this world is wearing a mask. You will rarely meet someone who isn't. Sometimes it's intentional, and sometimes it's not. Sometimes it's because of society and the stupid-ass gender roles we're conditioned to follow. The world is constantly screaming at us to act like a girl. They say we're supposed to look a certain way and that we're born backstabbing, emotional, jealous bitches, when in fact, that couldn't be further from the truth."

"Could you please tell that to all the mean, shitty girls at my school?" Geneva said while rolling her eyes.

"I'd love to but the last high school I spoke at in Helensvale asked me to not come back because I said the words porn star!", I replied.

Completely in my element, and feeling like I was on top of the world, I carried on.

"They say we're born the weaker sex girls, but let me tell you the facts. Women are fierce! Someone grew you inside of their body for nine fucking months, and then pushed your ass out of a tiny hole or had their guts cut open to pull you out! Like *how* is that *not* magic?" I shouted.

"I told you about my session world experience, briefly. When you're a bit older you can hear more details, but that watermelon smashing stunt has now become a symbol of female strength. I started doing it to show some guy how strong I was, and got paid four hundred to do it. Remember though, that four hundred dollars an hour did not fill that void which was all of you. You were the ones my soul was burning to talk to. That money just temporarily filled that void. Stay very aware that you don't fall into that trap of 'I'll be happy when', because that shit doesn't work out."

"But now, when I smash that watermelon, I remind you girls that this is your sacred space that is capable of magic! When we go out, we go out knowing if we decide we want to get laid. I'm sure some of you are there, and some of you are not- and as Em said, I'm not interested in talking about that, but as women, we have the power. When men go out and want to pick up, they go out thinking, wondering, wishing, hoping, praying. Us? We go out with one hundred percent certainty. So why is it that we end up getting raped and taken advantage of, or decide to give it up when we really didn't want to in the first place? Bitches, your body is a temple, not a visitor's center! Like I said, after my rape, I acted out sexually because I was hurt."

"We have the power, and it's up to us to protect that. We have the capability to bring life into this earth, and we have the power to taketh. Men can't smash these watermelons like us because their fragile balls get in the way. Think about your Dad or your brother. They get kicked in the balls and it's game over, right? Or they get the flu, and they're down for the count, huh?"

"Yes! Dad got a tiny little chest cold last month and he was literally the biggest baby," Jill touted from the floor.

"Exactly, Jill! Women push babies out of their vagina and jump up and get on with life. I've read that giving birth is the equivalent of breaking every bone in your body. We're so powerful, we go through that pain, and then some women decide to do it again! Like how many of you have a sibling? Raise your hand!"

As I looked around the room almost every girl had her hand raised.

"Ask any historian about women and they'll tell you we were fierce. The only time we fought was if we were provoked by someone threatening our children. Then you suddenly had one possessed witch on your hands. Fuck around and find out! Men historically fought for chivalry, girls," I said as I jumped up and assumed the position as if I was holding a sword.

"Har me Lady! Let me win thy love and joust some asshole off his horse," I said in my best macho voice.

"Whereas we, if we fought, it was ON! We're even equipped to be better fighters if taught properly- we're more determined, agile, fierce, and we have a much higher pain threshold! Not to mention we have a lower center of gravity- I mean look at these legs! If I had a dollar for every time a man told me, "I wish I had your legs", none of us would be here right now! I'd be chilling by a pool working on my tan. Being jacked and tan, eye on the prize girls! But really--think about it. Why do most of us have bigger legs?

As I waited for someone to answer, I moved my hips around in the air in a circular motion.

I pointed at Courtney, "Because we have bigger hips for childbearing?" she said.

"YES! Yes Courtney, that is EXACTLY why!" I shouted while jumping up and down.

Seeing that Courtney was elated with her answer, I kept on.

"We have wider hips which is where ALL of our power comes from!"

"How many of you have seen Happy Gilmore?"

As I looked at Jessica with her hand raised, I asked her, "Remember the part where he's golfing and he sings, "It's all in the hips. It's all in the hips!" Well, that's what's up! Swinging a golf club, throwing a punch, Olympic lifting. All of these movements are generated from the hips. We have wider hips, therefore generating more power!"

"Remember that a majority of men are probably wishing they had the "fat" thighs you wish you didn't have. Also, if and when a boy talks shit to you, remember that seeing a girl get pissed off is a turn on for them. Girls aren't supposed to get aggressive and angry. Plus, they like the attention. Remember I told you how I started out on a webcam getting paid to flex my biceps? I forgot to tell you that men sometimes paid me to actually just talk shit to them! I couldn't believe it!"

"There's SO much you're going to learn over the weekend. But if you take away even just ONE thing, you're winning. You girls are going to get an insight into everything we wish we were taught in school, and by the end of this weekend, you're going to understand why it's so important that we work together as girls. The cards are stacked against us, and by seeing each other as competition, we're only making it harder."

"So, let me explain what this all means and why you're all here," I said as I clicked on the slide containing the infographic of what

Kamp Konfidence looked like.

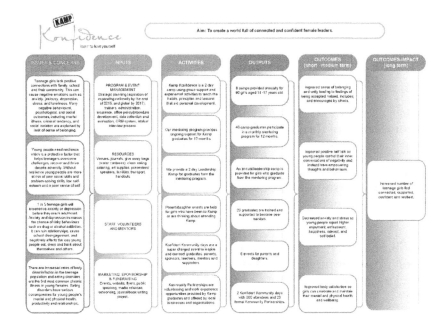

Aware that I was rapidly approaching their capacity to take any more info in, I asked the girls, "Alright... you girls still with me?"

Seeing their heads nod, I wrapped up.

"Once you girls start working on yourself and build some confidence with a K, you'll move up the pyramid and stop seeing other girls as your competition. From there, we have unity, thus building a sisterhood, and once we have that, y'all will help each other get to the tippy tippy top of the pyramid and reach your ultimate potential and goals without fucking stepping on each other! Capiche?"

. . . .

Noticing it was almost 10:00 p.m. somehow, I decided to reel the girls in despite seeing all of them starting to bond and open up with one another.

While standing in what is known as the "X" position, I turned on my boss voice. "Okkkkkkay ladies! I hate to interrupt, but it's time to stop bedazzling your futuristic vision boards and give us all a rundown of what you've been working on for the last forty minutes before we get our beds ready and fall asleep watching the best documentary on the planet, Killing Us Softly by Jean Killbourne!" I said.

"Why are you standing like that?" Courtney asked laughing.

"I was hoping someone was going to notice!" I replied while seeing a gleam in her eye. "This is what's called the X position. I was going to show you in the morning, but like I told you, after smoking so much meth and popping pills, I don't have a great memory and I'm worried I'll forget to tell you if I don't tell you now! Also, I'd set an alarm on my phone, but guess what?" I asked while still holding the X pose.

"What?!" the girls replied in unison.

Standing with my feet further than hip width apart, and my arms stretched out to the sides above my head with my palms facing forward, while thrusting my hips in the air, I energetically shouted, "My fucking cell phone has died and it feels AH-MAZZZZZZZING, ya heard!"

Feeling the power of the group, I was completely in my element. As their laughs bounced off the tile floors and metal tin walls, I interjected while continuing to air fuck the air but now on one foot. Dancing around like only a white girl on crack could, I found myself thriving off of their laughing fit.

"Hashtag, don't do drugs!'"

"Ok, but seriously! This is serious shit, seriously!" I said while laughing through trying to keep a straight face while standing on one foot and holding my arms up still.

"When you wake up, take two minutes to hold this position," I said as I put my foot down and confidently stood back in the X pose while flexing every muscle in my body and holding my head high.

"Ever heard people say the mind, body connection?" I asked.

"Yes!" replied Courtney while a few other girls nodded in unison.

"Ok, what the fuck does it actually mean?" I asked while assuming the position.

"I don't know, but I know you look hilarious standing like that!" said Courtney laughing.

"Exactly! Most of us don't know what the hell we're saying half the time. We just say shit without consciously connecting to what it actually means. We'll get more into that on Sunday when we talk about subconscious beliefs, but for now, think about this. Your body is physically connected to your head, right?"

"Yeah, I think so! Maybe not yours, though!" Courtney exclaimed with pride as the other girls laughed.

"Accurate! But yes. My head is actually connected to my body, and in my head, is my mind. When I wake up and hold my body in this posture, it actually talks to my brain, and subconsciously tells my body to release chemicals, aka hormones, to increase confidence, which is testosterone!" I replied. When we go over assertiveness training this weekend, we'll talk about how walking with your hands in your pockets and your eyes down on the ground can cause your brain to feel depressed subconsciously, but I had to bring this up in case I forgot!"

As I let my arms fall down to my side, I instructed the girls to take thirty seconds to share what they'd been working on.

Being completely confident that Courtney was going to be my teacher's pet, I knew she'd start with the right tone for the activity.

"Courtney, why don't you start us off while Soraya times us for thirty seconds each?" I said. "After Court goes, we'll go to the left."

"Oh! Alrighty then," Court started while waiting for Soraya to give her the head nod to start.

"Well, I cut out these letters to spell H-O-P-E so I don't forget. Down here I put a picture of girls laughing over coffee, because I want that in my life. My best friend died a few years ago, and all the other girls in my school are too busy doing drugs and partying," she said as the room fell quieter than a morgue. I have a picture of a new home because I'd like to buy my Mom a house for her and my baby sister to live in because we currently live in a one bedroom. But at least my step dad moved out after he threw a bottle at my Mom's head a few months ago."

Suddenly the sound of crickets chirping filled the room as Courtney sat down.

"Wow, that's pretty powerful stuff Court. Thank you for sharing. Go ahead Sarah," I said as I smiled and looked Courtney in the eyes, letting her know she did a remarkable job.

Standing up, Sarah started in with a wavering voice, "Ummmmm yeah. Well, I cut out pictures of different girls looking healthy and working out. I also have these on here so I can focus on eating healthier foods so I can stop getting fat."

"Yeah, hi. You're not fat!" Courtney bluntly interrupted.

"You're crazy!" said Jill. "You're perfect."

As she started talking again, I noticed her cheeks become flushed as I drifted off in thought.

How is this stunning fifteen-year-old girl standing here thinking she's fat?

She's obsessing on food right now.

She had like two bites of the yogurt and protein whip we made before they started on their vision boards.'

The crickets sounded off again as I pulled myself back into the room.

"Thank you, Sarah. Great job."

After leading the rest of the girls to share, it became very evident that they weren't going to have a problem opening up for the bonfire the following night. Once Jill had finished, I made a point to wrap up the exercise with a strong closing story to hit the point home.

"You girls did great. Remember I told you earlier tonight how I realized I didn't want to be some random bloke's fantasy anymore despite how much money I was making, and that I realized I wanted to be speaking to women and girls, ya?" I asked.

"Yeah we remember the Konfidence tattoo you showed us," said Missy.

Surprised that it was no longer just Courtney aiming to be the teacher's pet, I shouted back with excitement to Missy, "Yes! The tramp stamp as I like to call it."

"I kept focusing on my desire to empower girls and women by sharing the truth behind media and advertising, and that there were some guys out there that found hairy armpits *gorgeous*! Whaaaaaaaat! So, you see, when Big Brothers, Big Sisters called me and told me that I wouldn't make a good role model, my subconscious mind didn't let me fall victim to thinking my future was going to be dictated by some religious organization. Because I had been continuing to focus on the bigger picture, I was able to take Konfidence by Kortney and turn that into Kamp Konfidence! Now please don't take offence, but I'll probably hold off on getting Kamp tattooed above the Konfidence logo, keh!"

As the girls hung on my every word, I continued on.

"Y'all notice how Court stood up when she shared, yet I didn't ask her to, nor did I give you instructions to? You all just followed suit yeah?" I asked as I looked around at the girls nodding their heads. "You become the sum of the top five people you hang around. Not only do you start to mimic their movements, but you also start to mimic their energy, behaviors and patterns. So, stop hanging around assholes!" I said as I winked at Emily.

While Emily threw a pillow at my head, the girls started laughing as I ducked and missed copping it in the face by an inch.

"But seriously! Our subconscious minds are always taking in data. It's important to be focused on positive stuff and people so when things try and throw us off track, we can have our minds prepared to bounce back. It's human nature to focus on negative shit, girls. Watch," I said as I turned back to Emily.

Without taking a single breath, I quickly painted a picture.

"Em, look... I gotta tell you something. You have the most amazing energy. When you walk into a room, it instantly lights up. You have the greatest smile. It's totally infectious. You train so hard and are super strong. You even have the coolest outfits. I wish I could put outfits together like you. But I gotta tell you- your gold jewelry is *so* ugly! It totally takes away from everything else. It makes you look like a cheap hooker.", I said as we sat facing each other.

"Keh, love you, byeeeeeee!" I said as I chucked the pillow back towards Emily's head.

As the girls burst into laughter, Emily threw the pillow back at me, "You bitch! I fucking love my gold bling! You're just jealous!"

"Nahhhh, I don't get jealous anymore, I'm grown! Hashtag, not your competition!", I said back to her.

Now facing back towards the girls, I finished up my point.

"But you see girls... what's the *one* thing Em will keep thinking about?" I asked.

"Her gold jewelry," Jill said smiling.

"Yessssssss! That's exactly right! Never mind Em's amazing energy, infectious smile, strong body and cool outfits. She will sit and stew on me talking shit about her gold jewelry for the next several hours!" I said.

"Yeah Em, we all know you were a leprechaun in your last life!" shouted Soraya from across the room.

"So, girls! Remember to check yourself. Who are you hanging around, and what kind of messages are you taking on board? Now go get ready for bed and come back so we can lay this stack of crappy camping mattresses out on the floor and watch Jean's doco on the big screen," I said as I pointed at the projector screen.

After the girls were back in the shack with their PJ's on, I started to tell them about Jean's documentary while they laid their mattresses out on the ground.

"Ok, girls, listen up! The lady you're about to watch has been doing this exact same talk since the seventies--that's before I was even born! She's been cutting out pictures of ads in the newspaper and magazines since she noticed the first ad that was basically telling women we needed to look a certain way if we ever wanted to be married! This doco changed my life!

As the girls all crawled into their sleeping bags, I walked back to Soraya and Emily and made sure they were good to stand watch for the next couple of hours while I slept. Unlike most nights where I'd lie in bed spinning my wheels wondering how I was going to fix the world while simultaneously thinking about if I'd had too many calories that day, I fell asleep without a thought or concern about what I should be doing. The last time I could recall feeling this peaceful was the night I fell asleep on my cousin's floor tucked into my sleeping bag with a stomach full of pizza. Without any thoughts of guilt or shame from eating pizza, or worrying about not having the right outfit and feeling out of place, I fell asleep with a quiet mind.

I was exactly where I was supposed to be, doing exactly what I was supposed to do.

. . . .

When I launched Kamp Konfidence, you could say I was still a hot mess. Although I had a little over three years clean, I hadn't yet really worked out my issues. As you read in the previous chapter, I had only just acknowledged more buried childhood trauma. During the time of Kamp, I was unknowingly working through a new form of disordered eating. Because this behavior was masked as being healthy in my mind, I wasn't fully able to see it for what it was at the time. I maintained a heavily restricted diet of eating only Paleo safe foods, and looked at something like frozen yogurt as a once a week "sinful but excusable" treat. After having put too many shaved almonds on as toppings, I would walk around the house feeling my abdominal muscles to make sure they hadn't disappeared under the fat-free treat.

I was doing Brazilian Jiu Jitsu, Crossfit, and Bikram Yoga sessions all in the same day, five times a week, with a usual extra Crossfit session on Saturday and Bikram on Sunday. Relative Energy Deficiency in Sport (RED-S) caused me to stop having a period and decline in health. But even though I was struggling with freedom from diet culture, I talked about it with my peers and the teenage girls who came through our program. A lot of us think we have to have our shit completely together before we can start helping other people, but that is simply not true. As we say in 12-step recovery, someone with three days of continual sobriety, can absolutely help the person with only twenty four hours. And please believe the person with three days, is certainly not 'mentally well'. So, sometimes you gotta fake it (stumble, fumble, pretend) till you figure that shit out. Just make sure you're being authentic throughout the journey!

Do the F*cking Work

What images of women have you compared yourself to, or used as "goals" in your lifetime? Have you stopped to think about whether they're realistic goals, or if that person you're chasing/basing your happiness on is actually happy themselves?

In what ways have you felt like your worth is equated to your exterior? Describe how society and diet culture play into this.

Come to think of it, define diet culture in your own words! So often we regurgitate shit without fully connecting to the meaning of it.

Inspired by the dissonance-based work from Dr Carolyn Becker in The Body Project, write a letter to your younger self. Just as you would address a child who doesn't know a ton of worldly stuff, tell her what you know now that you wish you knew then.

What things do you wish you were taught in *school* as a kid?

How can you be responsible for furthering your education yourself and improving your sense of empowerment?

Intentionally spend an evening watching commercials on the telly. Observe how the ads speak to you and how that ties in to what Jean Kilbourne talked about in "Killing Us Softly".

For example, when watching a commercial from Jeep, how do they portray the driver and their lifestyle? What are they doing? How are they acting? What kind of subliminal message is the advertiser sending you/viewers?

I know in my experience there aren't any moments when the sun is shining through the windshield and straight down onto my perfectly made mocha with whip cream.I'm also not driving through unknown territory off-road on an adventure wearing a perfectly matched outfit that looks brand new with a full tank of gas, smiling at my passenger with perfectly straight, super white teeth!

In reality, the scene would look more like me wearing mismatched, heavily washed gym clothes that were slightly piling and now dirty from spilling my coffee in my crotch as I slammed on my breaks to not run a red light. Or perhaps me shouting at my husband for getting us lost because the GPS stopped working on our navigation, and he totally sucks at directions. Or better yet, us sitting in the living room talking about wanting to go off-roading, but not leaving the apartment because we'd be too concerned about getting eaten by a mountain lion and not having the extra money to justify the adventure.

Scan here for more good shit.

LESSON 19

GOALS NOT CONTROLS

*H*earing someone rustling by the side of the bed, I opened my eyes to find Dean setting down a fresh cup of espresso.

"Good morning Princess." he said in his husky, British accent as he kneeled down next to my head.

"Hiiiiiiii," I said, wiping my crusty eyes.

Having realised we needed to take an extended break due to Soraya hitting the thirty five-week mark with her first pregnancy, I was feeling emotionally drained after finishing our eighth kamp.

"My God you are so beautiful, Kortney Kay," Dean said as his eyes filled up with tears.

"I just woke up and my eyes are all swollen from crying last night!" I said.

"You are so sweet bringing me coffee!" I exclaimed, pushing myself up to a seated position.

"I can't believe how lucky I am," he said as he stroked my forehead.

"I'm sorry I've been so miserable. I think I'm just down about Kamp being over for a while."

"Honey I don't care. You're the only one putting pressure on yourself."

"Yeah, but I feel like I failed. I always start things and never finish them."

"It's just a part of the journey, sweetheart. Here, have your coffee," he said, edging it towards me.

"I'm going to the store, so text me if you think of anything else you want outside the norm."

After finishing the tart coffee, I slid out of bed and stood in front of our cheap, full-length mirror attached to the wall. It had been six months since I'd made the decision to get breast implants which provoked an Australian journalist to, once again, write a story with the sole purpose of selling a headline.

"One of Kortney's most passionate projects has been helping young women to build confidence and accept their body image. But a recent decision to have a breast enlargement has sparked questions as to whether the trainer herself has acceptance of her own body image? It would suggest that she does, after posting a story of her breast augmentation from an A cup to a D cup, on her online blog to tell fans what was going on and how the surgery has not changed her one bit.

'I can't begin to tell you how much more sexier I feel. How feminine..... having muscles, a half shaved head and small pecks have been great but there is definitely a side of me that has felt my femininity slipping down the drain,' she said.

The trainer, who got the breast enlargement last month has seemingly been very transparent with her decision to get the

surgery and has added a little humour to the situation.

'Girls make sure you marry a man who picks you up from a breast augmentation that he financed/paid for and a bouquet of gorgeous flowers.'

The blog went on to say, 'I fully intended for paying for my own job but my husband's main purpose in life is to find ways to create joys and happiness for me.'"

The months leading up to my decision, I was sick without *really* accepting that I was sick with hypergymnasia. Being beautifully shredded with the sides of my head shaved, I felt that taking my lopsided A cup up to a D, might improve my sense of femininity. But just like most things, I was bored after a few months and back to being dissatisfied with an empty void inside.

With Kamp now on the back burner and my new tits mending on the front, I could make a comeback in the bodybuilding world despite swearing I would never do it again. Pulling my shirt up, I stared at my bare chest while flicking my unresponsive nipple. I couldn't believe I hadn't spent more time researching surgeons and *somehow* managed to pick the shadiest man in the city. Although deep down, I knew my "somehow" was merely me just repeating the same old character defect of ignoring red flags.

For me, sometimes red flags were hard to miss. Then again, there were times where they practically had a spotlight shining directly on them, as in the case with my surgeon. Any self-respecting man in his fifties in a surgical setting, should avoid having his shirt halfway unbuttoned, sitting in an office full of gold, gaudy trim, and displaying heavily photoshopped, hardly-legal looking models on his website. Also, no one should be drawn to a cosmetic surgeon because their commercial plays on a cool EDM station.

Whilst charging down the path of competition prep, I was

determined to create some kind of Kamp Konfidence format for mothers. I started working on a new business model called Unconditional Self Love for Mum for months on end before Dean came to me with his brilliant idea one afternoon.

"Baby girl, guess what?"

"You're going to help me write a business plan, so I don't fuck it up?" I replied.

"No. This is much better."

"Oh, really?"

"I know it's been a year since we registered the company name, but I've been thinking about it a lot."

"Go on," I said.

"You and I were brought together from opposite ends of the earth. Never in a million years did I think you'd actually be a part of my life."

"Uh huhhhhhhh…"

"Remember when we met, and I said you were a golden child with something incredible to do?"

"Yes, of course. I mean, I can hardly remember what I was doing five minutes ago but I recall that as clear as day."

"So, I was thinking… since the day you told me that you wanted to speak to women, it's been on the back of my mind."

"Okayyyyyyyyy. Also, that's a long time to have something on the back of your mind."

"What you've built with Kamp Konfidence is incredible, but

rather tricky to duplicate as well as market. You can't really be speaking directly to teenagers when the parents are the ones paying. And you can't be speaking to parents, when the girls should want to be going. Plus, there is no one else in the world like you, my love."

"All sounds on point. So, what's the nut of it all!"

"Instead of reaching eight to ten teenage girls every other weekend in a tiny corner of Australia, why don't we take the same vision and mission from Kamp and roll it into a global clothing line! Plus, I know how many t-shirt ideas you've come up with since Kamp started."

"That's amazing, but how?"

"Leave that part up to me--I want you to keep focusing on growing and changing lives."

. . . .

About a year earlier, Dean had come home from work with a 'vision', as he called it. He said while driving, he had this idea of creating a clothing line for girls that was specific to whatever sport they were playing. Everything was centered around, 'like a girl'. Running clothes, fighting gear--anything you could think of to say "do it like a girl". A week after this vision ran through his head, the female hygiene brand 'Always', rolled out a campaign called 'like a girl'. Everyone on social media was tagging me and Kamp Konfidence. The next day we registered the company name, "Like A Girl Clothing, Pty Ltd.". It sat untouched for over a year.

Flying down to Melbourne to meet with a designer meant that this thing might be actually happening. After a brief cup of coffee in a hipster cafe, we all came to the conclusion that the name sounded very flowery, and we'd have to rethink our strategy. Walking back to the rental car, Dean was deep in thought.

"So, this just popped across the front of my mind. You ready?"

"Born ready."

"Grrrrrrl, like a growl."

"Oh my God that's genius! How do you come up with this stuff?"

"I thought about your name, and how it's spelled differently. Then I thought about the word and what the messaging was behind the brand, and the sound grrrrrr just appeared in my mind. Grrrl-"

I stopped in the middle of the sidewalk and felt a rush similar to the first time I smoked meth. But instead of throwing my life away, it was just about to start.

Over the next several months we took the concept and turned it into a brand with a revolutionary idea of ditching traditional sizing. Instead of using a chart that was created by a man in the forties from the department of agriculture, we would instead use athletes' names and measurements to guide our "sizing". Thinking back to one of the many lessons learned in one of my 'meaningless' network marketing conferences, I applied the 'everyone is waiting for someone else to go first' concept to our idea and held strong.

On top of convincing calf-loving Don to invest twenty thousand, I borrowed ten grand from Pop, five grand from my dad, and together, Dean and I created the magic which would make up why The Universe united us from opposite ends of the world. As I found sound suppliers who weren't exploiting children, built the website, and created the brand, I stumbled upon a talented fighter in the UFC who was due to fight Ronda Rousey in a month's time as the main event.

Holly Holm was the underdog by a long stretch. With the fight taking place in Melbourne, we decided it was worth a shot in trying to see if we could make it work. Finding out that it would literally take the last of our money, leaving a whole seventy eight cents in the checking account, caused us both more insecurity than Britney Spears post head shave.

Our videographer Gino and I managed to get two tickets for the fight along with our sponsorship. We flew Gino out to live with us in Australia to get as much content filmed for the launch as we could. With only five super basic designs created on shirts, I picked two that I thought would suit Holly best:

Fight Like A GRRRL

It's Leg Day, Bitch!

Her manager's assistant emailed to let me know that she wouldn't be wearing the leg day design; I had been unaware that Holly was "The Preacher's Daughter", both literally and figuratively. Dressed in my charcoal grey 'lift like a grrrl' muscle tee, I finally found my and Gino's seats on the floor inside the Etihad Arena. Every Tom, Dick and Harry were there to support Ronda Rousey, wearing their Ronda appropriate shirts.

Having little expectation around her winning or losing, the anticipation of the fight was more intense than appearing on live television with a case of gastro. As the lights went down in the massive arena, the crowd's cheering reverberated around the crisp air. Halfway between the cage and stadium seating, Gino and I had a perfect view of the massive monitors overhead, watching as the UFC played the promo video which showcased both fighters.

Introducing Holly, the announcer's voice rumbled through the crowd as I gripped the sides of my metal folding chair.

"What the fuck music is this!" I shouted to Gino.

Laughing, he shouted back, "Sounds like the Riverdance production!"

As we watched Holly enter the arena and walk out with her small team, we screamed in support as the neon green and blue laser lights flashed around the walls. Looking calm, centered, and focused, I suddenly had a feeling tug sideways in my gut, feeling like Holly could have a shot at winning. As Holly's music dipped out, the announcer hyped up the stadium and got everyone on their feet as Ronda appeared on the screen, entering the arena. After a whirlwind of introductions, both fighters were engaged in the middle of the ring with the referee.

Suddenly they broke apart and Holly reached out her grappling gloves to touch hands with Ronda. In the most horrific display of shitty sportsmanship, Ronda denied what we all expected, and started back peddling to her corner to start the match. As the crowd of over fifty thousand people gasped and murmured, Gino and I looked at each other with wide eyes.

"Oh my GOD, what a dick!" I shouted.

"Bro! Wow-", Gino shouted back.

Ronda came out swinging wildly with punches but was unable to really connect as Holly circled around her from the outside. After Ronda tried to get Holly in a clinch, Holly landed a few dazzling punches, leaving Ronda with a bleeding nose. As both fighters were in their corners, Gino and I assessed the stand-out attacks and counter attacks from the round, further proving to myself that Holly was in a prime position. The first round concluded in what seemed like seconds.

Then, shortly into the second round, Holly threw a kick that landed a stunning knockout. As Holly ran in a circle around the ring, I knew right then and there that The Universe had been guiding my life all along. Feeling like Gino and I were the only ones who resembled an action of just winning the lottery, we screamed in the moments immediately following the stunned silence that enveloped the entire stadium. Taking my shirt off and waving it around my head, Gino and I jumped up and down in elation.

Two days before the fight, Holly posted in her 'fight like a grrrl' t-shirt. Launching the next day, we sold in twenty-four hours what we anticipated selling in six months.

. . . .

I felt so utterly out of control not knowing where we were going to be living, I could hardly keep from ripping my skin off. I didn't know a single thing about the country of Thailand, let alone what side of the road I'd needed to get used to driving on again. The only thing bringing me any kind of reprieve from the surmounting fear, was knowing I'd no longer have to come face to face with another Huntsman spider again. Thanks to Holly, we had clear confirmation we were onto something. But unfortunately, that confirmation meant we needed money. Growing a global clothing line with zero background in fashion, fabrics, supply chain, or money, meant drastic measures.

A quick decision to move to Thailand and decrease our cost of living seemed like a no-brainer. Thanks to GumTree and all the Kiwis living Down Under, I was able to pretty much sell everything we owned to generate enough income to live off of for the next six months without drawing a paycheck. From my MAC eyeshadow collection to the roof off the Jeep, I took my experience from selling drugs and cars and hustled enough money to make it make sense.

As we were taxing to our gate, I asked Dean, "Wasn't there a massive tsunami somewhere in Thailand like a decade ago?" "Yes, you are correct. But it was on the opposite side of the island we're on," he replied. "Wait… you mean the tsunami was in this part of Thailand?" I asked. "Yes Hun," he said as we were standing up to join the crowd of people who had zero etiquette in disembarking a plane. As we shuffled down the aisle with our overflowing carry-on luggage, I started to remember back when the tsunami hit. Just like when September eleventh struck, I was incredibly high on meth. I recalled looking at the TV and shouting out to Billy, "That fucking sucks, but how funny is the name of this island? Sounds like fuck it!" Now reluctant to get off the plane, suddenly I was back to feeling fearful with an added side of shame.

I can't believe how up-our-own-ass Americans are. I don't know what's worse… thinking Phil Collins was American, not knowing Australia was in the future with a completely different time zone, or my absolute ignorance with geography. I bet I couldn't even point to Nebraska on a map.

As we walked into the terminal, I felt like we stepped off a time machine and into the eighties. *The only things missing are Ronald Regan and a Lunchable with a complimentary Capri Sun.*

With the familiar feeling of hunger turning over in my gut, I was now yearning for some kind of carbohydrates. Knowing I was going on America's Got Talent in three weeks' time, I decided to take drastic measures and was on my second day of a 'fat fast'. Similar to a Keto diet, the fat fast was a sure-fire way to kick my body into ketosis and burn the extra fat I'd piled on from the previous months' binge eating episodes after my last bodybuilding show. For ten days straight, I could only have a thousand calories, which ninety percent of were fat.

Why am I always craving something?

I feel like a fucking fraud trying to drastically lose weight just to go on TV.

410

Literally just launched a clothing brand that's about love yourself, and I'm out here eating a block of cream cheese for dinner.

I wonder if I will ever fully stop giving a fuck?

Like can I skip one day of training, and not catch the reflection of my disgusting, baggy kneecaps in the mirror and ruin the rest of my entire day?

Now containing the contents of our entire lives, we headed to grab our luggage. Feeling a tiny shred of excitement that my entire life fit into two large suitcases now, and somewhat torn over living in tsunami territory, we got our stuff and headed towards immigration. The only other time I'd been to Thailand was when Dean took me to Bangkok for what should have been a lovely little getaway, but as usual, I spent the entire trip obsessing over whether or not I was eating too much rice.

"Well that was easy," he said while laughing. "Yeah, I know! I don't think ol' mate even looked at my business visa," I said. Feeling a shitty combination of anxiety and hunger, we somehow managed to exchange some currency and find a taxi. Proud that I had pre-prepared the address in Thai, hestaredat the screen for several seconds, before simply saying, "can", as he opened the sliding door for us.

As we pulled out onto one of the main roads going through Phuket, I felt reality start to set in. We had moved to a third world country without a Westerner in sight.

During the first ten minutes of driving, I took in the scenery with shock and awe. Watching disheveled, dreaded dogs roaming around the streets, random cows in fields tied to trees, kids kicking cans in the streets, scooters with sidecars that were set-up as mobile food stands, and dilapidated rundown buildings stacked up against each other like a set of Legos that seemed to never end, I couldn't believe this was where we were going to be living for some unknown amount of time. Instead of romantic Thai styled landscapes and temples I was envisioning on the plane, my gaze looked up and locked onto the endless bundles upon bundles of dangerously low lying cables that seemed to be hanging between telephone poles appearing as if they were seconds from snapping like a matchstick.

I turned from looking out the window and enthusiastically said to Dean, "Maybe we can make it a goal to get our first round of funding and incorporate in Singapore within the next six months?" In an instant, his face shifted, and his eyes became cold.

In a sharp tone I rarely heard, "We just got here, and you already want to leave?" he said.

I'm sure he's thinking I'll never be happy anywhere we go. And he wouldn't be wrong.

I flashed back to the day Bubba told me how he didn't want to "live his life with such a miserable person any longer" as I sat sobbing on the closet floor.

"Noooooooo, I'm not saying that because I'm unhappy, I'm just saying we should set a goal," I replied defensively as I turned back around to stare out the window. But the reality was, I was gravely unhappy. I had no friends, no working phone, and not a clue what the future held. Instead of "let go and let God" bullshit, I was gripping onto the tiny threads of control I had left, which was currently about how my body looked. I was gripping harder than I'd gripped the sides of the toilet seat that one fateful evening in Miami when I couldn't go to the bathroom no matter how hard I tried.

For the next thirty minutes we sat riding in silence. I became fixated on the number of exposed electrical wires that lined the streets, feeling like they could all turn into Scarlett Johansson from the movie 'Lucy' at any given moment.

Maybe David Icke was right, after all.

Maybe the so-called Illuminati that's controlled by a race of grey aliens are trying to turn us all into machines and wipe out the human race.

Suddenly the van took a sharp left-hand turn onto a side road and pulled into a dirt driveway. Not having data on our phones to translate, we started in on a game of charades. "Here?" Dean said to the driver as he pointed to the address. The abandoned shack we were now in front of had a couple of cows aimlessly standing around and a rooster on the front stoop. The driver started speaking in Thai, while Dean started speaking back in English. Furiously flicking through some pictures on his phone, he found the real estate agent's phone number who had rented us the house and showed it to the driver.

As the magnitude of the possible scenario that we'd rented a tiny barn grew stronger, Dean and I shifted our bodies from polarizing magnets to now facing each other with despair in our eyes. As the taxi driver's voice got louder and more forceful, Dean looked at me. With his slate-blue eyes now filled with tears, he reached out to grab my hands. With his head tilted down like a naughty child who just got caught sniffing glue from under the kitchen table, he apologized.

"I'm sorry baby. Your happiness is the most important thing in the world to me. I only reacted that way because I feel like I let you down. I feel heartbroken and I had no other way to express it. Please forgive me?"

"It's OK, I get it Hun," I replied. How in the world could I ever stay mad at this man? Ever since that day I told him all I wanted in life was a platform to speak to women from, he was quietly masterminding what we were now embarking on. He quietly watched my feeble attempt at creating a brand through Konfidence by Kortney, to holding my hand into Kamp Konfidence, to supporting my decision to spend thousands of dollars on learning how to create a career through speaking to mothers and running retreats, and never once intervened.

Fuck, why does it feel so good to know that I was right, and that he in fact reacted instead of responded to my comment about getting the fuck out of Thailand as fast as humanly possible?

"Funny the only word I can pull out in Thai is the word 'crap'", Dean said as we laughed together.

"Yeah, I was literally just thinking that. I still can't believe we're here. Everything seems like it's happened so fast," I said as the taxi driver handed back his phone and said something in Thai with a smile on his face.

"At least our new residence isn't this three-sided wooden shed with a cow out the back, hey!" Dean replied while giving my hands a little squeeze with a new shred of hope in his eyes.

After reversing back onto the road, we were off again. After another short minute, we were again turning left and driving through some kind of rusted-out, yellow iron security gate with an abandoned guard shed that looked like it hadn't been operated or occupied since the Cold War. The taxi driver turned around and once again started talking in Thai with a big smile on his face to signify his pride in finding our village.

Overtired from the planning, selling, packing, jetlag, and absolute inability to let go of control, I fought back tears as I thought another thousand thoughts that I could never seem to switch off.

In a blink, we were wheeling our lives up the tiny driveway and towards the stairs into our new house. As soon as we walked through the door, my heart dropped as the reality sank in that we'd just left our beautiful, renovated piece of heaven in Queensland. A house where everything matched and was brand new, quietly sitting upon an acre that we used to own, to this tiny house that had not one appealing thing about it.

Now seeing why the rental website referred to the house as 'The Cloud House', I looked up to see the ceiling had a set-back for aesthetic purposes. However, far from aesthetic, the box was painted aqua blue with white clouds that reflected the artistic ability of that same six-year-old that gave me my scorpion tattoo.

Noticing I was blankly staring at the ceiling, the agent reached over and flipped a switch. Turning on a hidden neon purple strip of light that lit up the cotton ball "clouds" she said, "Very nice touch. Owner very proud of this addition. You like?"

Making a heart shape with my hands, I replied "Yes, I love purple."

Why do you fucking lie, Kortney?

Who cares if you hurt someone's feelings?

As Dean and the agent continued towards the back door, I walked into the 'master bathroom' and was met with my worst nightmare. Affixed to the walls were fire engine red, chive green, and mustard yellow tiles donning some kind of tapestry-styled design. Affixed to the floor were slate cement tiles around a plastic toilet that was basically inside the shower that not only lacked any kind of curtain or closure, but also had the heating electric-box openly exposed on the wall.

I tried to quelch the growing discomfort my OCD was causing me by shifting my focus inwards to stop myself from staring at the myriad of different styled tiles. Slowly walking closer so I could examine the bags under my eyes, I could feel the deep rumble in my stomach as I stared back at my reflection, I realized that the mirror was a dead ringer of the exact same mirror I was gazing into right before meeting Miguel, except this mirror wasn't encased in a frame.

I thought I was supposed to be moving forward in life.

This mirror reminds me of something I'd snort a line off of inside a crack house.

I can't believe I had a steam room built into the guest bathroom, and only used it three times in nearly two years.

Now I have a bathroom that looks like a pinata threw up on the walls of a jail cell

This is all just temporary.

All the kids we passed in the street kicking cans and riding scooters.

All the people working in their shop houses.

All the drivers riding their mobile food shops.

All of them looked happy and content, and here you are being an ungrateful, shitty little cunt.

The next day, Dean arranged for a rental car company to drop us off a two door Honda Jazz.

Slower than old mate at passport control, Dean reversed onto the street while I tried to find the website highlighting one of the closest places that offered massages by the blind community. Being a common practice in Thailand, a friend from Australia had told us about their experience. Thinking that a massage by a blind person might be one of the odder things I've ever done, aside from pissing in a vase when there was a perfectly good toilet down the hallway, I was clearly wrong. As we turned the corner, what we saw next, practically caused both of our buttholes to cinch up tighter than a Kardashian's waist trainer.

Slamming on the brakes, the white Honda Jazz skid to a stop in the middle of the road as Dean and I sat speechless.

Are we on the set of a movie?

Do I have fucking heat exhaustion from walking to the house to the car?

Surely this isn't really happening right now.

About a hundred feet in front of us, a woman wearing a baggy t-shirt and black cotton knee-length shorts was sobbing on her bare knees on the pavement. With her hands resembling the prayer emoji, she was screaming and pleading with the man twice her size who was towering behind her holding a brown leather belt in one hand, and a can of Tiger beer in the other. Dean and I sat frozen with our jaws wide open as he started walking around the woman as if he'd captured a prisoner of war. Now facing her straight on, he pounded the rest of his beer and crumpled the can in his hand before throwing it on the ground in front of the chain-link fence.

Suddenly the sound of a whip cracked through the as the belt hit the ground next to the woman. Sobbing now even harder, the man reached in his pocket.

"Oh my GOD, what the FUCK is happening!" I screamed. "Park the car, park the car!" I shouted as I slapped Dean's arm. With a wavering quiver I'd never heard in his voice before, Dean shouted back, "I am! I am! Fuck! For fuck fucking sake!"

After Dean pulled into what must have been some kind of visitor's parking spot, he threw the car into park and turned the car off. With both of our hearts beating out of our chests, we were once again sitting in silence, not knowing what the fuck to do.

Now parked, we watched as the man pulled a cell phone out of his pocket and proceeded to waive it around his head, screaming at the woman with tears streaming down her face.

"What the fuck do we do?" I said.

"It's better to ask for forgiveness than to ask for permission," he replied.

As Dean reached his hand over to open the car door, I flashed back to the only other time we'd encountered a domestic violence situation, which was back in Australia. We both immediately crossed the street and without a second thought jumped in between the drunk couple and started rough housing the man who we'd just witnessed shove his assumed girlfriend. The rush from feeling heroic stayed with us for hours afterwards.

But for some reason, today was oddly different. Completely unlike me to pause when agitated, restless or discontented, I abruptly reached out and put my hand on Dean's arm and said, "Hold on! Give me one second. I'm just going to message Derrick really quick." Derrick and I hadn't met yet, but a friend connected us on Facebook as he was in the program and had been living in the area for over a year. Just like when I quit drinking in 2007, my hands were trembling from the adrenaline pumping through my veins as I tried to open up Facebook messenger. As fast as I could type, I explained the situation:

Hey man! Can't wait to catch up and hit a meeting. Def need one right now. But really quickly, we're heading out and there's some woman getting her ass beat in the middle of the street. I'm shocked I'm even messaging you right now, but for some reason something told me to ask you if it was safe to intervene. Thanks brother and let me know when and where you'll be for a meeting!

Noticing that Derrick's status was showing 'online', I sat and stared at the blue box containing the message I had just sent. "What are we doing?" asked Dean. Feeling like I was about to combust from a combination of rage, sadness, and helplessness, I replied, "Waiting to see if God has a message for us."

'What the fuck did I just say?' I thought as Derrick's little circular Facebook profile picture dropped down and landed next to my message. "I beg your pardon!" Dean said.

"Fucking hold on! Derrick just saw my message!"

Sitting there waiting for him to start typing, I could feel my level of anxiety grow thicker than an ivy bush; no matter how many times I pulled it out by its roots, it seemed to grow back.

I wonder if he thinks I'm crazy.

Maybe he's in the middle of something important and is super annoyed I even messaged him?

He's seen my message, why hasn't he started typing yet?

Fuck I should know better than to feel this way.

I feel like a fraud once again.

I used to tell the girls that came through Kamp Konfidence to not take it personally if someone read their text message or Facebook message and didn't reply straight away.

It didn't mean shit. Firstly, no one owed them anything, let alone in any amount of given time. Secondly, maybe they had their phone open to your chat message and weren't even by their phone. Thirdly, maybe someone else had their phone.

I used to tell them that just because someone hadn't looked at their message, but you could see their status showed they were 'online', didn't mean that they were purposely ignoring them. Maybe they have ADHD like I do and get distracted very easily!

Wonder if Thailand sells ADHD medication over the counter here?

Suddenly Derrick's little blue bubble appeared and the three moving dots started dancing.

"I can see he's typing. Just hold on a sec," I said. Seconds later, Derrick's reply popped up:

Do NOT intervene. I highly advise you go about your business and not play God right now. I know it'll be incredibly hard, but what often happens is the authorities will get called and the Thai police will somehow corroborate with the abuser, and it will somehow turn out to be your fault, and you'll be left having to pay off the cops so you don't get taken to jail. Or he'll more than likely have a knife on him. I have a black belt and train in several different martial arts and have had to talk myself out of similar situations because I've seen it happen to a handful of Westerners. Good luck and see you soon.

Although I felt completely defeated that I wasn't going to be a hero, I had enough clarity to realise that I'd finally listened to my intuition. As much as I wanted to play God in that moment and save the woman who was kneeling on the hot concrete, I also knew that I could only control myself. Controlling other people, places, and things were no longer my job.

. . . .

The concept of 'goals not controls' came to me when writing a keynote for our first live event for GRRRL. I realised that all of these things I was "supposed to be", were just stepping stones to lead me to where I am today. Konfidence by

Kortney was the vision of a brand where I'd speak to women and let them know about my time in the muscle fetish industry. I wanted you to know that the world is not what we think it is, and that the world finds beauty in everything that isn't on the cover of a magazine. I wanted you to know that it's ok for men to cry and for women to lift weights. But of course, that brand turned into Kamp Konfidence, and eventually, that turned into GRRRL Clothing (not to mention there were three other brands between Kamp Konfidence and GRRRL).

The overall goal between these three brands was teaching women and girls the tools that lead to the development of self love and building a sisterhood throughout. But had I gotten caught up with the controls (trying to control the detail of everything, and assuming I knew how it was supposed to look, feel, sound, smell, etc), I would have quit along the way. The details of the overall goal looks very different from when I first started. The 'Konfidence by Kortney' logo (which unfortunately is tattooed on my lower back!) has a cyan color and script font, whereas the GRRRL logo is black and montserrat font. The challenge most of us face is because we have no visible proof constantly in front of us that there is a power greater than ourselves that will help guide us to where we want to go, we repeatedly try and take back our control (our will) and do this shit through the power of our ego. So, remember to stay focused on the overall goal of what you're trying to achieve, and let go of the microscopic detail of what you think things are supposed to turn out like.

Do the F*cking Work

Do you feel like you're failing at executing your mission in life?

Describe a situation where you thought you were failing but it turned out you weren't.

If you're currently in that situation, have you figured out what your main overarching goal of your mission is?

If so, can you commit to focusing on just that and trusting that The Universe will provide you with the right path to achieve that goal?

If not, what is it?

Describe a time you find yourself playing "God"? (i.e. thinking you often know what's best for other people)

According to Stuart Wild and Robert A. Schwartz, author of "Your Souls Plan", our souls signed up for all this shit before they came down. For people who belong to religious bodies that only believe in one life, this can be a challenging concept to grapple with. But for me, it completely resonated. The homeless person begging on the corner with a small child. The woman who opened a box with a pipe bomb inside that blew off her legs and disfigured her face upon exploding. The drug addict who ran over and killed her own daughter in a drunk driving accident. Our souls signed up for these 'horrible' experiences before they came down in order to learn the deeper meaning of something.

Write about an event in your life that at the time was horrible, but eventually you turned into a blessing or great learning experience.

If you haven't figured out how to turn your horrible event into a blessing or learning experience yet, think about how you might be able to one day in the future.

Thinking back to assuming Derrick had seen my message on Facebook, let's reflect on how you're showing up on virtual communication.

Do you respond right away to every single text message, or do you purposely wait to reply to non-urgent texts to remind people that you are not required to respond instantaneously?

On the flip side, do you take it personally when someone doesn't reply straight away?

Studies have shown that effective communication is only 7% dependent upon the actual words themselves. The rest is based on body language, pitch, tone and speed. Recognising that virtual communication often only relies on written words, how often do you engage in online communication?

Do you have important conversations via text message or direct message instead of waiting to see the person in person, or picking up the phone to call someone?

Describe a time you interpreted someone's text message the wrong way because you got the tone wrong.

Describe a time when someone misunderstood you because they took your tone wrong.

Scan here for more good shit.

THY WILL BE DONE, NOT MINE

*B*ack in familiar stomping grounds, I did what every good addict does--I found a meeting.

"Hi! My name is Kortney, my favorite flavor is more, and I'm an alcoholic/addict visiting from Thailand."

As usual, my peers were excited to have someone attend their fellowship from a faraway land.

Without fail, I heard exactly what I needed to hear from the speaker. With the floor now open for sharing, I opened my mouth after a long period of silence.

'I fucking hate silence.'

"Hi, my name's Kortney, and I'm still a crazy alcoholic!"

"Hi Kortney!" sang out in unison from the room.

"I feel like I'm about to explode! I loved hearing your story John, because of course, it was exactly what I needed to hear to remind myself that I am not in control. I know the absolute root cause of all of my misery is my inability to let go, and it's amazing how we come into these rooms and hear from a complete stranger who we can absolutely relate to, and suddenly feel like family."*

I let the vibration from the rooms' applause's wash over me as a complete sense of relief and bliss hit me. I hadn't shared something that passionate in some time, and immediately started to question if I had talked for too long and whether I'd slipped too much into my ego.

I hope I don't turn out to be one of those people in the rooms who talks a great game on a group level, but in their personal lives remains fucking miserable.

Before I could have another self-centered thought, several people immediately attempted to share at the same time following all of the shit that just came out of my mouth. For what little time was left in the meeting, I sat and felt accomplished as each person who shared thanked me for sharing something they considered profound. As I sat and listened to everyone, I questioned why I loved this feeling of being liked.

As Martha continued to talk about how deeply she related to how easy it had become for her to forget the gift of desperation that had brought her into the rooms just a few months prior, my mind started to drift back to self-obsession.

Why do I crave this acceptance from other people?

At least it's not attention I crave anymore.

I mean, there's some level of me that still craves attention, but nowhere as nearly as bad as I used to be.

But what started it all?

Still staring directly into Martha's eyes, I nodded my head as if I was hanging onto every word she was saying and not stuck in my own head. Just like the dreadlocks on my ex, white pot-growing boyfriend's head, I shouldn't have been there. I just couldn't stop thinking about myself and why I needed this approval.

After what seemed like the longest day of my life, aside from the day I detoxed off of Oxycontin, or the day my Dad drove me to rehab, or the day Adriana crashed my Honda Accord, or the day I crashed my Honda Civic, or the day I crashed my second and third Honda Accord, or the day I wrecked my Honda CBR600, or the day UFC 193 arrived, or the day we landed in Thailand, I made it back to the hotel and crashed hard. But this time I was crashing into a bed, clean and sober, and next to one of my best friends who I always used to leave hanging, waiting for me to no-show somewhere when I was drinking and high.

. . . .

When my alarm went off at seven a.m., I'd already been awake for nearly two hours listening to my brother saw logs while I lay there thinking about what the day ahead was going to hold. After turning my alarm off, I bolted out of bed and got into the shower. I had my hair and makeup artist arriving at eight a.m., and still needed to do some air squats and my ab routine. Clearly, I was going to end up like one of those people who just sounded great in meetings, but miserable in their daily life because I had zero fucks to give, and even fewer attempts at developing some kind of morning spiritual ritual of prayer and meditation.

Although I had just ranted on from a soapbox the night before about 'needing daily medicine or I'd surely die', I did the square root of fuck-all that morning to connect with my higher power. Other than to say a five second prayer before my feet hit the industrial carpet, I made my bullshit attempt at asking The Universe to guide and direct me throughout the day.

I thought back to what my last sponsor had boldly told me. In regard to my inability to spend any significant amount of time working towards deepening my relationship with a higher power, he said:

"I imagine you didn't fall in love with your husband by waking up every morning and spending five short seconds saying some gibberish bullshit to him, without any kind of conscious connection. Furthermore, without listening to what his reply might be, I doubt you would still be together unless the sex was just out of this world."

Whatever. I'll get there in the end. But just for today, I'm not going to drink or use drugs, and potentially be seen by millions of people across America who think my legs are disgusting and fat.

As time often does, the morning had flown by and I was standing in the lobby with my brother waiting for Shavone and her grand plan to arrive.

After what seemed like eternity, Jeff, a frail looking boy sporting a plastic badge and lanyard greeted us.

From that point on, it was the game of 'hurry up and wait'.

Starting to get annoyed that it was now almost three p.m. and my hair wanted to do anything but stay in its PiNK inspired blow-out, I started to outwardly show signs that I was no longer interested in being the teacher's pet. I was hungry, exhausted, and beyond bored. Reading my energy, Jack promised they'd get back to me with an update soon, and that the audience was being filtered into the theatre and filming would begin shortly after.

Once I heard the word audience, I suddenly felt a little surge of energy reappear and decided to go back to my corner and do some more air squats and lunges.

After twenty minutes of pumping up my legs, I picked up my phone and sent my brother a text to find out if our aunts and two size athletes, Size Ali and Amenah, had found him.

Within seconds, my brother had texted me back to let me know they were all together as a group and in line waiting to go inside.

Another hour had gone by, and my original handler Jeff had popped back by to say sorry for having to wait for so long, and that hopefully I would be in one of the first groups of acts to go out on stage.

"No worries. Keep me posted," I said as I sat back down.

Saying 'sorry' doesn't fix the broken plate you just dropped on the floor, Jeff. Aimlessly tossing the word 'sorry' out doesn't magically glue the pieces back together, Jeff.

Another hour and a half passed, and I was now at a boiling point.

Since ten a.m. I'd been sitting in this giant building with my dick in my hand for absolutely no reason. I could have at least slept in until ten a.m.!

Trying to figure out what to do next, I once again sent my brother a text for an update, and immediately wished I hadn't.

"Damn Kort! This auditorium is massive! There must be about two thousand people here! We've seen a few acts come out that were pretty cool. Looks like they interview you for about one minute before you "perform". Any idea when you're on?"

Suddenly feeling like I had a football covered in barbed wire stuck in my throat, I wanted to speak, but had no one to talk to. Stuck with my own thoughts and stuck without any kind of definitive answers or control, I continued to sit while I started to feel my heart pounding out the side of my neck.

Fuck.

Two thousand people?

I was thinking two hundred.

Holy shit.

Maybe I should pray?

As soon as the word 'pray' entered my mind, the words "write it down and let it go" followed.

Not knowing who or what put that thought there, as it certainly was not KO, I walked over to my backpack and pulled out a notebook and erasable pen. Thinking back to how long I waffled on the night before at the last meeting, I felt even more pressure trying to figure out what I could possibly say that would be impactful in sixty seconds or less.

Ironic that we used to play the game I made up at Kamp Konfidence, 'if you knew then you'd know that...' where the girls had sixty seconds to try... ughhhhhh there is no such thing as the word try, bitch! You're either pregnant or you're not! But they got sixty seconds to attempt to tell their life story. My Higher Power must be one funny sonofabitch.

After a few moments, the words came out on paper as smoothly as the words rolled off my tongue when the incident with Gary resurfaced. In as little as five paragraphs, I crafted something eloquent, powerful, and punchy in the event I got the chance to just talk. I read and reread my five paragraphs over and over again while walking around, until I had realized another hour had passed. With my newly found lighter grip on an attempt to control what was going to happen next, I felt a sense of ease flow in.

Huh… imagine that. One second I think I'm failing, then the next I think I'm growing. I was speaking last night about developing self-awareness, and now I'm seeing that by taking action and letting go, things have shifted. How is it you can think you know something, but clearly don't know it--because you're not doing it? Maybe that's where the term 'sometimes quickly, sometimes slowly' comes from. Fuck, who knows. All I know is I'd kill for some sweet potato fries right now.

The time was now eight fifteen p.m. and I was trying to find the meaning of life. One thing I knew for sure is that I never wanted to go to prison because I would surely, surely die. But not of an alcoholic death or drug overdose, but from boredom. Just as I put my legs up on a table adjacent to me and closed my eyes, Jeff came speeding towards me, clapping his hands together.

"Ok, Kortney! It's finally your call time!" he shouted enthusiastically.

Suddenly the adrenaline was back for the umpteenth time that day, and I jumped up.

"Follow me backstage and we'll get you out there, champ!" he said as I trailed close behind.

Did this motherfucker just call me Champ? Haven't heard that one in a while, I thought as I stayed close on his heels. As we briskly walked from one side of the giant building to the other, I could feel some level or resentment now starting to creep in.

I know resentment is an unspoken expectation, so what expectation did I have today that wasn't met? I should have known by now that this is how TV works until you're some kind of star. Sit in a room all day on edge when we know you're a control freak… it'll be fun!

But what's my part in this situation? Do I expect everyone to know that I'm a control freak with an out of control ego? Or did too many teachers tell me I was someone special from a young age and I've got it all wrong? Or did the word 'champ' just strike a nerve somewhere deep in my brain that makes me want to knockout every single person in this building?

I imagine I still have more work to do around that. Although I feel like I've forgiven that sonofabitch, I'm like that little boy who cowered in the corner, terrified while his father beat the shit out of his mother. He swore he'd never hit a woman, but at some point in his young adult life, he involuntarily repeats the same actions of his father. Just like I swore I'd never drink like my mom. We think we clear shit out, we clean shit up, but does it ever really go away?

At least I don't have gastro right now. Fuck I have to pee. I always have to pee at an inconvenient time. Fuck my legs look fat and puckered right now.

Another forty minutes dragged on, and I was finally getting pulled to the actual backstage. After briefly getting an introduction to the host Nick Cannon and shooting some b-roll of us talking and me "warming up", it was nearly go-time. Next on deck to finally take the stage after almost eleven hours of waiting, I was close enough to peer through an opening of the floor to ceiling ruby red velvet curtains. Catching a glimpse of the endless sea of bodies spread across the historical looking theatre, I saw the panel of celebrity judges and realized it was indeed about to go down.

'Show time motherfucker,' suddenly went through my head. I was immediately brought to the thought of how the last time that thought went through my head, coupled with this level of intense anxiety, was the moment I had just finished putting eyeliner on in the rearview mirror of Bubba's truck and managed to chew up fifteen pain pills on the drive down, before going in to take part in my first, and last, enema session.

As my heart started pounding in my neck again, I paused and realized how great it felt to not have a single desire to checkout.

I don't need a shot of tequila.

I don't need a handful of pills.

I don't need to pound half a bottle of Robitussen.

Sure, I wasn't satisfied with the way my legs looked. And yes--I still give a fuck what these people might think of me, but thank God I don't have the desire to get fucked up right now!'

Right then and there, I paused. As if it was something instinctual that I'd been doing my whole life, I finally remembered to stop and pray when irritable, restless, or discontented.

With my eyes open, I looked up at the grandiose cathedral ceiling, and more or less repeated the same words I had said fifteen hours earlier from bed before setting foot on the carpet. The only difference was that this time I consciously connected to what I was doing and saying. I wasn't mindlessly just saying some shit without any kind of intention behind it. I purposefully and intently asked my higher power a question and made a simple request.

Dear God.

Please guide and direct me out here tonight.

Let me be an instrument and your voice to spread positivity and love.

Please remove me from my ego.

I trust everything is exactly as it's meant to be.

Let me do your will, not mine.

Thank you.

In an instant, I immediately released any fear, worry and anxiety, and felt five foot seven inches tall and bulletproof.

Like clockwork, Jack and Nick appeared by my side.

"Hey grrrrrrrrrl! Looks like we've saved the best for last! You're literally the last act!" Jack said as Nick followed up with, "You ready to do this or WHAT!" in some kind of an attempt to get me fired up after sitting around for twelve hours.

"So, as we discussed earlier, Nick will call you out from the stage," Jack said before I interjected. "You must be thinking of another grrrrrrrl, although there is only one of me! But no, we haven't discussed any of this," I said with a smile. Feeling proud of myself for stating the facts, Jack apologized, "Oh I'm so sorry. It's been SUCH a crazy day. But that's really all you need to know for now. You'll just head out when you hear the crowd. The crew will set the watermelons up, five on each side of you."

With a genuine smile, I joyfully said "Copy that!", as they headed off in different directions. As Nick slipped through the exact spot in the curtain I was peering out through just a few minutes earlier, the b-roll guy joined by Jeff and came up to wish me well and to "Knock em' out, KO!"

Like I'd been in a time warp, suddenly I heard the crowd erupt like a volcano while everyone backstage was shouting "go, go, go!" As I stepped through the faint slit in the curtain, I felt the velvet brush against my legs. Shocked that my mind didn't immediately pull up to KO's front door by the trigger of something touching my legs, I was clearly being driven by Kortney, who was prepared, stepping onto the stage, ready to do God's work.

Dressed in black laced-up combat boots that came to the middle of my calves, dark blue jean shorts, and a GRRRL POWER slate grey tank top, I walked out onto the stage waiving like Princess Diana greeting her adoring fans as I approached Nick Cannon to take the mic and take my space.

The spotlights were shining so bright, I could hardly see into the crowd of faces watching behind the judge's panel. The same wattage that was blinding me, must have been shining down on them because they were so well lit, I felt like I could see straight into their souls. As Simon bent over and spoke into the mic, I assumed the 'power position', standing with my legs spread at shoulder width distance, my hands in front of my sternum like the one I busted on Clark. In the shape of a triangle, my fingertips touched between my right and left hand as I held a slight smile and slowly looked each judge in the eyes for a few slow seconds each.

"Uh…why hello there. Tell us your name and what brings you here tonight?" said Simon.

"My name is Kortney Olson, and I'm here to take the record of most watermelons smashed between my legs in sixty seconds back from a woman in the Ukraine," I said without blinking.

"Hmmm. Sounds delightful," said Simon.

"Well, I've got to admit, Simon… I was deathly afraid of you prior to coming out on stage," I said.

As to say I had it all backwards, in a very slow, drawn out tone of voice, "You're afraid of me?" Simon replied while looking at my legs.

With the audience laughing, I was instantly snapped into my element.

Having an opportunity to once again employ my stellar professional developmental skills I'd learned throughout my "wasted" hazy life as a sales professional, I made sure to use the judges' names as many times as possible.

"Yes, Simon. I don't watch a lot of TV, I'm too busy lifting weights. But the few times I've caught you over the years, "they" always portray you as some horrific asshole," I said with an adorable smile on my face. Once again, the audience was filled with laughter.

"Well Ms. Olson, tell us a little bit about yourself. Like how in God's name did you come across this talent?" Simon said as he sat back in his chair with a grin on his face, but arms folded. Feeling like I was getting some kind of vibe from Simon, I kept going. "I mean, look at you now! Your body language is telling me that you could care less what I'm about to say, but that adorable smirk on your face is telling me otherwise. Like you're soooooo mysterious," I said back.

As laughter once again filled the air from the crowd, I started looking at the other three judges while I quickly caught myself wondering if I was attempting to become Simon's teacher's pet.

Was I crossing that incredibly thin line of using my charisma to flirt and obtain a man's approval?

Was I simply being entertaining?

Was I trying to win him over when I should be focusing on the two women sitting in the center?

After the crowd stopped laughing, I came straight from the heart, "Long story short, I grew up hating my legs. I was supposed to be the first female president of the United States, but I got sidetracked by drugs because I was desperate to lose weight," I said before pausing and turning my gaze straight into Supermodel Heidi Klum's eyes before carrying on. "I so badly wanted to look like Supermodel Kate Moss, that I lost sight of everything else," I said before moving my eyes to Mel B. "By the age of twenty one, I was diagnosed with depression, an eating disorder, and as a full-blown drug addict and alcoholic, all because I wanted to be skinny. After finding the gym as a new obsession, a boyfriend challenged me to "try" and pop a watermelon between my legs. I never back down from a challenge unless it's related to alcohol, because then I just get naked and start punching people in the mouth," I said now looking straight at Howie Mandel.

"So, after that day, it's become my thing. I've since been crowned the 'Woman with the world's deadliest thighs' by *the* Stan Lee and have gone on to create a revolutionary clothing line to empower women and girls to be strong," I concluded while fixing my gaze back towards Simon while maintaining my stoic power stance.

Suddenly, Howie Mandel chimed in. "Ok… sooooo, are you married? Have kids?" he asked. "No kids. I believe there are too many on this planet already that need parents, and yes, I'm married to an older Englishman. Hence my weak knees for Simon's accent," I said while looking back at Simon.

Hearing over two thousand people laugh was giving me some kind of high I'd never felt before.

"Ok… and what does your husband do?" Howie asked.

"The dishes," I replied.

The laughter was at an all-time high, but I could see that Mel B, Heidi, and Howie were ready to go home.

Taking charge, Mel B leaned into the mic and calmly said in her British accent, "Well let's get on with it then, shall we?"

Leaning in with his forearms on the table, Simon leaned into the mic and said, "Are you ready?" I nodded and turned around to walk to where the watermelons were lined up on the ground, five on each side. As instructed in the hours prior to stepping on stage, as soon as the remake of ZZ Top's, "Legs" came on, the timer would be starting the sixty second countdown.

After sitting on the ground, I rolled my shorts up a bit, causing my skin to bulge and dimple as it seemed to be pouring out the sides of my shorts. Shockingly, I was unscathed. I bent down and quickly laced up my boots a little tighter, did a few forward stretches with my legs extended straight out in front of me for a dash of added entertainment, then got ready to reach for my first melon.

As soon as the song came on, I immediately reached out for a melon. Shoving it between my legs, I squeezed with every force in every cell of my body. I was exerting so much energy that I felt like I was about to pass out. I released the melon, turned it one hundred and eighty degrees to get a different angle on it, and went again. With my butt up off the ground, my knees pushing in towards one another, my ankle bones smashing together, and my hips thrusting straight forward, I could hear the watermelon start to squish and move around inside, but nothing was exploding.

With the audience screaming their heads off, I knew I was running out of time and went for one of the watermelons I knew was the ripest of the bunch. I shoved it in, gave it a hard squeeze and watched it explode. As soon as it popped, I tossed it off to the side and went for another one, only to hear the obnoxious timer drill my ear canals. I was out of time.

Fortunately, no one had pushed their "X" button in the middle of my attempt, but at the same time, a rush of disappointment briefly washed over me. I had so much belief that these watermelons would've all combusted without too much effort, and yet I somehow managed to pick the hardest one of the lot to start with.

Grabbing the cotton towel behind me, I stood up and brushed the extra bits off my shorts before wiping the sticky juice off the inside of my legs and walked back to the middle of the stage.

"What happened Kortney!" Simon said.

"I truly have no idea, Simon. I must have picked the one spawn of the devil to start with," I said.

"Well, I want to send you onto the next round, but these clowns needed to see the record broken," he said as he nodded his head down towards the other three judges.

Still feeling immense disappointment, I pushed it aside and apparently did God's work by concluding with a small pep-talk.

"At the end of the day, for any girl or woman out there watching, I hope you realize that your worth is not equated to your exterior. We are built for strength and power, and that it's OK to have big, giant legs. So many of us never try new things and spend our lives in fear because we think we're not good enough. I could stand here and feel disappointed, but what matters the most is that I gave it a go. I did my best, and that's all I can ask of myself. I doubt you're going to go home thinking what a shameful failure I was tonight, and if you did, that's none of my business what you think of me. Just know that you are perfect and more powerful than you could ever imagine. If Simon or Howie got the flu, or kicked in the balls, it's game over. But women? We push tiny humans out of our bodies and get on with life the next day like nothing happened!"

As soon as I stopped speaking, the crowd hit a new height of decibels and energy. Simon stood up and clapped along with the sea of bodies for a few seconds, then grabbed his mic off the table before saying, "Well Kortney, I want you to promise me that you'll come back and audition for us and bring that record back here to the United States."

"Ok, Simon. You got it," I said.

"Come give me a hug," he said.

With my headset bouncing on the back of my shorts, I lightly jogged across the stage and down the four short stairs to reach him. Reaching out from the bottom stair to keep my legs as far away from him as possible, we hugged and kissed each other on the cheek. I skipped a step and stepped back to the top of the stage and paused to wave back at the crowd as they were still cheering, jogged across the stage and disappeared behind the same slit in the curtain I'd previously walked out from.

Everyone backstage came over to congratulate me and comment how great my speech was, but all I could think about was failing again. Through forced enthusiasm, I thanked everyone for having me on, and started to head back up the stairs to get my belongings. As soon as I started to walk, my thighs stuck together from the dried watermelon juice. In an instant, I was straight back to self-loathing and feeling incredibly sorry for myself.

After getting my stuff, I met my aunts, my brother, and my two size athletes, Ali and Amenah, outside. After giving everyone a hug, we headed up to the room so I could change and have a short visit with everyone. Now surrounded by company, I was able to stop feeling the depths of my disappointment because I had five other people telling me what a wonderful appearance I had. Minus one aunt who basically laughed and said, "Yeah, like what were they thinking bringing you out anyway? What were you going to do for the next act?"

Brushing it off, I smiled and gave everyone a hug, thanking them for driving out to come and support me.

After saying goodbye, I went into the bathroom and held back tears as I took off my shorts and stuck a white hand towel under the sink to wipe off the remaining juice.

Why do I always fuck up?

'I missed my opportunity to inspire so many little girls.'

After getting cleaned up and my bottoms changed, I came out to my brother sitting on the corner of his queen bed. He always knew what to say to me.

"Kort, I know you're disappointed, I know you."

"Yeah I'm having a hard time letting it go. I really thought those watermelons were going to be so easy," I hesitantly replied.

"But no one, and I mean no one could have said what you did, and how you said it. What you said was so powerful, and you were so on-point. People hardly remember what you said, they just remember how you made them feel, and I guarantee you made so many women and girls feel better about themselves," he said sternly as an older brother does when he lectures his baby sister.

"Thanks babe. Shall we go get some food? I'm fucking starving!" I replied with a lighter heart and outlook on it all.

As we headed on foot to find the closest spot that was still open, we walked into BJ's along with what seemed like the rest of the entire audience from the filming. As we were leaning against the wall waiting to be seated, up walked a man that appeared to be in his forties.

"Hey! I was in the audience and just had to tell you how amazing you were. I have a daughter and really wish she would have been with me," he said with gentle eyes. "Ahhhhh thank you, man! I truly appreciate it," I replied with a smile while I reached out to shake his hand. "Do your best to relay the message to her for me!" I said as he headed out the front door.

Before another minute passed, a hostess was calling our name, "Olson- party of two!" Practically falling off the wall, we walked up with a smile, and followed the young woman to our table. After navigating around a sea of tables, our hostess stopped in a booth and set our menu's down on the table. Just as she started to ask for our drink orders, up walked a mother and daughter.

"Hi! We're so sorry to interrupt, but we had to come and tell you how much what you said on stage meant to us both tonight," she said. Dressed like a conservative Mom, she looked like she was probably around my age. "Why thank you! I'd be lying if I said I wasn't a little disappointed, but like I said, all we can do is our best!" I replied. I looked down at the little girl and asked her age. "Well hello Miss. How old are you? Eight?" I said. "Yes," she replied bashfully. "Awesome! That's a great age! In a couple years you're going to start asking yourself all sorts of silly questions around your body and whether or not it's good enough, but I'm telling you it's perfect just the way it is. All you have to do is focus on being strong, and that's it! Simple!" I said enthusiastically as I reached out to give her a high-five.

"Kort, you want an Arnold Palmer?" my brother asked.

"Sorry to interrupt. I know my little sister is kind of a big deal!" he said with a giant smile on his face.

"You know it!" I replied and then turned back to the mother and daughter and thanked them for stopping and saying hi.

I plopped down in the booth and perused the menu while I started in on the never-ending inner dialogue on food choices. Doing the Benjamin Franklin close on myself, I went back and forth on the pros and cons over the plethora of amazing choices that were making my mouth actually salivate.

In the midst of my inner turmoil, our waitress appeared with our Arnold Palmers and asked if we were ready. "You go first, Bri," I said to my brother as I frantically tried to make a simple decision. After ordering a club sandwich with fries, it was my turn.

Tacos.

Salmon with rice and broccoli.

"Mmmmmmmmm, nearly there," I said with a sense of panic rising in my throat.

Staring at the menu whilst wading through the feelings of disappointment I was already having, coupled with not being able to work out for a few days, I blurted out, "I'll have the salmon please with the salad and balsamic dressing on the side, and broccoli for my other side, thanks!"

Why couldn't I just eat whatever the fuck I wanted and not have this stupid conversation over and over again.

"Sounds tasty, Kort!", my brother said laughing.

"Better share a couple fries with me fucker!" I said.

. . . .

Coming back once again to this concept of a higher power, I constantly have to remind myself that I'm purely here to do God's will (again, whoever that is), and not my own. My personal will (created by my ego, which wants to be the best, wants to be comfortable, wants to be praised) wanted to crush every single one of those watermelons and "win" while on America's Got Talent. But God's will was clearly different. Because I prayed (another loaded word that most people equate to religion but simply means 'to talk to a power greater than ourselves) I was able to gracefully deliver a message to the world that was probably way more powerful, meaningful, and effective than me crushing ten watermelons.

This concept of 'let go and let God' is so challenging for me (and most people) that I even got part of the ninth step tattooed on my forearm, thinking that it would help me remember. It reads: Please remove me of the bondage of self, so I may better do thy will.

'Bondage of self' means the ego. On a daily basis, I simply ask my higher power to help me break free from my ego, and let me serve human kind.

An analogy that has helped me infinitely, is God (however you define him/she/them/it) is like wifi. You would never walk into a Starbucks and ask for the wifi password, then ask for someone to explain to you how it works before you can access it. Even though you can't see the wifi, you know it works, and you never question it. The 'Spirit of the Universe' is the same. Just because you can't see it, or necessarily define it (yet), there is something there if you remain open-minded and willing to ask for guidance.

Do the F*cking Work

Spend some time analyzing your connection to a power greater than yourself. Is your higher power the energy of a group? Do you feel most connected to the unknown when you're in nature? In a church? Completely lost with it all (been there, done that!)?

In what ways have you experienced "God shots" (aka coincidences, or luck, or hearing exactly what you needed to hear at the exact right moment).

How does the word "God" and "prayer" make you feel?

If you're struggling with finding purpose right now, describe how by showing up as your authentic self that you're being a leader and living with purpose?

My Ted Talk for extra credit reading (my continued share from the AA meeting)

* "Tomorrow I'm due to film in front of a live studio audience for America's Got Talent, and I'm anxious enough to give myself a cold sore. I've been on TV a handful of times, so this isn't my first rodeo, but I'm scared shitless of this Simon guy and full of fear that I'm going to disappoint people if I don't pull off what I'm supposed to do. And I don't even know exactly what it is I'm supposed to be doing yet! How stupid is that? It's a long story as to how I got started smashing watermelons between my legs, and at the time when I first did it, I certainly wasn't clean. We're talking about alcoholism here, so I'll keep it to that. But this little act has morphed into some symbol of women's empowerment. As someone who grew up absolutely hating her legs, to now being crowned 'the woman with the world's deadliest thighs' by *the* Stan Lee, this is all surreal because a majority of my using and drinking stemmed from having such poor body

445

image and self-esteem."

"So after several years of continual sobriety, it's remarkable that I'm now living my dream and have a platform to speak to women and girls from about being powerful and strong, but all day I've been obsessing on my legs not looking lean enough, and dwelling in the "what if" land over failure."

"I've felt like a fraud all day and nothing is ever good enough. I was pissed off that I wasn't flown over in business class because I think I'm special. I was pissed off that I'm not as lean as I wanted to be after half-ass dieting for twenty days because my new country doesn't sell anything Western that I'm used to. I was pissed off that I ate the dessert on the flight over and that I simply couldn't leave it alone because I hate wasting food. I was pissed off that I had to spend the day shopping for watermelons without any kind of forewarning. I'm annoyed that I still don't have clear instructions as to what I'm even supposed to be doing tomorrow. How absolutely stupid does all of this sound?"

"The reality is, I'm being an ungrateful asshole because I've lost sight of how bad it got, and how desperately I wanted to quit drinking and using but couldn't on my own. Once the obsession went away, and life started getting better, I began putting my recovery on the back burner. I mean, yes at least I haven't picked up a drink or a drug in many years, and that shit is a miracle, but I could be full of serenity and peace if I just worked a better program. But instead, I'm too worried about whether or not you all, along with Simon Cowell, will end up liking me or not. I'm too worried about controlling the outcome of a company I've just launched in an industry I know nothing about."

"My only job is to stay clean and sober, and ask God, whoever that may be, to guide me to do their will. That's it!

And yet I make everything into such a fucking spectacle! Constantly in my head, over-thinking every little thing. Setting a goal, reaching it, and not even stopping to acknowledge and appreciate what I've done. I know this journey of recovery is something that takes time and is different for every single one of us. I've heard in these rooms all over the world that there is no wrong way to stay sober, but I guess I'll start working a more serious program when I get in enough pain."

"I know I've probably talked way too long, but I'll end on this analogy that I heard in early recovery that really resonated with me. Someone pointed out that what we're dealing with when it comes to alcoholism, is the equivalent of stage-four bone cancer. The severity of our "dis-ease", and I say that in two words because all disease means is 'dis' and 'ease', the opposite of ease... it's not something like a crusty, puss-infested penis that's about to fall off someone's body! When I first came into the rooms and was told I had a 'dis-ease', I wanted to die. In rehab when I was told I had a 'mental illness', I wanted to die. It never occurred to me that everyone has mental health, and all mental illness means, is that my mind isn't really healthy! It didn't mean that I was a crusty old penis with an insane mind that might cause me to strip my clothes off and run down the street naked or light someone's car on fire- although I've done all of that while drinking."

"But what I'm saying is, people with stage-four cancer have to take their medication every single goddamn day. If they don't, they die. The same goes for us. Although we aren't visibly sick on the outside, on the inside, mentally, we are at the same level of risk as having that stage-four diagnosis- at least for this alcoholic and addict. Whenever I drink, I blackout and get behind the wheel with no regard to who I might kill. I sleep with people with no regard to that crusty penis I might break off. Unlike people who have a physical terminal illness, we usually look pretty well put together. We haven't had to endure chemo or radiation and we have our hair. Well except you John, you're looking pretty bald my friend!"

I paused while the room of sixty or so people erupted with laughter before I continued on.

"We haven't had to have blood or bone marrow transplants and haven't lost so much weight that we resemble a skeleton. I mean, don't get me wrong, some of us are pretty tore up from the floor up by the time we find our way into these rooms. But, in general, we look semi-ok. But if I don't work some form of a program on a daily basis by staying connected to you guys, talking to my higher power, and turning my will over to the best of my ability, which clearly isn't great at the moment, by helping someone who is out there struggling with this illness so I never forget how bad it actually got--I'll be dead."

"It will only take a second for my mind to tell me I'm cured, and that I can handle just one drink if I don't stay connected to you. Somehow this dis-ease remarkably gives me amnesia and I forget about every single time I wanted to kill myself because I couldn't stop drinking, no matter how hard I tried to control it."

"I should be so grateful that I even have the opportunity to go on national television. I get to fly on an airplane. I get to go pick out my own watermelons. I get to work out despite the number of times I've driven in a blackout and woken up not remembering being behind the wheel. I get to experience living in another part of the world. Most people will never even get an opportunity to own a passport and step foot on a plane. Some people are confined to a wheelchair because they were hit by a drunk driver, by one of us! They can't even get on a leg press machine because they had to have them amputated!"

Throwing my hands up in the air, I shouted the next statement.

"MY GOD, HOW DO I ALLOW MYSELF TO GET INTO SUCH A STATE OF UNGRATEFULNESS AND SELF-PITY?"

Reading the room, I could feel this was hitting home.

"I used to look at this program like a death sentence. What possibly could be glamorous about holding hands and saying stupid prayers with people I had nothing in common with? I hated all of you at first. I focused on all of our differences and ignored the one similarity that ties us all together: We cannot drink alcohol like normal people. As I always say when asked if I want a drink, 'I get naked and punch people in the face!'. People outside of these rooms, those "normal people", will never understand you like I understand you. We have something people with all of the money in the world cannot buy, and that my friends, is unconditional love. I know a lot of rich people who are miserable. They keep trying to fill that void with material things, and it never stays. But in these rooms, we can go anywhere across the world, and we have family. I may not know you from a bar of soap, but if you needed to pull up a chair and talk this obsession out at three a.m., I would gladly do that. And what's even MORE remarkable, is that you'd not only be saving your own life, but you'd be saving mine as well! There is something utterly magical when we come together and share our stories straight from our hearts. Nowhere else in the world can you find this level of raw, unadulterated truth shared, and no one judges you!

And if they did, then they probably belong in a different fellowship, and aren't in fact a true alcoholic."

"Look, you simply cannot buy what we have in these rooms! Unlike a majority of the rest of the world who only spend five minutes analyzing their shit on New Year's Day, we're given precise instructions on how to stop drinking, stay sober, and live happy and joyous lives, if we so choose to. My misery of late is all because I've made the choice to put my program in the corner. And no one puts baby in the corner! We're shown how to accept life on life's terms. We're shown how to cease fighting other people, places, and things. We're taught how to thoroughly analyze our past and dissect our behaviors and actions. We're guided on how to take responsibility for the wreckage of our past, make amends, work on our character defects and then shortcomings when we fail to attack those defects. We are given the steps to take daily inventory of ourselves, both positive and negative, so we can continue to grow and develop spiritually, mentally, and physically. We are shown how by being of service we can find a direct pathway out of self-pity and self-centeredness. All of which has helped this alcoholic develop a deepened sense of self-awareness. I no longer am a bull in a china shop, crashing into everything and everyone in my way. I no longer would steal your wallet, then help you look for it. But I am alive, and so grateful for each and every single one of you for showing up tonight and listening to me ramble. If you weren't here, and I was stuck talking to this wall behind me, I don't think it would have the same effect."

"We aren't bad people who need to get good, but sick people who need to get well. And I can't get well on my own. I know I was going to wrap up with the stage-four bone cancer analogy but, I hope I've said something that made sense to at least one of you.

I love you all, and again thank you for letting me take the floor for a hot second. Clearly, I have some shit to sort out! I'll be sure to take it out on Simon tomorrow!"

Scan for more good shit.

THE GRASS IS BROWNEST WHERE YOU DON'T WATER IT

I was so excited to move to Singapore…until we actually got there.

I'll be so happy when we get to Singapore!

I can flush my toilet paper.

People use blinkers.

No children on scooters without helmets.

There's public transport.

I'll be able to understand people.

There's a ton of 12-step meetings.

No worrying about dodgy cops.

As usual, my heart sank once I realized that my 'I'll be happy when' bullshit was in fact just that: bullshit.

I still wasn't making my recovery a priority.

Public transport was a pain in the ass.

People speak Singlish, which is more difficult to understand than Thai, and although there's no dodgy cops, I suddenly felt trapped pounding pavement in a concrete jungle.

We'd finally gotten our first angel investor onboard, with one of the stipulations being that we incorporated in either Hong Kong or Singapore, due to capital gains tax purposes. Feeling like Singapore would be slightly more Western than Hong Kong, off we went.

Singapore was so unbelievably hot and humid that it felt like I was tied to an industrial dryer perpetually spinning soaking wet towels on a one hundred and fifteen-degree day, minus the freshly scented Bounce dryer sheets. I wasn't sure what was going to give me cancer first, the abject boredom or the stress from running a global clothing line with no cash flow.

Though I couldn't imagine dragging my dogs to another round of quarantine again, from the minute our taxi left the airport in Thailand and landed in our new country of residence, I wanted to leave.

When we arrived at our new house with our four suitcases to meet the real estate agent for a welcome tour, I thought Ora was just a co-worker of the agent. While Dean was searching for rentals from Thailand, he mentioned that this particular one "seemed to have a maid that lived out the back". Based on all the other rentals he'd shown me previously, I assumed this was another 'shop-house' with some kind of community cleaner that lived in a unit of some sort "out the back" in the middle of the compound. But come to find out, the whole "lived out the back" statement couldn't be further from what I envisioned.

After shaking hands, the agent briefly introduced us to Ora before he continued to show us around. After a short ten-minute tour, the agent started saying his good-byes, though Ora didn't seem to be going with him. Suddenly, all of the little parts of the tour were starting to click. Without opening her bedroom door as he passed, he pointed out the back bathroom and laundry facilities as the 'helpers quarters', but somehow it hadn't registered that we would have someone living with us. When he was showing us the kitchen appliances and mentioned "Ora could make a simple breakfast or fresh juice", I was too busy marveling over the majestic black, wrought iron circular staircase to put two and two together.

While the agent was wrapping up and putting his shoes on, Ora sat at the kitchen table. After we said goodbye to the agent, I walked over to Ora and flat out asked her.

"Oh! I think I misunderstood, Ora. Do you actually live here?" I asked.

"Yes Ma'am," she said in her Filipino accent behind her glasses.

"Oh my gosh! I didn't realize that! So, is that your room right there?" I asked as I pointed towards her sliding door.

"Yes Ma'am," she replied.

As I laughed, I gave my first plea, "Ora, you can call me Kortney. Calling me Ma'am and being from California doesn't really feel right," I said.

"You from California, Ma'am?" she asked.

Noticing this wasn't going anywhere fast anytime soon, I asked Dean to come upstairs with me, while I replied to Ora and excused ourselves while we unpacked. Dragging a suitcase each up the twenty five steps, I suddenly fell out of love with the majestic appeal of the iron stairs as I tried to catch my breath inside our open, floor-plan bedroom.

"So, when you said, 'out the back', you really knew that we had a maid living with us?" I asked with a clear tone of annoyance.

"Yes. I told you that. We didn't have a choice. We couldn't rent the property without her living here, as she's employed by the landlords," he replied. "OK, "*Sir*". My apologies, I must have somehow missed that detail while trying to get our lives into four suitcases again," I said.

"Well, it was either this place, or living across the street from the power plant which you strongly opposed. I'm not sure I could have done any better. I'm sorry," he replied.

Standing there in the sweltering heat, I knew this resentment was just like any other resentment; an unspoken expectation in which I played some kind of part in, but was unwilling to admit fault.

The first three months of being a resident in one of the most expensive countries in the world without a pot to piss in, was gruelling--and it took a toll on our marriage. Unsure of whether it was the entreprenurial lifestyle causing a lack of sex, money, and hope that was causing my health to rapidly decline, or if it was the surplus of decades of illegal stimulants, I knew I needed to do something different. As I laid on Ted's tiny guest bed waiting for Dean to call, my teeth chattered while the tips of my toes remained numb. Pulling a sock off to examine my feet, I felt my heart start to beat out of my chest.

After living in South East Asia for nearly two years, it had been some time since I was exposed to proper cold weather. Flying over to attend the Arnold Classic Sports Festival in central Ohio in the dead of winter seemed like a good idea at the time when booking a month prior. Once I arrived, that good idea seemed more problematic. Feeling like a sharp razor blade had cut the fleshy tips of my toes open, my opal-white digits stung like a million bee stings as I lay in discontent. In an attempt to get the blood flowing back, I vigorously rubbed the soles of my feet before standing up to examine the next problem on my list.

As I pulled the last layer of clothing off the top half of my body, I stood in the mirror and examined my lopsided chest. Unlike most of my life where I'd miserably stared in disgust at how little and lopsided my breasts were, I was now marveling in shock over how big and lopsided they were now. Three years prior, the surgeon who did the install told me there would be little chance of me experiencing any complications. Following directions, I managed to sit on the couch for seventy two hours post implant surgery, but by day four, I was power walking up and down hills and doing hundreds of air squats a day.

Adjusting from training at the level of an Olympian, to sitting on the couch, was challenging to say the least, but I managed to spend the six months post surgery doing everything I could to not use my chest in daily basic movements. But regardless of my attempt, my right breast, which used to be the smaller of the two before the implants, started filling up with fluid underneath.

Just like everything else I thought would fill some kind of void in my life, the excitement of having a boisterous D-cup rack quickly wore off. Running my fingers around the outside of my right breast, I could feel the rippling edges of the implant as I stared at my chest in the mirror. Since having them put in, I had to see a doctor twice to have the excess fluid drained with a fine needle.

Suddenly the distinct tone of Whatsapp messenger filled the air.

"Hey Hun," I answered solemnly.

"Hi baby girl. How was your flight?" Dean asked.

"Oh my god, I can't even."

"Really?"

"We were almost two hours late departing Hong Kong, so by the time we got to our gate at LAX, I had forty minutes to clear customs and get to my next gate."

"You're kidding me? I didn't realise we had booked the flights so close together."

"Yeah me either. But when I landed, I managed to get ahold of Drake and asked if he was working."

"Drake.... Oh right- your cop friend whose beat is the Los Angeles airport. Same guy who used to pay you to act like a giantess and step on little toy soldiers in videos and worship your feet in person, right?"

"Yup that's the one! He came and met me outside of arrivals before driving me to domestic with his lights and siren on and then escorted me to security!"

"No way! I bet KO enjoyed that little escapade."

"Yeah, I felt like Lady Gaga. But come to find out, my flight to Cleveland was delayed and there was no reason for me to almost have a heart attack."

"Oh my-"

"Oh but it gets better."

"Go on...", said Dean.

"Well- because the flight was delayed almost 2 hours, I was

looking at having a half hour window to get to my next gate once we landed."

"Jesus H bald headed Christ!"

"As soon as the seatbelt sign turned off, I sprinted to the front of the plane, which you know I hate, and as soon as that door opened, I sprinted non-stop for what seemed like fifteen minutes to the next gate. Two shuttles later, and almost missing my stop, I finally got to the empty terminal with seconds to spare."

"I can't believe you made it after all of that!"

"But WAIT! I'm not yet at the grand finale!"

"More?"

"I was so tired by this point that when I got to the end of the ramp, I turned left instead of right, and boarded an empty plane. Not even thinking that the plane shouldn't be empty as it was about to take off, I sat down and caught my breath for a few minutes. I even looked out the window at the other full plane next to me!"

"You boarded the wrong plane?" Dean exclaimed.

"Yes! I'm literally fucking dead!" I said as I could feel my heart pounding in my neck.

"Hun I'm so sorry."

"It's ok. It was my idea to come to The Arnold festival."

"So you and Ted are driving up there tomorrow?"

"We sure are. On a totally random side note- I wish we would have held off on doing this live event. It's causing us so much stress."

"I know hun. I know how badly you wanted to recreate Kamp

Konfidence though."

"At least I finally get to meet Jean Kilbourne! How crazy is it that I emailed her back in 2013 with the vision of bringing her out to Australia to headline some kind of event with all the graduates from Kamp, and instead she's coming to do her talk at our first GRRRL event."

"I know, right? It's just a reminder that we have to remember that The Universe has a plan for us," Dean said.

"It's so hard to not give up right now. I keep thinking back to some stupid meme I came across when I was doing Isagenix."

"Which one was that?"

"It was a cartoon of some bearded guy standing in a tunnel he'd dug with a pickaxe. There was like a little strip of dirt in front of him with a giant pile of diamonds on the other side he obviously didn't know he was so close to."

"Ah yes. I remember that. Well, at least you're not using a pickaxe to try and destroy someone's car these days, darling."

"I told you that story, did I?" I said laughing.

"Get some sleep hun, we'll figure everything out."

After saying our goodbyes, I crashed back on the bed exhausted, ready for the best night's sleep in my life. But instead, as soon as I switched the light off the bedside lamp, my thoughts started racing as if I had just hit a meth pipe.

In the span of seven days, I had flown thirty two hours one way to attend a sports festival in Ohio (which sucked), traveled to Tennessee and Kentucky to conduct meet-ups with our grrrlarmy members, followed by flying back to Los Angeles to then immediately drive six hours to Joshua Tree with one of my best friends to do a photoshoot, before flying twenty two hours back to Singapore. I had spent the entire time feeling completely out of mind. Not only was I not sleeping, which I contributed to jet lag, but my body felt like it was shutting down. What was even worse than feeling horrible, was looking horrible. My legs had gone from retaining a slight amount of water, to now looking like waterlogged orange peels.

In the space of two weeks upon arriving back, I could no longer workout, sleep, hold a coffee cup, or feel any amount of joy. Every day I was drowning in a shallow puddle of irritability and anxiety. Any time someone opened their mouth, I immediately wanted to slap and slash them. Although a control freak mentally, I was still usually an outwardly happy-go-lucky person.

After taking a labored five minutes to walk up the spiral staircase, stopping every five stairs to catch my breath, I sat on the edge of my bed and held my arm out straight. Shaking more violently than the crackhead taking a dump in the D.C. subway back on my High School leadership trip to visit Congress, I knew that quitting stimulants for a month wasn't going to be the answer. I had quit taking pre-workout and drinking coffee for a few weeks, but my symptoms kept rapidly worsening.

. . . .

Our live event was a whirlwind.

The day before we departed Singapore for Las Vegas, I managed to see a doctor to review the results from my physical. Just as the chiropractor I'd seen a few weeks prior had concluded, my thyroid was "way off". Although the general practitioner got an endocrinologist to prescribe me emergency medication over the phone, it was going to take several weeks before it started working.

It was a relief to now know the root cause of my debilitating symptoms, however, I was still sicker than dog shit.

My skin was pale, my face was sunken in, and I'd lost close to twenty pounds in the month prior to being diagnosed with Graves' disease. My hair had drastically thinned, my nails looked and felt like plastic warped by the sun, my arms burned trying to press five pound dumbbells, and I was averaging around two hours of sleep a night.

The three days leading up to the event were unfathomably the hardest days of my life. Quitting meth and oxycontin seemed like a walk in the park in comparison to being an entrepreneur in the apparel industry.

On the flight over, I discovered through a single Facebook message that all of the leggings we were selling at the event (and in three different countries) were one size too small. Upon landing, the hotel we had bought out for the weekend where our attendees were staying, somehow went from eight grand in total, to thirty five thousand dollars. Not only did we fail to read the misleading fine print regarding the food and beverage inclusions, we somehow overlooked the fact that the 'hotel' was actually a swingers hotel for people over eighteen year olds. To top it off, although we had 'bought out' the hotel for the weekend, the bar and club was still open to the public.

As Josie walked us around the premises of The Artisan hotel, she cheerfully pointed out the hideous artwork throughout the interior, acting as if we'd never had a quarrel. As soon as we landed in Las Vegas two days prior, I put the desperate plea out to our grrrlarmy group, asking for any connections with a pro bono lawyer. Within a matter of minutes, we were on the phone with one of our member's husbands, planning to meet at Josie's office to contest their bullshit contract. After much back and forth, we had the option to either make the contract null and void, or take five grand off the total.

"And this is the bar-club area, which is open from ten p.m. until three a.m.," she said.

"You mean on other nights of the week, right?" I asked.

"No, this is still open to the public. And I believe there's a big party planned for a stripper tomorrow night!" she exclaimed.

"Wait- I'm sorry. We bought out the property Friday through Sunday. So what do you mean open to the public?" I asked.

"Well, there's a clause in your contract that states the bar and club area are an additional charge."

"Josie- you've *got* to be kidding me? One of my main speakers is in her seventies and showing up tomorrow night. You mean to tell me she's going to walk into the lobby to check in and there's a party happening in the next room over that doesn't have a door? Until three a.m.?" I said as my fists tightened.

"Well, we do provide complementary ear plugs in every room."

Before I could say another word, my phone dinged with a Facebook notification from our social media manager.

Someone's shooting a porno in the room next to mine, and Tori just messaged me to say she found a used condom in the desk drawer in her room.

Fucking perfect.

. . . .

After four days of absolute insanity, we had over one hundred women immeasurably happier, but were now close to thirty thousand dollars further in debt . From UFC fighters Rose Namajumas and

Cris Cyborg, to scholars like Jean Kilbourne, the conference was a huge success as far as our community was concerned. But as far as I was concerned, making it to Denver to audition for Shark Tank the day after everything wrapped up, was our calling from God.

Although I started the conference delivering my keynote on "Goals Not Controls", I just *knew* that we were destined to be on Shark Tank. Still not having slept more than two hours a night for nearly two months, I felt like I was going to come out of my skin as we stood in line waiting to make it in the building. I had a vague idea of what I was going to say in my sixty second pitch, but was feeling even more anxious and overwhelmed than usual. I was grasping onto the idea that this was all a part of God's will.

Immediately following the event, a long time customer and massive fan, decided to get the word "GRRRL" tattooed above her eyebrow. She was so moved by the conference, she felt compelled to show the ultimate form of respect. Armed with a watermelon under my left arm, and her face-tattoo-picture on my phone from the day before, I walked in to deliver my pitch. After waiting in line for four hours, I was finally face to face with a junior producer.

"Hi there! My name is Kortney Olson, and me and my brand GRRRL are here to *crush* gender stereotypes!" I shouted enthusiastically, slamming the watermelon down on the table.

"Have you ever seen the woman that crushes watermelons between her thighs?" I asked the young girl.

"Ummmmm yeah, come to think of it, I have," she replied.

"Well that's me, and I'm here along with my brand, to tell the world that women and girls are capable of anything! We're told our whole life that we're supposed to look a certain way instead of *feel* a certain way, and we're here to change that. We don't use traditional sizes because that crap was made up by a man in the nineteen forties.

We don't use photoshop or airbrushing, because we're normalising all bodies. And we're creating a sisterhood because we believe women are held back as a gender by our own doing due to seeing each other as competition!"

With my forehead now beading with sweat, I slammed my phone down on the table and delivered my final line.

"We have over twenty women who've gotten our brand tattooed since we started a year and a half ago. Now tell me- have you ever seen someone with a Nike swoosh tattooed on their *face*?" I asked. Before she could reply, I wrapped up. "No, you haven't. Because they'd probably be in an institution. Nike isn't a movement- it doesn't stand for anything concrete like we do. We started with a *why*! To change the way the world views women, and how women view themselves. That's what's up!" I said as I picked up my phone and slid it in my leggings pocket.

"Well then!" the young girl replied, "Thank you so much for auditioning, Kortney. If the producers are interested, they'll reach out to you within the next six weeks. Great job."

Six hours later, I received a call that we were onto the second phase.

. . . .

I'd made it to the final round after three months of ongoing submissions and calls with producers. Out of thirty thousand plus applicants, we had made it down to the forty fourth place. I just *knew* this was our meal ticket out of debit card Russian roulette. To get some real practice in, I decided to enter a pitch competition for start-ups. Held by an angel investment company based out of Australia, the terms and conditions were about as clear as The Artisan's hotel buy-out contract. By time I discovered the pitch opportunity, I had missed the local competition in Singapore, but decided to take the short flight over to Bangkok to compete.

With four minutes to pitch GRRRL in front of a panel of four judges, I had the flashcards down like the back of my old corner liquor store. With my medication starting to work, I looked awake thanks to sleeping more than two hours a night.

After a week of practice, it was time to head back to Thailand. Finding the cheapest flight possible meant we had very little time to get from the airport to the city center in time. As soon as we deboarded the plane and entered the customs area, I knew it was going to be impossible to make it in time.

Scan to see the chaos.

"Holy mother of God!" I shouted as Dean and I scurried amongst the sea of bodies filtering towards the official area. Knowing that Thai culture lacked a sense of urgency, my heart sank as I thought about how far we'd come.

"Try that line and I'll try this line, Dean said.

As we stood in opposite lines, we dually shifted in our shoes in anticipation and anxiousness. With both of our lines standing perfectly still for five minutes, Dean decided to take matters into his own hands.

"We're never going to make it standing in these lines. I'm going to go find a diplomat lane or something," he said.

"We can't do that!" I replied. Unlike when I was fucked up, I hated breaking rules sober.

After what seemed like an hour, Dean reappeared around a corner. Standing a good five inches above the sea of people, it wasn't hard to spot his bright bald head and arms flailing around. Motioning me to follow him, I reluctantly left my line and pushed through the crowd of people.

Grabbing my hand tight, he told me to hold on as he barreled through the crowd towards an empty line at the very end of the customs hall. Telling me to wait, I stood in the position that was next in line while he talked to a Thai woman in uniform. Before I knew it, we had our passports stamped, and somehow avoided a two hour plus line to enter the country. With only a few minutes to spare, we found our way to the competition. Looking around the room, I was the only woman with the exception of one other who was also competing.

Next to last, I stood in front of the panel of four Asian men, and emotionally delivered my broken lines within the four minute time limit.

After answering some questions about scalability and supply chain, I was given a round of applause and sat down to listen to the last competitor before the judges dispersed for a short break to decide the winners. First and second place were going onto the final competition which was held in Beijing three weeks from now.

Against the odds, I placed second after the only other woman competing who took first. Proud of our accomplishments, I congratulated her, and made our way back to our hotel for the night before flying back to Singapore. As Dean and I sat in the bed eating all of the chocolate we could scavenge from the minibar, we marveled at the fact we'd managed to make it in time.

"We have zero intention of going to Beijing, right?" he asked.

"No, definitely not! Besides, I think filming starts for Shark Tank around that time. They're supposed to be emailing me the day after tomorrow with a date so we can book our flight!"

"Well, I'm surprised how this all turned out. The angle of China having the highest rates of eating disorders built into the pitch was perfect."

"I know it's a total trip. Didn't you tell me that Japanese women will forego eating for weeks just so they can buy a Gucci bag?"

"That's what I came across in my research. But you do know that Japan isn't in China, just like Phil Collins isn't American, right darling?"

"Sue-sue-sussudio your mouth shut!", I exclaimed. "Well, I'd much rather be going back to Los Angeles instead of Beijing! But at least I got some practice in!"

As I finally dozed off, I briefly thanked my Higher Power for getting us there on time while I imagined how great it was going to be when I crushed a watermelon that had a sticker of Mr. Wonderful's face (the bald judge with little man syndrome) affixed to the side.

A day had already passed since we returned back from Bangkok. As I stood at the top of the stairs, I thought crossed my mind.

I bet they're going to email and tell you that they ran out of spaces.

Unlike most of the times I got a faint whisper from my intuition, I heard this one loud and clear. Pushing the thought aside, I continued my descent down the spiral staircase towards the kitchen counter where my phone was charging. After opening the email app, as expected, the newest message sitting at the top was from Shark Tank.

'Hi Kortney,

I hope this finds you well. I know you were recently traveling again, so hope that went well. Normally I would call someone to deliver the news, but since you're out of the country temporarily, I've resorted to email. Unfortunately we've run out of filming spaces this season. I know we were so close to getting this wrapped up, and I am so sorry. We're hoping to carry your application over season ten. Take care and thank you for all your work so far.'

Similar to the feeling I had after getting the call from Big Brothers, Big Sisters, I sat down on the bottom stair to try and process what I'd just read.

We've been working on this for like four months.

This was supposed to be our way out.

We were supposed to be booking our flights today!

I can't fucking believe this!

I hated lying about not actually living in the United States though. So at least that's over.

After taking a breath, I sat in silence while I held back tears. We were so far in debt it seemed impossible to keep carrying on, let alone breath. My fear of financial insecurity was drilling down into my cells until I suddenly realised that I had a fall back.

Holy shit.

God's will is not Shark Tank.

God's will is being big in China!

Everything is exactly where it's supposed to be.

FUCK!

God just stopped me from all sorts of potential drama.

I mean after all, we're based in South East Asia so it only makes sense that we're supposed to be pitching to the Beijing Government for this grant.

"Hey hun! We're not going to Los Angeles. We're meant to be big in China!" I shouted from the bottom of the stairs up to Dean.

. . . .

It wasn't until *after* we borrowed money from my Dad to book our flights to Beijing that we learned second place winners from the Bangkok and Malaysia competition weren't *actually* entitled to pitch for the million dollar grant from the Chinese government. Only the second place winners from the Singapore and Australian competition were entitled to pitch. It turned out all I had won us was free accommodation at a two-star hotel and the chance to pitch to the angel investment company who had organised the competition. All for a whopping two hundred and fifty thousand dollars. Which in the world of an established start-up company in a cut-throat market, is the square root of jack dick.

Unable to get a refund on the flight, we decided to go anyway.

After a three and a half hour flight, we had landed in Beijing and managed to get a taxi to our hotel. Barely able to pay the deposit, we got to our room. Heading straight into the bathroom to pee, I slammed down on the toilet seat in anger and started surveying the amenities. Noticing there wasn't any shampoo, conditioner, or lotion on the vanity, I ripped back the shower curtain assuming I'd find a stash in the bath. Staring at the vacant landscape, I turned my attention back to the task at hand, and wiped.

In disbelief, I once again looked for the toiletries. Glancing across the empty, chipped wooden shelves under the vanity, I came up short until something else caught my eye.

Is that a fucking scale!

How in the world can these a-holes not afford to put toiletries in a hotel but they can afford to put a goddamn scale?

Listening to my gut, I kicked the scale back under the vanity without stepping on it and proceeded to tell Dean about my findings. Feeling a bit more motivated to pitch after seeing the scale, we decided to give ourselves plenty of time to find the location of the competition and headed out an hour ahead of schedule.

Without a translating device or a Chinese SIM card for one of our phones, we hailed a bicycle cab and attempted to show him the address in Chinese. After thirty minutes of peddling while the sun casually started setting, the man stopped in the middle of a six lane road. Turning around to face us, the man started talking to us in Chinese. Knowing we were about to be fucked from past experience, I watched as Dean continued repeating back, "We don't speak fucking Chinese, mate!"

After ten minutes of back and forth, Dean and I were out of the rickshaw and walking around the streets of Beijing lost without a hope in the world.

. . . .

As the back of my legs stuck to the white leather couch, I sat in the disgusting heat thinking about Pop. I couldn't figure out why I kept making such stupid business decisions. A few years prior on my visit before last, she'd made a comment that seemed incapable of leaving my mind. She told me that I needed to focus more on the products and less on the women we were empowering. As far as she was concerned, if we didn't have a solid product, then we didn't have a leg to stand on. She fully knew that I was way more interested in fixing people over fashion and business.

The last time I saw her was just a few months ago. I'd spent almost half the year back home in the United States. My trip started out by attending the Arnold Classic, but this time as a vendor. With our shitty little pop-up exhibition stand, I felt like a total clown amongst the bigger, more sophisticated companies who had fifty to hundred thousand dollar booths set up. Although Kortney felt lucky to have Arnold himself make a guest appearance at our booth, watching her crush a watermelon while filming it for his millions of Snapchat followers, KO was utterly pissed off that she didn't have a VIP line of people wanting to get her autograph.

The sad thing was, I'd even tried getting rid of KO. About six months prior, towards the end of 2017, I decided it was time to close the door on her. Thinking that if I tattooed a picture of Prince over my infamous KO tattoo, I'd suddenly somehow bloom like a bouquet of long stem roses, I hastily picked a picture of Prince off the internet and asked a friend to cover her up. After KO was buried by Prince's wavy hair, nothing really changed. The big, little husky girl inside was still screaming to be loved.

After the expo was over, I flew back from Ohio to San Francisco to stay with Pop for several weeks. The next task at hand was launching a crowdfunding campaign. We had our second live event coming up, and once again, no way of paying for it. And like the first event, it was too late to back out. Not only would we disappoint the women who had been planning on attending since shortly after our first event, but we would disappoint the two customers (who met in our online community from opposite ends of the world) we were planning on marrying as the grand finale of the event.

After a few short weeks at Pops, I stayed busy over the next several months until I'd see her again. I'd been invited to speak at the FBI headquarters in Los Angeles for International Women's Day, followed by a flight to Alabama to wrap up our distribution center, where I narrowly avoided a tornado. Then, drove across country from Bama to Las Vegas for our second live event, then back to Fortuna, California to stay with my Dad while packaging up all of the orders we made through the crowdfunding campaign (which by the way, we only just enough money to pay for the inventory we sold-whoops), and back down to Pop's where I stayed for a few weeks before heading down to Los Angeles again to appear on Jimmy Kimmel Live for National Watermelon Day. Like I said, I stayed busy.

Trying to convey how great the brand was, the brand that she helped me launch with a ten thousand dollar loan, I showed Pop pictures from the event. Sensing she was unimpressed, I moved on to show her all of the screenshots of the life-changing testimonials from women within the grrrlarmy community I'd been collecting over the last two years.

 I have allowed myself to love myself for the first time in my life. I no longer hate my legs, my and I no longer feel any desire to restrict foods or beat myself up over a bit of fluff.

I see the world a different way, a more caring and understanding way. My thought processes are completely changed for the better.

I also have a donut and watermelon obsession.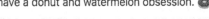

Like · Reply   7

I discovered Grrrl 3-4 months ago. I follow a lady on IG who (I'm assuming) is an ambassador and has a discount code. I saw her cute gym clothes and checked out the website. The sizing freaked me out at first. I wasn't expecting that. Christmas Day, I had my measurements taken. I had those, I had Christmas money...dammit, I was ordering. Posted on a FB fitness page about Grrrl and I had 2 gals RAVE about the brand, the clothes and the army. I ordered and I'm so happy I did.

Grrrl makes me feel sassy and a badass. It makes my feel like there's this underground woman led army and I'm a part of it. Tapping the grrrl tags on IG leads me to so many inspiring women, from all walks of life & I'm grateful for Grrrl.

Like · Reply   2

Ever since taking the pledge at the AGIG camp in 2014, I have been away of how judgemental
I was of myself and others appearances.
I still have that blue band.

Like · Reply   4

I no longer am on my psych meds, I have had courage to do things I normally wouldn't. I found courage to take the plunge and now in less than 2 months I'll be following my dreams and moving to another state.
TERRIFIED to do this but I know you and these grrrls got my back and I will be just fine! THATS what grrrl did for me!!!

females together. I never liked hanging out with women or becoming friends with them bc the few I have, have done me dirty in some way or other. I'm so happy to have met Misty and been introduced to GRRRL I know you say I helped create it but honestly GRRRL helped create a better me. Since I found grrrl I have not only gotten my power back but I suffer from mental illness something real

horrible... little by little it has helped me grab my mind back and shake off the shit that would normally make me sink down into the dark depression abyss. Fast forward to now and I am now off of the many Meds I was taking. Bc you ladies have helped me so so so fucking much! I still have anxiety here and there but I can handle it and I even can sleep without medication. So just want to say thank you. Thank you so much. I 6

Like · Reply

This is How Grrrl has changed my life.
I use to be so ashamed of my Body and how it looked. I always tried Covering Up. Since losing 34kg in 12 months I am a different person. I'm currently on a 2 week holiday. The first week I wear a Bikini on the Beach. This week I wore it With Shorts But 12 months ago there is no way in hell I'd be showing my stomach in anyway! I literally don't care what I look like now.
I feel great and am loving All the adventures and Wonderful moments with my children.
Grrrl has given me the confidence to Love My body no matter what size and that I can Enjoy my life without worrying about people Thinking I look horrible.
Thank you to all my fellow Grrrl and Our Main Mumma Bear KO. We all have our Personal demons to fight but if we Stand as One we Will change the World

Like · Reply

475

Expecting her to suddenly leap out of her chair with amazement, my thoughts quickly ran downhill when she showed little interest or enthusiasm.

She literally seemed like she couldn't have cared less about the impact.

She probably thinks I'm just on some kind of pipedream and she's probably right. Every time I've seen or talked to her, we're on the verge of going out of business.

A year ago, she said I needed to focus more on the product and less on the movement, but I can't help it. I knew we shouldn't have had an event again.

I couldn't help feeling like I kept failing her. The worst part of the trip came crashing down when I had returned from a short business jaunt over to Sedona, Arizona trying to meet a potential investor. A successful female entrepreneur and business coach had invited me to her members' weekend seminar after showing a tiny spark of interest in what we were doing with GRRRL. With my dad helping by paying for my flight (yet again) and accommodation, I made my way out to this 'sacred vortex of energy' for the weekend in hopes that someone would rescue us. Trying every person with a deep pocket to raise our first round of substantial funding, I somehow thought this was going to go somewhere.

Sunday morning before the second day of the seminar was to start, I woke up early enough to get a jog in. After all, this was my first time in Sedona, surrounded by magnificent scenery, and I wasn't about to succumb to saying I didn't at least touch a rock. Since being diagnosed with Graves' disease, my interest in pumping weights or sweating in general had almost completely vanished, but with the prospect of a potential investor, I felt like I could run to the moon and back.

As the sun slowly inched its way up the sky, I jogged my way up a steep hill until I hit the trails. With my fist-pumping a hundred and eighty beats-per-minute eighties playlist blasting through my ears, I managed to run nonstop all the way up the switchback trails until I reached the top. Feeling elated for the first time in months, I was suddenly inspired to snap a nude selfie with the glowing Sedona scenery behind me. Knowing that I had very little time before the family I passed on the way up would be closing in, I set the timer on my camera, and quickly pulled my sports bra off and my shorts down. Hitting a back-double bicep, I flexed as hard as I could until I counted to eight, and quickly got my gear back on seconds before someone's head popped up over the ridge.

As I made my way back across the flat rock to head down the trail, I smiled at the family and wished them well as I considered what inspirational shit I should post with my picture. Once I hit the pavement, I pulled my phone out and started typing.

It's called Mother Nature for a reason. Mother Nature is the most powerful force on the planet. And she gives zero fucks as to whether or not you have cellulite, dimples, wrinkles or stretch marks. She only cares that you keep showing up aggressively with a dash of compassion, empathy, and a giant dollop of love.

Deciding that posting a picture of myself completely nude from behind was questionably risqué nowadays, I opened the picture in the stories app. Feeling like a mastermind, I carefully placed the corn cob emoji right up the center of my butt, perfectly covering up the crack. Saving the photo to my camera roll, I then posted the picture to my wall before heading back inside to get ready to slay.

The next day, I was back at Pop's attending to the support emails in customer service when 'the scolding' happened. In a tone that I'd never heard before, Pop stuck her head into the office/guest room.

"Kortney, I need to speak to you."

"What's up Pop!" I asked as my nerves stood on edge, knowing something wasn't right.

"Well, it's about that *horrid* picture you posted on Facebook," she said as her face twisted up.

Unsure of what picture she was speaking of, I questioned what she could possibly be talking about. There were plenty of old 'horrid' pictures of me on the internet.

"Ummmmm… which picture are you speaking of, Pop?" I asked, feeling like I used to when I woke up from a blackout and not knowing what I had done the night before.

"The naked photograph with a corn cob over your buttocks!" she stammered.

Feeling my face get beat red, I had forgotten that Instagram was set up to populate to my Facebook page.

"I have friends on Facebook. I don't want them seeing my granddaughter's back side."

Feeling mortified that my eighty eight year old grandmother was scolding me, a thirty seven year old grown-ass woman, I briefly thought about raising the argument around how nudity empowers some, while modesty empowers others.

"Ohhhhhh…. I know what you're talking about. I posted that to empower women, Pop. Did you read the caption?" I asked.

"No--I clicked off of it as fast as humanly possible."

"So many women think they're not powerful because they have cellulite and dimples. I wanted to remind women that what our bodies look like, shouldn't matter."

"I don't care what you *thought* you were doing. It was distasteful and unnecessary."

"I'm sorry. I'll take it down."

"Thank you," she said sternly as she turned and walked out the door.

So, there I sat on the couch.

Unable to get my Grandmother's approval.

Unable to get someone to see the potential of a brand that has the capability to be bigger than Nike in ten years' time.

Unable to feel well.

Unable to stop stressing over keeping everything going.

Yet able to put my recovery as a priority, but choosing not to.

When. Will. I. Learn?

. . . .

The grass is brownest where you don't water that shit! As soon as we got to Singapore, I wanted to go back to Thailand. As soon as I got to Queensland, I wanted to go back to Melbourne. As soon as we got to Thailand, I wanted to go back to Queensland. And on, and on and on. Everywhere I've moved in my life, I was running from something. The reality is, had I put my recovery first and focused on taking care of my soul, over taking care of my body or my bank account, I would have been content being wherever I was.

At our first live event in 2017, I opened up on stage with a keynote talking about the concept of 'Goals Not Controls'. As you read, as soon as I left Las Vegas and headed to Colorado for the Shark Tank audition, my higher power

(God, whatever-) gave me multiple opportunities to practice what I was preaching (aka 'eat my words'!). From the disappointment of Shark Tank, to then not being able to pitch in Beijing, I stayed clean and sober but was absolutely miserable. Had I been working my 12-step program (or focusing on basic principles of gratitude and being of service, for those not in 12-step recovery), the ride would have been so much more enjoyable.

Also, even to this present moment, I still find myself packing my schedule full and find that I'm always 'busy'. No matter what, I'm always going and doing, but hardly being. I love action, and I hate slowing down. The ridiculous part about all of this, is that I know in my heart of hearts if I slowed down and committed to a regular morning meditation ritual, I would find a lot more serenity in my life.

Do the F*cking Work

In what ways are you distracting yourself from taking care of you first?

What types of activities are you making a priority in your life?

Is that helping you find happiness?

Who or what do you need to cut out of your life in order to help yourself flourish?

By cutting said things out, will you be allowing more time to slow down and process things and see how you can make things happen, instead of things just happening to you?

Scan here for more good shit.

WHAT DOESN'T KILL ME MAKES MY LEGS STRONGER

*T*he air outside was sweltering. Although the level of heat was similar to that of Singapore, the humidity was bearable. It's what white people call "a dry heat".

Finishing one of the most brutal workouts in my life and higher than a kite flying off Mount Kilimanjaro, I skipped out of CrossFit Las Vegas and headed back to my apartment downtown. After spending two years in the concrete jungle and not finding a single investor, we decided it was time to submerge ourselves where eighty percent of our market was, The Divided States of America.

It wasn't as bad as the fireman-carry WOD with Tony, but it was up there.

Fuck my legs are amazing.

Kneecaps are baggy, but still amazing.

With a matching neon yellow sports bra and rainbow cheetah shorts, I strolled down Las Vegas Boulevard while Prince serenaded me via earbuds.

I couldn't carry a tune if you strapped that shit to my back.

Tired of dicking around with the fabric rolling up my rocking thighs, I folded my shorts under. Aware that my legs were doing all of the talking, I sang along while making eye contact with every vehicle passing. I had only been back training for a little over a month at this point. After having my implants taken out upon moving back to the US, for the first time in my life, I hadn't seen the inside of a gym for nearly three months.

I vacantly stared at the downtown United States Postal Service branch while waiting for the lights to change. Out of tune and out of fucks, I belted out the words while playing the air trombone.

You sexy mother fuckerrrrrrrrr' … 'Bomp Bomp Bomp!

Noticing a dilapidated wedding chapel with a building permit nailed to the front door, I instantly started feeling anxious.

Fucking longest light in history!

I used to despise this flashing red pedestrian hand sign until I learned that a Black man invented traffic lights.

Anyone or anything telling me what to do could piss off.

Perspective is such a magical tool.

Wish the federal government could call some of that into its life.

Somehow overlooking it, I noticed a giant sign in front of the chapel as I finally started to cross the street:

Vegas' Best Marijuana Distribution Joint Coming Soon

As I glanced back to make sure no one was behind me, I caught sight of the Post Office once again when suddenly it clicked.

CRUSHING IT

I'm feeling anxious because my family is fucked.

Coming from a long line of Post Masters, Brian, my childhood hero and older brother decided to carry on the torch. After thirteen years of slaving for the government, he went postal (figuratively) and transitioned into weed cultivation with the hopes of sending my niece and nephew to college without them having to incur crippling debt.

My stepbrother, head of the drug task force for the Sheriff's department, had, unbeknownst to him, started surveillance of our brother's operation. Not a huge deal, but Christmas and family gatherings definitely became a bit awkward. Like most people who are over forty without a degree as a fall-back, Brian returned to doing what every other redneck and hippy was doing in Humboldt County and turned his soil to start a grow with a cousin.

The day after Thanksgiving, two days after his probation was finished, the Feds rolled up with men in black and assault weapons and raided my cousin's operation.

Twenty four months later sentencing finally arrived, but because no one would roll, both cousin and brother were sentenced to two years in Federal prison.

Wow, that's some woke shit.

Don't say woke- that belongs in the Black community.

We're always taking shit from them.

Bitch, you have Prince tattooed on your arm and you've never been to a march.

This waking up shit never seems to end.

The USPS building to the weed storing, linked me to feeling out of control by not being able to help.

The Constitution was written on hemp.

Why is he serving time and I never did?

He's gotten like one traffic ticket in his life.

He has more values and morals than the Pope and yet here we are.

From the post office to the new dispensary, I felt consumed with feelings of injustice and frustration. With only two blocks to go, I fought off the anxiousness while practically stepping over a few bodies living on the street without shelter. Taking a deep breath, I remembered the nine key words I once heard from a wise fellow drunk that had seemed to become my mantra as of late.

There is a God, and I am not it.

Rounding the corner towards the front of my building, I noticed a man with his head in his hands sitting on the sidewalk.

Fuck, Kortney--go over there and ask him if he's OK.

By the time I'd crossed and was within five feet of him, I paused. Trying to figure out if the man was sleeping or crying, I started second guessing whether or not I should intervene. Mentally feeling like I'd just ran a 5K in the space of ten seconds, I noticed a black town car slowly turn the corner and drive past directly in front of me. As I stood frozen trying to make a decision, I caught a glimpse of the man driving as he crept down the street. Deciding that the man was probably sleeping, since he hadn't moved in the slightest, I decided to 'let go and let god'. Out of my peripheral, I noticed the town car had now pulled over into a shuttle bus area about thirty feet down the road.

Don't walk back to your building.

That guy is watching you.

Listening to whatever was bubbling up from my gut, I decided to walk straight by the car instead of turning around and going back towards my apartment.

You are such a self-obsessed idiot, Kortney.

This guy is probably an Uber driver.

Why do you always think people give a fuck what you're doing?

You need to stop watching Forensic Files before bed every night.

Aggressively walking, I purposely pulled my lats out and made myself look as large as I could. Prince had rolled over to Kenny Loggins just as I came up behind the car. Noticing there was no license plate and that every window was darker than the deepest part of the Pacific Ocean, "Danger Zone" was blaring in my ears. I hastily looked over at the driver and made eye contact as I stormed past the passenger side window at a pace similar to being late to your own wedding.

Because the man looked relatively close to my age, I gave him a head nod up. Just as I taught the girls at Kamp Konfidence, I made eye contact with everyone. Any man looking around the same age or younger, received the nod up. It was my way of saying, "I see you. Respect me, and I'll respect you, and no one gets kicked in the dick." If a man appeared twenty years older or more, they got the head nod down. It was a way of saying, "You probably served in the military and are completely disrespected by the government, so thank you for your service, sir. And also, I see you. If you attempt to rape me, I know exactly what you look like."

Feeling my heart rate pick up with the anticipation of a confrontation, I stopped at the next crosswalk and waited for the walk sign to appear. Along with the crowd of tourists, people waiting for the bus, and the buskers living on Fremont Street, I stood baking in the sun like a loaf of bread.

Thinking about my brother and everyone else living on the street, I felt tears rise up in my eyes.

I must be getting my period at the rate of emotions I'm feeling today.

I wonder if I'm bi-polar?

As I looked over to see if the town car had moved, I thought about how every song I listened to made me think of my brother.

I can't believe the amount of homeless people sleeping on the street.

I can't believe I didn't stop and just say "are you ok" to that man back there.

I can't believe I didn't stop and check on the woman I'd seen yesterday on my walk back from training. She was just standing on the corner, disheveled, holding a plastic grocery store bag full of clothes. She kept walking out into the street then getting back on the corner.

Where the fuck are these people going?

Who is taking care of them?

Where do they go at night?

How come they ended up here and I didn't?

Suddenly the herd I was standing amongst started crossing the street, snapping me out of my revelry. I knew I needed to hurry the fuck up and get to work, but something was telling me to pull my headphones out as I noticed the town car hadn't moved.

As soon as I slid them in my pocket, I heard *the* sound from across the street. It was the noise I'd make when calling me dogs.

Conveniently, I had my phone in my hand.

This motherfucker is about to cop it

Shockingly, there was only one car coming towards me. It was as if God had parted the automotive sea for me to cross the busy boulevard.

"Did you just hiss at me?" I shouted across the street. Not hearing a word he'd said back, I waited for the car to pass and headed towards the island in between lanes, and once again, had a clear path to cross straight towards him and his beat town car.

"Were you cat calling me?" I asked as I approached the window. Due to the traffic now whizzing behind me, I couldn't hear him. Completely overcome with adrenaline, I came at him again.

"What were you doing when I was across the street?" I said. "I was blowing you a kiss," he said.

"A what?"

"Blowing you a kiss."

"Yeah but why?", I replied.

"Because you're sexy," he said.

"I know, but why?" I said back.

My heart was pounding so fucking hard I could hardly speak.

Seeming somewhat shocked I was standing at his window,

"Latinos we just do it like that," he said.

"Ok, well I'm just gonna tell you right now. A lot of women get intimidated by that," I said as I held my phone straight at him.

"Really?" he said.

Without taking a single breath between sentences, the words rolled off my tongue just like they did when I told Tony about Gary.

"Yeah--it can be seen as intimidating. I'm married, so it's all good. I dress like this because it's hot as fuck outside, and I work out really hard, *but* what I'm saying is, a lot of women would get intimidated by that. You have blacked-out windows, you don't have a license plate... and women can feel really vulnerable. You know what I'm saying?" I said.

Before he could even say a word, I went on.

"You ever see *the* girl that crushes watermelons between her legs?" I asked. Trying to keep my video rolling, and hardly being able to hear him with the traffic exceptionally close flying by behind me, I said.

"POW!" whilst simultaneously slapping my legs together.

"That's you?" he said incredulously.

"Yeah. Like I'm strong and powerful and I'd fuck you up, but most women don't have that mentality. Most women are thinking this motherfucker is gonna throw me in the back of the car. You know what I mean?"

"Yeah, but I don't need to," he said.

"Yeah, I know, but you get what I'm saying? There's a lot of fucked up people out here in the world, so next time you want to holler at a girl, try giving her a thumbs up man. Catcalling is so nineteen nineties!" I exclaimed.

From under his weathered, rounded bill cap, he bashfully smiled a bit.

"Look at me out here trying to help you stay in the game homeboy! What's your name man?" I said.

"Jason."

"Alright, cool. Nice to meet you Jason, I'm Kortney," I replied as I stuck my fist out to give him a fist bump.

"I gotta get to work, but play it cool man," I said as I walked towards the back of his car and stepped back up onto the same sidewalk I was just on a few minutes ago.

With my heart pounding in my face, I felt a sense of accomplishment.

This Sexy Motherfucker walked right into the Danger Zone and fucked shit up.

I walked past the front desk and gave the concierge a head nod up and smiled as I headed up to start working on our third annual live event.

. . . .

I was the only one sitting on the burnt-marshmallow Chesterfield in the VIP reception area of The Palms. Looking around the dimly lit space, I contemplated whether or not I *really* wanted one of every free macaron and finger-cake on offer, or if I just wanted to stick it to the man. Specifically, two men – the Fertitta brothers, who owned this place and plenty else besides.

While waiting for my name to be called, I thought about all the times in years gone by that I'd butter up bougie hotel receptionists. It was my tried and trusted line: 'Despite what it might look like with all these men coming and going from my room, this isn't *Pretty Woman* part two.' The receptionists always laughed when I told them that I made hundreds of dollars an hour to pick men up and carry them around or choke them with my legs. But today, I didn't need to explain myself.

I'd been meticulously planning our third live event for nine months. You'd think that owing US Bank seventeen thousand dollars from our first one would cause me to consider this a poor business decision, but when you hate fashion and you hate shopping online, bringing women together for a weekend of magic had to be done. Maybe that's why there are fewer female entrepreneurs – we have a tendency to make decisions based on emotions and ideology rather than just following the money. But I was willing to take the risk. Again and again.

Choosing an 'I'm here, bitch!' venue like The Palms seemed like a righteous choice. So why do I still feel like Julia Roberts when she went dress shopping in the Regent Beverly Wilshire? I don't think I'll ever stop feeling like a Best Western girl. Constantly torn between 'fake it till you make it' and 'fuck being fake', I righteously declared 'be a boss' and yet couldn't recognise a P&L statement if you slapped me upside the face with one. Even knowing that *Forbes* called my business 'the billion-dollar brand in waiting', I'd flip flop like a fortune-teller fish, backslapping myself in a dizzying carousel.

Take responsibility and learn all aspects of your business, don't rely on your husband.

Just focus on what you're great at, that's why you build a team. You hire people to do what you don't know how to do.

But you can't build a team with Monopoly money. Also, can I just stop using the word 'just'? As a woman, it makes me sound like I feel obligated to justify what I want. Unlike when Nike uses it. Just do it. Fuck Nike! Globalist dick-wanking fake frauds. I can't believe their bullshit empowering-women ads. The number of people who tagged me on that subpar 'Show them what crazy can do' clip was shocking. Do you realise that there are only three women on their board of directors? At least I put my money where my mouth is. Or I would, if I had any.

Twenty minutes have gone by.

Fucking hurry up, for the love of GOD! I still have so much to do before this shit kicks off tonight.'

As I stand to walk over to where the free shit is, I made a point to look annoyed. I *am* annoyed. I'm annoyed because I'm lining the pockets of two rich white men by making the poor choice of using their casino resort as my venue to empower women. I'm annoyed at the fact that both of the receptionists are wearing miniskirts and uncomfortable-looking low-cut blouses. And I'm annoyed that I have everything I wanted and yet I'm still unable to be happy.

Obviously picking up on my body language, one of the receptionists made eye contact.

"Good afternoon, Mrs. Olson. Your room is almost ready."

"Great. Thank you."

Leaving the macaroons, I grabbed some purple grapes from the fruit platter and rage-ate the handful.

But I really need to cheer the fuck up. I don't have to do this. In fact, I get to. And stop judging what these women have to wear. First of all, it's Vegas, and second, if they were really bothered by it, they could go get a job somewhere else. I'm just spiteful because these casino cocksuckers spent over thirty million dollars on some giant statue of a naked man in their hotel pool when all I need is a million dollars to grow my business. And yet these fucks couldn't even reply to an email about giving me four minutes to pitch for investment. Four minutes, after four years of bone-grinding, soul-sucking hard work and choosing their hotel to host my event in! Yeah, I'll find my own fucking path, thanks anyways boys.

I shifted on the couch and tried to feel like I had the right to be here. Smoothing down the fabric of my GRRRL samples – matching tiger-striped hoodie and tights – I made sure I ate the grapes with my mouth closed. Across the enclosed private room, a glass door opened, and a crew of young black men walked in. Trying to figure out who these boys were, I eavesdropped as they set down their luggage and started filling the seats, talking about some conference. Not my conference, clearly.

It's a million degrees outside, and I wore long pants and a hoodie that make me look like I walked off the front of a Tony the Tiger cereal box. Jackass...Does this boy really have a matching three-piece Gucci luggage set?

Realising that I am sitting amongst a professional football team, I entertained the thought of making conversation with the three-hundred-pound man sitting next to me, not paying me a shred of interest.

Maybe I could find some way to bring up the watermelon crushing. Maybe I could get one of these guys on the Kortney Olson leg program. Then I could stop chasing rich white men for investment. But I lost so much muscle after the Graves' Disease diagnosis, I'll look like a fraud.

"Mrs. Olson?"

Suddenly embarrassed by my mismatched luggage, I leave it concealed at the side of the couch and head towards the reception desk.

"Hi Gwendolyn," I said, pulling the velvet armchair back from her desk and crossing my legs longwise as I sit, in the event that the boys need something to look at. I could usually charm the pants off hotel staff like Gwendolyn, but today my cortisol levels were too high to be helpful. I've got meet-and-greets to do, speeches to rehearse.

'Thank you so much for your patience. I'm just going to need some form of ID and a credit card."

"You guys have my credit card on file. I've already paid you thirty grand. We have an event here this weekend," I said, with a sense of entitlement.

"Okay, no problem Mrs. Olson," she smiles, unruffled. "So, it looks like we have you staying in a penthouse, checking out Tuesday morning. Is that correct?"

"Yes, that sounds accurate," I reply, looking over to see if any of the Gucci-toting boys are looking my way. No.

As she handed me my key and explained which set of elevators to use, I decided to start acting like the tiger I've dressed as and take whatever I want.

'Thanks Gwen, I appreciate your help," I said, rising and heading towards the plate of macarons. After grabbing as many as I can comfortably fit in my hand, I returned to the couch. As I sat and ate the first macaron, it dawned on me that at some point over the past few weeks, I have somehow arrived at not giving a single fuck about what I was eating. That, at least, is progress.

Three weeks prior to me sitting in the VIP area of The Palms, and wondering if I had a right to be there, I was at the headquarters of the National Eating Disorders Association. It was there that I had the realisation that I had basically zero happy memories of my life because my mind has historically been too busy obsessing over food and my body to fucking make any. And yet here I was taking part in facilitator training for The Body Project so that I could spread the message of body acceptance to other women.

The last time I'd eaten a macaron had been in Paris, the night after Dave proposed to me in a horse-drawn carriage in front of the Eiffel Tower. I hadn't enjoyed the macaron because I was terrified of getting fat; terrified even as this man was expressing to me his unconditional love. I didn't take in any of the incredible sites on that entire trip, because my mind was held hostage by my diet. From the Sistine Chapel to the Pompeii Ruins, The Colosseum, Palatine Hill and the Roman Forum, I talked myself out of eating pizza and gelato, despite being in the birthplace of both. The only thing I really wanted to do was use the small gym inside our suite back at the hotel and not feel disgusting. And yet I decided to launch a clothing line whose total identity was rooted in being inclusive of all body types.

Now, as I sit slowly eating the salted caramel macaron in the Palms VIP area, I let the crumbs fall down the front of my tiger stripes and let loose the inner critic. Actually, it's more of a committee.

You devote yourself to teaching Australian teenage girls about confidence and yet decided to get a boob job because some no-nothing at the gym told you it would improve your physique.

You call yourself 'the woman with the world's deadliest thighs', but actually all women can smash watermelons with a bit of practice.

You were Australia's first female arm-wrestling champion but there were only five competitors.

You get a 'KO' tattoo, leading the world to think you're some kind of world champion boxer with several knockouts under your belt, but all you were was just a fucked-up, broken, hurt, little girl.

Hey – less of the 'just'.

Yeah, fuck that. You were a fucked-up, broken, hurt little girl. But a girl who had such high hopes for herself.

Letting my head rest against the back of the couch, I pushed the remaining bits of the macaron around my mouth, making sure I painted every crevice, nook and cranny with the taste. With three left in my hand, I decided to get a move on, since I had a keynote to practice. With over three hundred women attending and twenty-one different presenters and speakers flying in, my level of patience was running thin.

I grabbed my black GRRRL gym bag, flung it over my shoulder and, for the third time, walked past the athlete packing the Gucci.

Bet you don't own your own global brand that's creating a revolution, do ya? And achieved all without bullshit endorsements of diet tea or shapewear.

As I pushed the glass door, I caught a glimpse of several grrrl army members (aka 'customers', I guess) in reception and made a beeline to the elevators, hoping that none of them would see me. Learning the hard way from the last two events, I knew I needed to protect my personal space and not let too many women into my heart. Through the hundreds who reach out via direct message on a monthly basis, with their stories of struggle and hurt, I seemed to start the day feeling like a block of rock solid cheddar cheese but by the end, I was nothing but Swiss.

Cutting through the rows of slot machines, I made my way to the bank of elevators and once inside, repetitively hit the number eighteen button with force. With a straight shot to my floor, the elevator stopped, and the doors opened for me to come face to face with myself. In front of a giant framed mirror, there I stood.

Kinda buff. Super tough. Short black hair, slick and sharp. Tiger stripes.

Surrounded by all this affluence, I could feel my confidence starting to boost back up again bit by bit, with its intoxicating effects.

It's showtime, bitch! Don't need eyeliner, that shit's tattooed on.

Waving my key in front of the ten-foot-tall door, I stepped inside and onto the white marble floor. With the sun shining straight through the panoramic windows, illuminating the giant shuffleboard in the corner of the living room, I glanced around the penthouse and felt confident that I could easily fit twenty-five women in the space for our post-conference special event. After undoing the laces on my black velvet platform shoes, I drug my bare feet across the carpet to the audio system. With Aerosmith playing faintly across the speakers, I turned up the volume before walking into the bedroom for further inspection.

I remember hearing that Steven Tyler was a closet schmoe.

After eyeing the purple velvet chaise lounge in the corner, I ran over to the king bed and leapt backwards in the air to test out the firmness. Catching my breath, I stared up at the vaulted ceilings and thought about whether or not we didn't belong back at the Golden Nugget like last year. Knowing I was about to descend into a pit of pity, I jumped up to head to the toilet. After dragging my feet across the plush beige carpet, the white marble floor felt cool and refreshing.

Taking in the beauty of the bathroom, I briefly imagined Dave and I making love in the garage-sized shower. Knowing that we wouldn't have the time, nor the interest, I laughed out loud to myself before spinning around and locking eyes with the woman in a large print framed on the wall. With her entire body stretched out across a white leather couch, she held a rotary phone to her ear while laying on her stomach. Propped up on her elbows, her dark blue long sleeve blouse made her arms look even more frail then I could remember. Wearing a rose-gold sequined miniskirt and black high heeled pumps, her incredibly long, thin legs reached right to the very edge of the couch as she looked out of the frame.

I couldn't believe the odds. As I stood there staring back at the frail-thin body that had caused me so much grief growing up, I thought about the irony of where I was in that exact moment. Grinding through the unoiled gears of an arduous start-up, I had carefully structured our third conference to the same format as Kamp Konfidence. Every workshop, event, and speaker was modeled around the five habits, lessons, and principles that led to the development of self-love and nourished a strong sisterhood.

From transgender athlete Janae Marie Kroc, to All-American gymnast Katelyn Ohashi, I had truly lined up an amazing and diverse group of women to preach the message of empowerment. Sitting down on the love seat beneath the framed print of Kate, I suddenly realised that I'd been so busy trying to bust through glass ceilings, that I no longer recognized the trampoline I was jumping off of.

In that moment, I realised that what I'd heard in a meeting days earlier, applied directly to me. I just wasn't ready to make the connection until now.

Gratitude and a sense of entitlement cannot occupy the same space.

Dumbfounded, I sat and processed what felt like a bag of bricks dropping out of the sky onto my face.

I have exactly what I wished for, and yet it still feels like it's not good enough. All because I feel entitled to have money from the government and investors to make this seem easier. But I know that having more money doesn't make shit easier. It just means that I'm losing focus on doing God's will and being here to help people. I'm trying to make shit happen how my ego thinks it's supposed to happen. Because you take back your will and stop focusing on doing God's work, you feel entitled instead of grateful. It's one hundred percent on you for feeling this way.

Right up until the moment he was murdered, Dr. Martin Luther King, Jr. prayed for God's guidance, and expressed gratitude for having the opportunity to make change. And here I was, feeling sorry for myself because I was playing debit card roulette with plastic across three different countries. I never had to fear not having a toilet to use, shoes to put on my feet, a mattress to sleep on, water to brush my teeth with, or food to eat. More importantly, I wasn't having to fear for my life.

Deciding to step into my power, I made the conscious decision to let the anchor of Kate Moss slip off into the sea where she, Gary, Rob, the journalist, and Big Brothers Big Sisters could all teach each other their tips on how to crush watermelons.

I fell onto my bed after getting back from a twenty four hour whirlwind trip to New York. I'd spent a full day sitting in a green room just to make a five-minute appearance on The Match Game. Having Alec Baldwin take a piece of watermelon that was served up from between my legs was worth it. Other than eating, I had one last thing to do before crawling into bed; call Pop and wish her a happy birthday. Asking the GRRLarmy in our closed Facebook group to send handwritten cards to Pop's house, I explained how it was her eighty ninth birthday and I was too broke to get her anything. Sharing that without Pop's loan, we wouldn't have been able to sponsor Holly Holm, and hence, GRRRL probably wouldn't have given birth to this community of powerful women, several cheerfully agreed to write.

Unsure of who and how many would actually write to a woman they'd never met, I prepared to pick up the phone and find out. Staring blankly at my home screen, I checked the UberEATS app for an ETA on the chicken alfredo and cheesecake I ordered from The Cheesecake Factory. Eating a plant-based diet for the last several months, I was craving something "bad" and managed to place my order from the back of the cab.

Just as I opened the app, a faint knock interrupted my thoughts. Shuffling in fluffy house socks, I skidded down the hallway and joyfully flung the door open to receive my goods. Thanking Carmen, I let the door slam behind me as I ran towards the kitchen with the paper bag bouncing off the side of my thigh. I hadn't eaten something substantial in what seemed like forever, and was prepared to deal with the backlash of guilt, shame, and remorse that would soon follow. Ripping open the bag, I pulled out the plastic container of fettuccine and started chowing down.

As the thick, rich, cream-based sauce hit the back of my tongue, my body immediately felt satiated.

I know someone could cook this vegan and make it taste just as good. I really should learn to do that. You really should learn to just chill the fuck out, Kort.

Unlike pain pills, I deliberately chewed through every bite unrushed with appreciation for my savory alfredo before moving onto the cheesecake. Making it halfway through, I started to feel full. Instead of powering through the sweet dessert with a mindset of making sure nothing was leftover to tempt me later, I closed the lid and placed the container in the refrigerator before heading back to my room to call Pop.

"Hey Pop!"

"Hi doll. How are you?"

"Can't complain! But also, I'm sure I could if I wanted to."

"Well, what gives?"

"I just got back from New York, appearing on an episode of The Match Game."

"Oh, yes. I'm shocked that the program is still around."

"Yeah, me too."

"So what was the problem?"

"Well, it wasn't a problem so much. More of an annoyance. I sat in a room for six hours with the world's worst selection of craft services!"

"Ohhhhhh oh oh! You poor thing!" Pop exclaimed sarcastically.

"Yeah! It was just me, my phone, and a bunch of chip bags!" I laughed.

"How did the filming go?"

"As usual, no one had a clue as to what I was supposed to be doing, but once I actually got backstage and was given instruction on when to walk out on set, I heard exactly how this was all being framed."

"Uh huh," Pop said.

"All I knew was that I was the supposed daughter of Gallagher with some kind of rendition on crushing a watermelon."

"And you crushed it?"

"Of course!"

"Then what was the issue?" she asked.

"Well, Alec Baldwin, the host, said 'Gallagher's daughter performs her father's watermelon crushing trick with a sexy new twist, but instead of a mallet, she uses her blank."

"And you didn't like the sexy part?" she asked.

"Nailed it!" I shrilled. "By the way, happy birthday! Did you get some nice cards in the mail?"

"Why yes, I did! They were just marvelous, Kortney."

Feeling a slow build of satisfaction, I sat up on the bed. "That's great! How many did you get?"

"Oh my heavens, too many to count. I just couldn't believe the stories of these brave women. I'm truly, truly impressed." she said, oozing pride.

"Ahhhhh that's outstanding!"

"Yes. I read every single one of them and enjoyed them very much. You've really seemed to have done something special with GRRRL."

After a long pause, I choked down the lump I was feeling in my throat and replied."Thank you, Pop."

"And thank *you* for organising the lovely cards. I want you to keep crushing it, my dear."

With some additional small talk in the books, I hung up the phone and, for several minutes, sobbed uncontrollably. Standing up to get a Kleenex, I caught my reflection in the free-standing full-length mirror in the corner. As I gazed at the skin above my knees, the most disrespected part of my body, a new thought crossed my mind.

Fettuccine alfredo and cheesecake aren't bad.

They have no morals.

Neither one of these foods are awaiting trial for stabbing someone.

Their calories are more beneficial than a vodka-laiden screwdriver.

It's going to be ok, toots.

. . . .

In the end, Kate didn't kill me. Whatever we experience makes us stronger (so as long as we don't die along the way). The reality is, far too many of us are suffering from childhood trauma, which often turns into addictions, which clearly distract us from being of service and useful to the rest of the planet. Beyond childhood trauma and various addictions, our societies in The West are designed to cause us to feel like we are never enough (as a person), and we'll never have enough.

Once again, all life is, is one big-ass learning experience. We can't take anything with us to the grave. As I heard in a meeting the other day, you'll never see a Brinks truck following behind a hurst.

With that being said, what are we doing to make the planet a better place, for everyone?

All we are is energy. After doing the effing work, you may have noticed how smiling at a complete stranger in a car passing by may have caused you to feel overwhelmed with positivity when they smiled back. Or you may have started realising all the previous times you thought were pure "coincidence", were in fact a synchronicity. So if all we are is energy, and all of us are connected (that's science, sister!), then wouldn't it be safe to say that if one group of people are suffering, we are all inadvertently suffering?

Do the F*cking Work

Taking a break from stuff allows us to reset. For me, I believe taking a break from working out was the key to helping me to stop obsessing over my body. (Mind you I still wore GRRRL leggings every day!)

What things do you need to take a break from?

What areas of the world could use your focus instead of wasting energy over bullshit like cellulite?

Are you too busy being obsessed over counting calories to step in and speak up for protecting the lives of BIPOC? (Even if you're a theorist and think George Sorros is part of the swamp, there is absolutely no denying that racism and injustice is alive and well.)

Are you too busy getting hammered and chasing dick to question things like prison reform and why fracking is legal?

Are you too busy worrying about your boyfriend (who potentially isn't treating you like the queen you are in the first place) being attracted to someone else when on average, five women a day die in the United States from domestic violence?

When I first heard the term 'white privilege' in early 2017, I nearly came unglued. I immediately felt attacked (which in retrospect is *fucking hilarious*). I felt like all of these stories you've read about were suddenly being invalidated and minimised because I held privilege. After a slow series of conversations, or better known as 'uppacking', I had the 'ah-ha' moment in realising that I indeed have privilege on many levels. (Which will more than likely be a different publication in the future. I cannot concisely write about how blown away I am that it took me *so* long to recognise that I have privilege. I was still tossing around saying 'my ni**a' up until a few years ago.)

Where do you have privilege in your life that others do not?

How can you use that privilege to help others who are marginalised?

We don't know what we don't know. Until I lived with a deaf man for a few weeks, I never thought about what deaf people struggle with on a daily basis. Until I met a sensational interpreter, Amber Galloway, I never understood how soul-destroying it must be for the deaf community to not enjoy a concert. Until Alexandra (sponsor turned best friend) made me hangout in a mall all day with her and her friend that's confined to a wheelchair, I never realised what people living with disabilities have to endure (this woman developed a debilitating brain tumor that completely leveled her life at the age of thirty six).

Do you use the ADA bathroom when other stalls are available, or do you kick the ADA automatic door-opening button instead of using your elbow or shoulder?

Are you making a consistent effort to use an app to add closed captions to your videos if you share publicly on social media to help the deaf community feel included? (I'll admit I need to do better with my efforts, but when I do, I use the app Clipomatic)

One important micro lesson that I learned this year was that gratitude and a sense of entitlement cannot occupy the same space. Because I felt like I deserved investment to make my business run more smoothly, I could not find moments of gratitude because I had a sense of entitlement.

Do you hold a sense of entitlement anywhere in your life that needs checking?

Now that you have done a significant amount of work, write yourself an empowering letter, summarising what parts have stood out to you the most, as well as congratulating yourself for taking the time!

Scan here for more good shit.

EPILOGUE

Acceptance is the Answer to All of My Problems

As you've read, my journey to finding self acceptance has mimicked that of a frenetic heart monitor-- a screen with massive highs and lows. I started using the term self acceptance over self love, just as I've started focusing on body neutrality instead of body positivity, because loving yourself or being positive every day about your body is basically impossible.

In my experience, being freed from the prison of self pity brought on by diet culture, addiction and the patriarchy was an arduous and very gradual process. But there seems to be two main tools I always rely on when sharing my story to help others; awareness and acceptance.

Without awareness of a problem, there is no problem to solve; and without acceptance, I'll just continue to battle against every person, place and thing when really, that's God's job (again, whomever God might be).

To this day I want to solve every Tom, Dick and Harry's problems on the planet, but my *only* job is to simply do the next right thing and not pick up a drink or a drug. It's really just that simple. But when you're complicated like me, it's easy to forget and slip straight back into self centeredness and self obsession, feeling about as useful as the venom in a daddy long leg spider. I'll never forget the day years back when my step-mom sarcastically said, "Kortney, I think some guy has already come along and died on the cross for everyone's sins. Some guy named Jesus, I think it was?", in response to me floundering on about how more needed to be done in the world, not yet realising that the work that needed to be done was inside of me.

I know when I look around at people who are deemed "influencers" with large followings, I can easily think "what's the point- no one will see my post anyway". That is one hundred percent self-centered thinking. But when I focus on the opposite, I'm thinking of myself as an agent for this 'God' entity and out to simply do one's job, which is to leave this planet better than I found it.

God's will might be for me to post a video that only one person sees. And that one person, the exact person God intended to have seen it, then takes that inspiration and heads off to a stage where they share it with a group of a thousand people who'll exponentially bring the message from that one video to millions of others. Or maybe it just helps a single, solitary person. Either way, it's a win.

We can't all help everyone, but conversely, we can all help someone (That's a play out of Ronald Reagan's handbook by the way). And by helping someone, we find a direct pathway out of focusing on ourselves. Self pity, self centeredness and self obsession are the primary roots of our self perceived problems. When we move away from a me-me-me mentality and start thinking of 'we', you can consider yourself to be having a spiritual experience.

It's important to note that there are many of us who have clinical depression and anxiety who are unable to access medical help. You simply cannot tell someone with a clinical mental illness (or even a hormonal woman!) to think positively or to "buck-up". Just like you shouldn't tell a Black woman to stop being angry because she has to worry about getting shot by the cops due to the color of her skin, or you shouldn't tell a fat person to harden up, train harder, and eat right to lose weight. (By the way, I still have a difficult time using the word 'fat' to be descriptive as I was raised believing that in doing so, I was being hurtful and hateful. However, today we are evolving and listening to women who are a part of the fat liberation movement and taking the power back behind the word itself.)

We aren't here to compete in the Olympics of disadvantages, but we must recognise that we cannot possibly tell what other people are battling or experiencing. This is why it's imperative that we focus on our own shit, and when we're trapped in self, we reach out to help others who need it.

To think that I've spent thirty five years of my life being so utterly miserable solely because I never addressed my trauma properly, amazes me. I allowed it to manifest into various forms of disordered eating and full blown alcoholism and addictions without consciously knowing I was even really damaging myself. But as I've said when talking about Kamp Konfidence, prevention is so much cheaper than cure. And by sharing our stories with others and having these conversations, we are creating more awareness, which in turn will prevent others from having to travel down the same road we have, and hopefully, they'll not suffer the same traumas.

If we can spread more awareness and acceptance around the world, we'll move ahead victoriously.

I'd like to point out while we're here that some of us are more empathetic than others. It's a characteristic of being a woman. We want to fix shit! But we must create enough self-awareness to catch ourselves when we go from aiming to be useful and help others, versus wanting to fix others and do God's job. One of my good friends Natalie spoke at our last live event in Las Vegas. At the end of her talk, she instructed three hundred women to stand and take the piece of white, thick string they were handed upon walking back into the room after the break, and place it in a circle around their feet. After everyone had roughly one foot by one foot in diameter of string on the ground, she simply said, "Look- anything outside of this circle is none of your fucking business!"

Other people's opinions of us are none of our business. So if that's the case, how do we decide what is our business, and what is not? When do we get involved, and when do we let people be people, or God be God, and do his/her/their job? I wish I had all the answers, but obviously I don't. Sometimes I feel like I'm seconds away from having the vision if I could just slow down enough to visualise it.

I start to envision what I should be doing with my brand, and within a matter of minutes, feel overwhelmed and stressed out about not having a great plan. But then, as soon as I let go of control (the details of it all), and focus on the goal (empowering women and girls to accept themselves and creating a sisterhood), followed by a short prayer (something that sounds like, "Yo God! Yeah hi! Ummmm look- can you take this shit off my plate and fucking figure it out for me, please? I'd appreciate it. You just put the people and experiences in front of me so I can figure it out, keh? Thanks a bunch! Over and out sharp shooter!"), then everything seems to just flow. Remembering that I only need to keep showing up and doing the next right thing (and of course not get hammered or high!).

In the subtitle of this book, I wrote, "how I smashed addiction, the patriarchy and diet culture". But I'd like to point out that this is not a past tense action, despite what the word implies. How I'm "smashing" them just doesn't have the same impact as how I've "smashed" them. The truth is, it is a daily, ongoing fight. Just like finding self acceptance is an ongoing action.

Just because I've managed to consecutively stay clean and sober for a decade now, I'm even in more danger of relapsing because I forget how bad it got. Time causes me to think "I'm cured" if I don't stay plugged in to recovery. Just like someone with stage four bone cancer has to take medication every day to stay alive, alcoholics and addicts are in the exact same position. Every single day we have to take our spiritual, mental, and physical medicine in some way, shape, or form, or we will inevitably relapse.

Considering we have the first woman vice president of the United States about to take office, we haven't smashed the patriarchy by a long stretch.

Because I started fiercely posting unedited pictures of myself on the internet, rolled out a brand that empowers women to focus on what their body can do and not so much on how it looks, and started eating whatever the fuck I want without guilt or remorse, doesn't mean diet culture has ended. This would basically be saying "I have Black friends so I can't be racist" or "I don't see color."

But all of this is a start, and hopefully you have found a new level of awareness around these topics that will help you crush this shit as well.

We don't arrive at an ending in this thing called life, until you're dead, and then it's too late. I guess that's why that obnoxious self-help quote of "life's about the journey, not the destination" is absolute truth. But if you're like me, you get tired of hearing happy-clappy bullshit that just seems to get thrown around without any context. Then again, the only person that can give me context most often is myself. If I catch some influencer posting a fancy designed quote of this on their social media and it annoys me, then that is my perception and thus my problem! If I actually paused and consciously connected to what the motivational quote was expressing, I'd sit back and reflect on all the shit I just wrote about in the previous pages and see that this journey will forever continue to go on until I die. I will never reach the destination of figuring it all out.

However there is one thing that I have figured out and that is women are not born catty, backstabbing, jealous bitches that are the weaker sex. We are born to lift up, empower, and love on one another. And when we do this, we create a collective group of women who are unstoppable. It takes a squad of united women to change the game and create a new normal, and I believe we are doing just that. We are at that tipping point in humanity where we must evolve or die.

So where to from here?

Imagine for a second that this is your purpose in this lifetime--
to step into your power and make the conscious decision to start
accepting yourself and other women with the ease and quickness of
simply snapping your goddamn fingers. From there, we will
collectively be able to fight for all women and shake down the veil of
untruth, so every person on this planet can have access to basic rights,
freedoms, and liberties. We will dismantle debilitating stereotypes
around gender, free our minds of judgement, and stop looking
outside of ourselves to fix the insides.

What would your life have been like all of the times you
unnecessarily felt unworthy, not good enough, gross, disgusting,
shameful, and guilty all because of the way you perceived yourself?
Then think about how by doing the work on yourself, you'll be able
to start creating that world for those who come after you.

When I think back to meeting Peyton, the eleven year-old
daughter of one of our customers, I remember that there are millions
of girls just like her who are out there needing to hear our voices, as
opposed to those who are sucking on "skinny pops". When they're
eight years old, they primarily need to hear from someone outside of
the house that their exterior is not equated to their worth . The world
needs us strong, healthy and powerful now more than ever. It truly
does take a village to raise our girls into grrrls. If you've read this far
I'm going to congratulate you on joining the revolutionary group of
women we call the #grrrlarmy.

Scan here to hear Peyton's story:

Everyone is waiting for someone else to go first, and that person is you.

Take 'The Pledge' like Peyton did and testify to the world that from here on out, you are going to do your best to stop being negative towards yourself as well as other women.

grrrl

I solemnly swear, to the best of my ability,
to refrain from talking negatively
about myself, as well as other grrrls.

I am an equal amongst my peers,
and see myself as neither better than,
nor less than.

Through this pledge of non-judgment, I
understand, and embrace, that i am having a
positive impact on the world, and furthering
the global revolution of body acceptance.

I take this pledge.

And Do the F*cking Work.

Scan here for the last of the good shit.

Made in the USA
Coppell, TX
13 February 2021